The MINISTRY OF MUNITIONS in the FIRST WORLD WAR

The
MINISTRY OF
MUNITIONS
in the
FIRST
WORLD WAR

The MINISTRY OF MUNITIONS in the FIRST WORLD WAR

Doing Their Bit

ANDREW RAWSON

Pen & Sword
MILITARY
AN IMPRINT OF PEN & SWORD BOOKS LTD.
YORKSHIRE – PHILADELPHIA

First published in Great Britain in 2025 by
Pen & Sword Military
An imprint of
Pen & Sword Books Ltd
Yorkshire – Philadelphia

Copyright © Andrew Rawson, 2025

ISBN 978 1 03611 538 8

The right of Andrew Rawson to be identified as the Author of this work has been asserted by him in accordance with the Copyright, Designs and Patents Act 1988.

A CIP catalogue record for this book is available from the British Library.

All rights reserved. No part of this book may be reproduced, transmitted, downloaded, decompiled or reverse engineered in any form or by any means, electronic or mechanical including photocopying, recording or by any information storage and retrieval system, without permission from the Publisher in writing. NO AI TRAINING: Without in any way limiting the Author's and Publisher's exclusive rights under copyright, any use of this publication to "train" generative artificial intelligence (AI) technologies to generate text is expressly prohibited. The Author and Publisher reserve all rights to license uses of this work for generative AI training and development of machine learning language models.

Typeset in INDIA by IMPEC eSolutions
Printed and bound in the England by CPI Group (UK) Ltd, Croydon, CR0 4YY

The Publisher's authorised representative in the EU for product safety is Authorised Rep Compliance Ltd., Ground Floor, 71 Lower Baggot Street, Dublin D02 P593, Ireland.
www.arccompliance.com

For a complete list of Pen & Sword titles please contact:

PEN & SWORD BOOKS LIMITED
George House, Units 12 & 13, Beevor Street, Off Pontefract Road,
Barnsley, S71 1HN, UK
E-mail: enquiries@pen-and-sword.co.uk
Website: www.pen-and-sword.co.uk

or

PEN AND SWORD BOOKS
1950 Lawrence Rd, Havertown, PA 19083, USA
E-mail: Uspen-and-sword@casematepublishers.com
Website: www.penandswordbooks.com

Contents

Acknowledgements   vii
Introduction   ix

Part I: Going to War

Chapter 1	Mobilisation	3
Chapter 2	Trouble Ahead	9

Part II: Organising Industry

Chapter 3	The Administration	19
Chapter 4	The Ministers	25
Chapter 5	Financing the Munitions Industry	31
Chapter 6	Commercial Control	39
Chapter 7	Programming Munitions Output	45
Chapter 8	Research, Testing and Inspections	49
Chapter 9	The Railways	55

Part III: The Raw Materials

Chapter 10	The Coal Industry	63
Chapter 11	Iron and Steel	67
Chapter 12	Non-Ferrous Materials	73
Chapter 13	The Explosives Industry	79
Chapter 14	The Chemical Industry	91

Part IV: The Factories

Chapter 15	The Royal Arsenal	99
Chapter 16	The Ministry Steps In	101
Chapter 17	The National Shell Factories and the Cooperative Schemes	105
Chapter 18	The National Projectile Factories	113
Chapter 19	The National Filling Factories	117

Chapter 20	Tools of the Trade	123
Chapter 21	American Imports	127
Chapter 22	Canadian Imports	131
Chapter 23	Cooperation with the Allies	135

Part V: The Workforce

Chapter 24	Increasing the Workforce	141
Chapter 25	Agreeing Wages and Hours	151
Chapter 26	Dilution of the Workforce	161
Chapter 27	Welfare Arrangements	173

Part VI: The Weapons

Chapter 28	The Artillery	183
Chapter 29	Making the Shells	187
Chapter 30	Personal Weapons	195
Chapter 31	Machine Guns	199
Chapter 32	Small Arms Ammunition	203
Chapter 33	Trench Warfare Weapons	207
Chapter 34	Optical Munitions	213

Part VII: Mechanised Warfare

Chapter 35	Shipbuilding	217
Chapter 36	Tanks	225
Chapter 37	Lorries, Cars and Motorcycles	231
Chapter 38	The Aircraft Industry	235

Part VIII: The War Ends

| Chapter 39 | The Armistice and Demobilisation | 249 |

Bibliography	252
Notes	253
Index	263

Acknowledgements

Several people have helped me turn my ideas into words and my words into this book. Most of them have helped me with many of my projects over the past twenty-five years. I would not have completed many of them without their encouragement and support.

Professor John Bourne, Vice President of The Western Front Association, has encouraged me for many years, as I have worked my way through my various First World War projects. He gave many words of encouragement during the writing and guidance during the editing of this book. The same applies to Tony Bolton, Chairman of The Western Front Association, who I have known for over forty years. He too provided reassurance and advice as I worked my way through the masses of information. My brother, Fraser Rawson, a chemical engineer, checked the chemistry in the sections about the explosives industry and lethal gas production.

My research was made far easier by the unknown members of the Library of Minnesota in the United States, who went to the trouble of digitally scanning the twelve volumes of the *Ministry of Munitions' Official History* and putting them on the website https://www.archive.org. This website is a treasure trove of rare and out of print books, which have been made available to the public.

Any book needs a good editor if it is to succeed and I would like to thank Heather Williams at Pen & Sword Books Limited, who effortlessly guided me through the writing, editing and proofing process. I would also like to thank Lori Jones, who copy edited the manuscript, removing the errors I had left behind.

Finally, I might not have started on the long voyage of discovery into Britain's munitions industry without the encouragement and advice given by the late Rob Thompson. Rob's passion was the logistics of the British Expeditionary Force (BEF) and introduced many a First World War historian to this important but often ignored subject. The work of the munitions industry fits snugly against military logistics and we had many a conversation on social media during lockdown about them both. Rob was an inspiration to many First World War historians and to everyone who knew him.

Thank you to each one of them and to the many people who have assured me that the munitions industry deserved to be looked at in detail.

Andrew Rawson, 2025

Introduction

There is a well-known First World War recruitment poster where a man is sat in his living room with his young daughter on his knee and his son playing on the floor. He thoughtfully looks across the room, as she asks him the question 'what did you do in the war daddy?' It was released in March 1915 and was supposed to prick the consciousness of the men who had still not enlisted in the armed forces by making them feel guilty.

However, as the war grew from months into years, many men would have proudly given the answer 'I repaired warships, I made howitzers, I assembled tanks or I built engines for aircraft.' All of them considered to be essential jobs by the Ministry of Munitions after it took over Britain's munitions industry in June 1915. The children would have also been able to ask their mothers the same question. Tens of thousands would have proudly answered 'I made shell casings, I filled shells, I assembled gas masks or I made aircraft wings.'

The armed forces needed weapons and ammunition, particularly the BEF during its huge struggles on the Western Front. This book charts the history of the British munitions industry; its growth and those who administered it and worked in it. One important thing I have learnt is that few people even consider where the weapons and ammunition came from, nor the men and women who made them. I hope this book shines a light on their important work.

I became interested in industry when I returned to my home town of Sheffield in 2018. After a lifelong interest in the Sheffield City Battalion, I wanted to know why a city with a population of over 500,000 in the 1911 census, only raised one New Army battalion in the autumn of 1914, when other northern cities, such as Newcastle-upon-Tyne, Liverpool and Manchester, raised so many. Part of the answer lay in the fact that the city was world famous for producing steel, which was used across the country and around the British Empire.

A study of Graces Guide (https://www.gracesguide.co.uk) website, 'the leading source of historical information on industry and manufacturing in Britain', provided an insight into what the city was doing between 1914 and 1918. The number of men working with steel had risen five-fold to over 75,000, while the female workforce had risen ten-fold to over 25,000. The men and women of Sheffield were 'doing their bit' for the war effort: making steel plates for warships, barrels for artillery pieces, helmets for soldiers and parts for shells. As the Sheffield Munitions Committee reported at the end of the war, the men and women of the city had contributed 'over 11 million war items to the forces insatiable demand for armaments throughout the conflict.' One company alone, Thomas Firth and Sons, had made 9,000 tons of gun forgings, 10,000 tons of ship parts and 4 million shells.

After writing and talking about Sheffield's contribution to the war effort, lockdown gave me time to look at the rest of the country's contribution to it. The process started with the 1.1 million miners and the huge demand for shipping of Spanish iron ore and the nation's steel workers. Large numbers of workers were busy in the Clyde and Tyne shipyards, the Birmingham rifle and bullet factories, and the Bristol and north London aircraft manufacturers. Thousands more were producing explosives, making shell casings and then filling them.

The questions kept coming:

- Where did Britain get its raw materials from?
- What else had to be imported?
- Who organised all the factories as they switched from domestic to wartime production?
- Where did all the workers live?
- And were there issues over wage settlements or even strikes?

Fortunately, the Ministry of Munitions took the time to record the work it did between June 1915 and March 1921, as well as the War Office's efforts during the first ten months of the war. It published 12 large volumes, comprising around 8,000 pages, not long after it closed. All the volumes are available on the website https://www.archive.org for free if you want to do any further reading.

Much has been written about the men and the battles that the BEF was engaged in across France and Flanders and in theatres such as the Dardanelles, Salonika and the Middle East. Very often the words 'forgotten', 'overlooked' or 'lesser known' are used. I use the words 'taken for granted' when speaking about the munitions industry. Without the efforts of hundreds of thousands of men and women, the soldiers would have had nothing to fight with, there would have had no ammunition to use against the enemy and there would have been no ships to import everything from food to iron ore.

This book is a condensed version of the struggle faced by the War Office and Ministry of Munitions to arm Britain's armed forces. It also covers the coal industry and its 1 million miners, who did not come under the Ministry of Munitions' authority. It looks at the struggle for manpower, which had to be balanced between the armed forces and industry, and the introduction of women in large numbers into male dominated factories. The reader will also see how hard British industry had to work on many levels to keep arming the British Army, the Royal Navy, the Royal Flying Corps (later the Royal Air Force) and the Allies.

PART I

Going to War

Chapter 1

Mobilisation

Pre-War Industrial Action

British trade union membership had been on the rise in the industries that would become involved in making munitions. Eight out of ten coal miners had joined the Miners' Federation of Great Britain, while half the men working in the foundries, steel works and shipyards had joined a union. On the other side of the fence, 830 firms had joined the Engineering Employers' Federation to help them deal with disputes.

Wages were agreed in different ways, sometimes by industry, sometimes by district and sometimes by trade. For example, the wages in the steel and coal industries were set according to the selling price of the goods they produced. While shipbuilding wages were decided nationally, other industries made district agreements. Trades agreed their own district rates, while each factory determined its own piece rates. Altogether, it produced a complex wages system fraught with difficulties.

The years before the First World War were known as 'the Great Labour Unrest'. Trouble started with a banking crisis that led to the downfall of the Knickerbocker Trust Company in America in October 1907. That led to the New York Stock Exchange falling by almost 50 per cent in a short time. The depression that followed spread to Europe over the next two years, causing industrial unrest across Britain.

There were spontaneous strikes across the North East of England, affecting mills, engineering works and shipyards. However, the nation's attention focused on the South Wales coalfields in September 1910. Miners were paid for each ton of coal they dug and while consideration payments were supposed to cover difficult working conditions, they rarely did.[1] It led to men walking out of Ely pit after the men refused to accept a low price for a difficult seam.

By November 1910, 30,000 miners had been locked out of their workplace or were on strike; over 1,000 police were drafted in as blackleg labour was rounded up to restart work.[2] Home Secretary Winston Churchill even sent troops to the area, resulting in outbreaks of violence and threatening behaviour around Tonypandy. New payment rates were rejected in May 1911 but work resumed after an offer was accepted in August 1911.[3]

While the nation had been watching events in South Wales unfold, there was a mass walk out of 11,000 workers at the Singer Manufacturing Company sewing machine factory near Glasgow in March 1911. It was a huge show of solidarity with twelve women who had been told they must do more work for less money. While the strike ended a month later, 400 workers, including the strike leaders and members of the Industrial Workers of Great Britain, were sacked.

The trade unions now started to coordinate their actions, resulting in the first national strike in the ports and on the railways in June 1911. Before long, numbers swelled to around 250,000 with the focus on Liverpool. Churchill eventually deployed two warships to the River Mersey, while sending 5,000 soldiers and police into the city. Over 350 people were injured during a baton charge on 13 August 1911, which became known as Bloody Sunday. Two days later, soldiers fired into a crowd, killing two and injuring fifteen.

Unofficial action on the railways extended into the first national rail strike at the same time and soldiers were again deployed to towns and cities across the country to support the police. However, union leaders called off the strike after just two days when the government stepped in. It left the workers angry and undermined their confidence in the unions.

A maximum working day, as set by the Coal Mines Regulation Act 1908, known as the Eight Hours Act, left many coal miners short of money. So, the Miners' Federation of Great Britain asked their 560,000 members to vote for a minimum wage in January 1912, in line with the shipbuilding and engineering industries. Around 80 per cent voted to stop work and the first national strike began at the end of February 1912, resulting in 1 million miners going on strike within days.[4]

Prime Minister Herbert Asquith stepped in as every industry relied on coal. While he recognised that the demand was for the minority of miners who were earning too little, coalfield owners in Scotland, Northumbria and South Wales refused the government's proposal to grant a minimum wage. As factories went on short time and train services were restricted, miners wondered how they would feed their families on their strike pay.[5]

The Miners' Federation of Great Britain made proposals but there were arguments over the rates. So, the Coal Mines (Minimum Wage) Act 1912, which was given Royal Assent on 29 March 1912, stated that the rates would be agreed later.[6] While all pits were soon working, the miners felt they had been cheated by the government's intervention.

There were more strikes in the transport sector during the summer of 1912 with London Transport employees and dockers stopping work. As time went on, clashes became more violent as workers demonstrated that they were willing to fight for their demands. Around 3,000 strikes between 1910 and 1914 resulted in a 50 per cent increase in union membership; over 11 million days were lost to the strikes during 1913 alone.

Meanwhile, there was little union activity in the Royal Dockyards where the workforce relied on an antiquated practice called annual petitions to set rates and conditions. They were paid less money because their working week was forty-eight hours rather than the standard fifty-four hours, but their jobs were more secure and they had a pension at the end.

Around twenty trade unions were active in the private shipyards, including the United Society of Boilermakers and Iron Shipbuilders (USBISS) and the Shipconstructors' and Shipwrights' Association (SSA). Meanwhile, employers joined the Shipbuilding Employers' Federation and each area would negotiate its terms, conditions and rates. Although the USBISS agreed not to go on strike without negotiations, its members walked out over minimum rates in the summer of 1910, resulting in a national lockout.

The National Union of Railwaymen was formed in March 1913 and it joined the Miners' Federation of Great Britain and the National Transport Workers' Federation in what was called the Triple Alliance.[7] The plan was to stop militancy among the rank and file, coordinating action between the three large groups of workers. Only time would tell if it would work.

Support for women's suffrage had also increased dramatically in the same period; the National Federation of Women Workers alone expanding ten-fold. There had also been violent incidents involving the Women's Social and Political Union. It will never be known what would have happened across industrial Britain had war not been declared in August 1914.

Britain Goes to War

Britain was a naval power with a small Regular Army capable of policing the British Empire. Planning with France had agreed that an expeditionary force of six divisions, 150,000 men strong would be deployed to the Continent if there was a war with Germany. A reserve of time served soldiers would keep the BEF up to strength, while the Territorial Force would protect the British Isles.

The War Office relied on four factories to make most of its weapons, ammunition and equipment at the start of the war:[8]

- The Royal Small Arms Factory at Enfield Lock made pistols, rifles and machine guns. The Small Arms Committee carried out its research work.
- The Royal Gun and Carriage Factory at the Royal Arsenal, Woolwich, made artillery pieces and limbers, while the Ordnance Board carried out its research work.
- The Gunpowder Factory at Waltham Abbey in north London made the propellants and high explosives.
- They were all supported by the Royal Laboratory and the Research Department at the Royal Arsenal. The Chief Inspector supervised inspections at Woolwich and testing at the Shoeburyness firing range on the Essex coast.

While the factories could cope with peacetime production, they soon struggled to meet the wartime demands of Britain's armed forces. They may have had over 200 years of experience but they also had cramped layouts with little room to add new buildings or expand. It was too expensive to move to a new site, so the managers struggled on with outdated working practices and old machinery.

The aircraft industry had a much better start. A balloon factory had been established in Farnborough, Hampshire in 1905.[9] It became the Army Aircraft Factory in 1911 and was renamed the Royal Aircraft Factory a year later. Airships were transferred to the Admiralty at the end of 1913 but Farnborough carried on making aircraft. The factory had a modern design, plenty of space and up to date working methods.

The Army Council relied on two departments to deal with the supply of weapons and ammunition:[10]

- Department of the Master General of the Ordnance bought items.
- Department of the Quartermaster General transported them.

The Deputy Director of Ordnance Stores dealt with the receipt, storage and issue of what were called warlike items before the war. It stored ammunition on the nearby Plumstead marshes or in Chislehurst caves.

The War Office also employed a handful of private contractors, which the Director of Army Contracts dealt with.[11] He was also responsible for checking new applicants who wanted to make munitions and competitive tendering was used to make sure the best price was found. He complied with the budget set by the Chancellor of the Exchequer and the Treasury in peacetime. However, war meant that short-term rolling contracts were issued to maintain production; contractors had to be ready to increase or decrease output at very short notice.

The Director of Army Contracts issued patterns, specifications and drawings, supervised modifications and dealt with failures to comply. The main contractors on the outbreak of war were:

- Armstrong Whitworth's of Newcastle-upon-Tyne.
- The Projectile and Engineering Company of London.
- Cammell Laird's of Sheffield and Birkenhead.
- Thomas Firth and Sons of Sheffield.
- Hadfields Limited of Sheffield.
- Vickers of Sheffield and Barrow-in-Furness.
- William Beardmore and Company of Glasgow.
- Watson, Laidlaw and Company of Glasgow.
- Kings Norton Metal Company of Birmingham.

Once they were working at full output, it was time to find new companies to meet the increasing demand.

The Reaction to War[12]

Within days of the outbreak of war, Britain was recruiting tens of thousands of volunteers in response to Field Marshal Lord Herbert Kitchener's call to arms in his role as Secretary of State for War. Men from all walks of life enlisted in the armed forces and they were signed up with no regard for their peacetime occupation. As the BEF fought hard along the River Aisne just one month later, Lord Kitchener correctly predicted that Britain's 'chief difficulty is one of material rather than personnel.'

By the time the War Office was looking for new contractors, in October 1914, the BEF was fighting for its life at Ypres in Flanders. Pre-war estimates of the amount of munitions it would require were woefully inadequate, leaving the army's stores low on ammunition. Meanwhile, the New Army's volunteers were training without weapons, equipment or even uniforms as industry struggled to equip them. Even so, unrestricted enlistment continued over the winter and 2 million men, many of them from the coal, shipbuilding and engineering industries, had joined up by the summer of 1915.

The Territorial Force divided its men into fourteen service divisions, which started to deploy overseas, while another fourteen home divisions would guard Britain. The volunteers had been formed into four New Armies, each with six divisions; they would follow as soon as they had completed their training. However, disasters on the Western Front demonstrated that the nation's munitions industry was struggling to supply even the Regular Army. It resulted in the Ministry of Munitions taking over the munitions industry in June 1915.

Lord Kitchener and Prime Minister Herbert Asquith returned from the Calais Conference with French Prime Minister René Viviani on 6 July 1915. They told the new Minister of Munitions David Lloyd George that Britain had promised to deploy seventy infantry divisions to France and Flanders. It meant the Ministry of Munitions had to find new sources of raw materials, ask companies what they could make and look at importing munitions.

A New Supply Policy[13]

A new Cabinet Committee on Munitions met to discuss the supply of weapons and munitions on 12 October 1914. It then spoke to the armament contractors, only to hear that they could not cope with the War Office's orders. While they were offered money to expand their factories, they were busy dealing with inexperienced subcontractors and overzealous inspectors.

Securing supplies of explosives were the Committee on Munitions' first concern. The High Explosives Committee was appointed to safeguard all sources of guncotton, cordite, picric acid (TNP), trinitrotoluene (TNT) and other explosives, so none left the country. An amendment to the Defence of the Realm Act, on 27 November 1914, meant that a company could be forced to make munitions or come under government control. Rainham Chemical Works in Essex, the only TNT purification plant in the country, was taken over the following day.

Shell production was falling behind by December 1914, so the Committee on Munitions again spoke to the main armament companies to ask what they needed to increase production. However, the discussions raised more problems than they solved. As the year came to an end, the Committee on Munitions discussed the high explosives situation, the escalating labour shortage and how to coordinate army and navy supplies. It appointed the American banking company, J.P. Morgan and Company, to buy raw materials, steel and munitions across the United States, on 1 January 1915.

During the early months of 1915, many contractors offered their services but none had any experience nor had any idea what to charge, so only nine were invited to make shells. On 15 March 1915, just after the BEF's first attack of the year at Neuve Chapelle, Lord Kitchener told the House of Lords that the country would struggle to make enough munitions, so American and Canadian companies were contracted.

Chapter 2

Trouble Ahead

A Diminishing Workforce[1]

An emerging problem was that key workers in engineering and mining were enlisting in large numbers. Part of the issue was that the state of war had caused many factories to shut down or go on to short time. It also resulted in lower demand for coal and steel, and a lowering of wages because both industries paid men by the ton of product produced. The amount of rail traffic also decreased as leisure travel came to a halt, so railway employees were joining up too. Men were joining up to be patriotic, for financial reasons or due to peer pressure as the public demanded that every man must do his duty. These are the numbers of men who enlisted during the first twelve months of the war:[2]

- Coal mining: 200,000 or 20 per cent
- Railways: 90,000 or 15 per cent
- Iron and steel: 47,800 or 18 per cent
- Other metals: 13,400 or 21 per cent
- Shipbuilding: 24,700 or 17 per cent
- Engineering: 90,700 or 20 per cent
- Electrical: 12,000 or 24 per cent
- Hardware: 15,400 or 21 per cent
- Motors: 27,400 or 24 per cent
- Rail carriages: 4,000 or 20 per cent

While it had been suggested that key workers could be given a ticket to show they were doing war work as early as September 1914, the Admiralty was the first to provide a badge for its workers in the Royal Dockyards at the end of the year. Meanwhile, collieries, steel works, shipyards and factories kept haemorrhaging skilled workers. One in five men who could have worked in an industry related to the munitions industry had enlisted by the time the Ministry of Munitions was formed in June 1915.

The problem was that the government thought there would be a surplus of labour when war broke out. It had also predicted that domestic production would fall and unemployment would rise. However, most of the men who responded to Lord Kitchener's call to arms came from the industrial areas. By November 1914, mass recruitment was disrupting all industries. The munitions factories alone reported they were 16,000 workers short and it was seriously affecting production.

Discussions at the Shell Conference on 21 December 1914 made it clear that the nation's labour had to be coordinated. The Army Council and the Board of Trade then told the Royal Arsenal and the armament firms that the Labour Exchanges were looking for skilled workers. The War Office had also been told to keep its recruitment officers away from munitions and food factories.

Meanwhile, the Board of Trade divided the nation's industries into List A, which made goods essential to the war effort and List B, which made non-essential goods. While it wanted List B factories to stop making items for the home market, they could continue to export items to keep the economy buoyant.

The Board of Trade also started asking the List B companies to hand over workers to the List A companies, only to discover that some were doing indirect work for the war effort. The rest of the companies were also asking if they could tender for munitions work rather than lose their key workers.

By March 1915, the Master General of the Ordnance's department had issued certificates to the factories on munitions work. Their employees were also issued with badges to show that they were doing war work. It did not take long because there were only the four government factories and four private armament firms; four aircraft factories were added later.

Relaxing Trade Union Restrictions[3]

Employers and employees had agreed to a truce of labour when war broke out. It was followed by agreements made on 25 August 1914 by the Trade Union Congress, General Federation of Trade Unions and the Labour Party to suspend ongoing strikes, lockouts and trade disputes. They also agreed not to start any new ones.

Prime Minister Asquith's government also wanted the trade unions to suspend their customs and practices, which limited workers to set jobs, to help increase production in munitions factories. He also asked them to use arbitration to settle any future differences.

The unions discussed Asquith's request over the winter, but they would only consider doing so if the Board of Trade assured them that their customs and practices would be resumed when the war ended. The Amalgamated Society of Engineers (ASE) also thought it was unfair that company owners would get higher profits because their members had relaxed their working rules. So, the government agreed to talk to the munitions companies about limiting them.

The unions asked for key men to be returned from the armed forces and for firms working on short time to transfer their key workers to munitions work. In return the unions agreed not to insist on who manned which machine, nor insist on any demarcations in the workplace. They would not object to companies employing non-union labour or female labour for munitions work. They would also refrain from using overtime bans to settle differences.

The Production Committee

The Industrial Council appointed in January 1915 soon learnt that the munitions factories faced shortages of labour, plant and materials. The main contractors were also struggling with their inexperienced subcontractors, while the winter weather had delayed work on factory extensions.

The Industrial Council wanted to stop workshops doing commercial work and transfer their workers to munitions work. It also proposed employing lesser skilled workers to do work normally done by apprentices, a practice referred to as dilution (as in dilution of skills). It would allow older men and women to replace younger men, who could then enlist in the armed forces.

The Industrial Council made a popular suggestion, which would let workers have Sundays and maybe Saturday afternoons off, so they could rest. It also made an unpopular suggestion, which involved reducing the opening hours of public houses.

The Industrial Council set up the Production Committee to monitor the progress being made on working agreements. It discovered that the enlistment of key workers was interfering in shipbuilding because their colleagues refused to work without them. While a suggestion was made to address what were called Broken Squads, employers did little to rectify the problem.

A second report said that skilled workers were worried that companies would employ cheap labour to meet urgent munitions orders. While they were prepared to work alongside semi-skilled and unskilled men and women, they wanted them to be paid the same for doing the same work. They also wanted assurances that the semi-skilled and unskilled workers would be dismissed first. In all these instances, workers would only tolerate these circumstances for the duration of the war.

The result was the Shells and Fuses Agreement, which was issued on 5 March 1915. The Production Committee went on to recommend removing demarcation in all government run factories, so anyone from a different union or non-union labour could be asked to carry out a task if they had appropriate skills. However, it was agreed that demarcation rules would only be suspended in factories when they were making munitions. The cooperation of the unions was assured during the Treasury Conference on 17 March 1915, which resulted in the Treasury Agreement.

Limiting Profits in Controlled Factories

Amendment No. 2 to the Defence of the Realm Act 1914 was given Royal Assent on 16 March 1915. One aspect of it was to limit the profits of controlled factories while on munitions work, so they did not benefit from the lifting of trade union customs and practices.[4] The Act also said that munitions work now included the making of weapons, ammunition, equipment and the machines required to make them. While it included coal mines and steel works, shipyards were exempted. The Act also granted the government the following powers to make sure that nothing interfered with production:

- Inspect or take over a factor.
- Direct, regulate or restrict work.
- Transfer workers between factories.
- Take over empty premises to make munitions.
- Make a contractor switch to munitions work or take over production.

The Production Committee's plan was to take control of forty armaments companies with an option to renew control every six months. It wanted to set their maximum profit at 10 to 12.5 per cent, while shareholders would continue to receive the same dividends as they had before the war.[5] However, the company owners rejected the idea of a central committee controlling their businesses because they wanted to continue running them. A suggestion by Lord Kitchener to pay workers a share of company profits was also overruled.

Two of the biggest armament companies, Armstrong Whitworth's and Vickers, eventually agreed to a profit pay out at 20 per cent above the average of the past two years. Any excess profits would be returned to the Exchequer or be deducted from their next bill. The remaining twelve munitions firms signed in May 1915, prompting the trade unions to relax their customs and practices.

The Treasury Agreement[6]

On 17 March 1915, Chancellor of the Exchequer David Lloyd George told trade union leaders that the amendment to the Defence of the Realm Act would suspend unions' customs and practices. There would also be a ban on strikes, while workers had access to arbitration in case of differences with their employer. In return, there would also be a ban on lockouts, while employers had access to arbitration in case of differences with their workforce. All sides agreed that the changes would only apply for the duration of the war.

Arthur Henderson, Chairman of the Workmen's Representatives, signed the Memorandum of Proposals on behalf of thirty-four unions on 19 March 1915. However, the representatives of the ASE refused to sign until its leaders had been assured that dilution would not undermine its members' jobs on 16 June 1915. The representatives of the Miners' Federation of Great Britain did not sign up either: they never would.

The Memorandum of Proposals became known as the Treasury Agreement and the National Advisory Committee on War Output was appointed to help carry out the measures. However, local committees soon discovered that the workforce was 'to a very considerable extent out of the control, of both the employers and their leaders.' For example, there would be over 225 new disputes between February and May 1915 because workers believed that company profits would continue to rise while the terms of the agreement would stop them asking for wage increases in the face of a rising cost of living. It would require further negotiations and the limitation on company profits to be made law under the Munitions of War Act, which received Royal Assent on 2 July 1915.

The Armaments Output Committee[7]

While the amended Defence of the Realm Act allowed the Ministry of Munitions to transfer workers between factories, owners pointed out that it was a false economy because subsistence allowances had to be paid. Instead, they asked for their own munitions contracts, so they could keep their workers busy in their own factories.

So, the Board of Trade decided to find out which companies were interested in war work. Those that were qualified to do so would be given a contract but workers would be taken from them if not. Sample shells and components were displayed in Labour Exchanges across the country at the beginning of March 1915; companies were invited to give their prices and confirm how many they could make and how quickly. A few companies offered to make complete shells, while others offered to make components for their local armaments company. Some companies even suggested other items they could make, while the rest offered their labour, satisfied that it was the best they could do for the war effort.

The Armaments Output Committee chaired by Lord Kitchener was set up at the end of March 1915 to look at making better use of the country's workforce. The North East Coast Armaments Committee successfully found 2,000 suitable men to work at Armstrong Whitworth's huge factory in Newcastle. However, other attempts across the country failed. For example, enquiries to over 400 firms across London only turned up a few dozen skilled men. Over 800 local authorities were also asked to draw up lists of spare workers but they only came up with the names of 5,000 skilled men and 25,000 unskilled men after 2 months of searching. Meanwhile, a survey of what labour and plant factories already had was stopped because it was taking too long to complete.

The project had, however, launched a successful idea when representatives from Sheffield's Vickers factory visited Leicester, looking to recruit workers.[8] Robert Dumas of Rugby's British Thomson-Houston Company told the Leicester Association of Engineering Employers how he had seen a group of French companies making components, so a central factory could assemble a shell. The idea 'set the local employers ablaze' and Major General Reginald H. Mahon of the Ordnance Board visited the town to meet the owners of over ninety local companies. An order was issued and a cooperative group was formed to arrange labour, plant and materials, as well as the finances to pay for them all. Representatives from other areas were soon visiting Leicester and they used the ideas to set up cooperative groups in their own towns.

The War Office continued to focus on the armament factories because they had financed and equipped them in the hope that they could make large quantities of shells. Over the months that followed, it became clear that most would default on their promises and the work of the cooperative groups would become important.

After only a week, the Armaments Output Committee was instructed to report to the new Munitions of War Committee, chaired by Lloyd George who had just stepped down as Chancellor of the Exchequer. He had been appointed to end the problem of Lord Kitchener directing the munitions industry. It meant the Secretary of State for War could focus on the armed services, while Lloyd George focused on the munitions industry.

In future, the Munitions of War Committee would decide policies, while the Armaments Output Committee would carry them out. However, after only six meetings, Sir Percy Girouard suggested separating the Armaments Output Committee from the War Office. This in turn led to the formation of the Ministry of Munitions with Lloyd George at its head.

Organising Industry[9]

The Armaments Output Committee initially divided the country into two types of areas: A and B. Factories with munitions contracts in place had a 20-mile exclusion radius put around them. No new contracts could be issued to companies in these A areas. Other districts were designated B areas; cooperative groups were allowed to bring together the efforts of the local factories in these areas.

Both Newcastle-upon-Tyne and Glasgow were designated A areas. The North East Coast Armaments Committee and the Glasgow and West of Scotland Armaments Committee started transferring labour between factories to help production. They were both looking at distributing work across their areas when they were disbanded in August 1915.

The problem in other A areas was that a 20-mile radius covered several complete cities and towns where lots of factories were asking for work.[10] For example, a 20-mile exclusion zone around Sheffield included Rotherham, Doncaster and Barnsley. Meanwhile, cooperative groups in the B areas were proving that they could make small calibre shells and components. George Booth summed up the situation when he said, 'the country will run itself extremely well, if it only gets the chance.' The small companies in the A areas wanted the same opportunity.

On 16 April 1915, the A and B areas system was dropped and the Armaments Output Committee divided the country into eleven regional area:

- Areas 1 and 2 covered the North of England.
- Areas 3 and 4 covered the Midlands.
- Area 5 covered Wales.
- Areas 6 and 7 covered the South of England.
- Areas 8 and 9 covered Scotland.
- Areas 10 and 11 covered Ireland.

Each area office acted as the Ministry of Munitions' regional headquarters.[11] They were run by a superintending engineer who was the chief technical advisor to the boards of management in its area. A desire for greater control resulted in sub-area offices being opened in other towns and cities. Staff were then able to keep a closer eye on the armament firms and National Factories, helping them to eliminate delays and problems.

Many towns and cities appointed munitions committees to find out what their local factories could make. Some sent a cadre of workers to an established armaments factory for training, so they could pass on their knowledge to their colleagues. They also helped factory owners acquire the necessary plant, tools and gauges.

The munitions committees also appointed boards of management, consisting of local businessmen who organised the factories into groups to make components for small calibre shells. Many set up a factory in an existing building, where surplus labour could assemble components. These National Shell Factories were financed with government money. The first one opened in Leeds in West Yorkshire in May 1915 and it became the working model for another fifty.

The committees disbanded once the National Shell Factories were open and the cooperative groups were up and running, leaving it to the twenty-five boards of management to run them. While it had taken just ten weeks to harness the country's output, it would take a similar length of time to iron out the teething troubles. Only then would the Ministry of Munitions be able to tell the War Office how many shells could be made.

A Shortage of Everything

By the spring of 1915, nearly 20 per cent of the workforce in key industries had enlisted in the armed forces. Even so, the War Office was still encouraging skilled men to join the army, so the Board of Trade told them to source unemployed men from the Labour Exchanges instead. Meanwhile, companies that had been given munitions contracts were anxious to get their key workers back, so they were told to compile lists of who they wanted. At the end of April 1915, Lord Kitchener ordered units still training across Britain to send skilled men back to their factories, where they would be allowed to work in uniform.

While active recruiting was being scaled down, men were still leaving their jobs, either for patriotic reasons or because they were fed up with being called cowards. So, the Ministry of Munitions' new Labour Department looked at how to balance the needs of the armed forces and industry. It made lists of key trades, which should not be recruited from, and tried to stop companies poaching key workers from their rivals.

An emerging problem caused by too much focus on labour was a shortage of tools and machines.[12] Tools carried out the drilling, grinding, cutting and shearing of the basic steel shapes. They are made from a specialist steel, known as high-speed steel, which was harder and tougher than carbon steel. Plans to make new machine tools involved the Ministry of Munitions' Raw Materials Department buying high grade iron ore from Sweden, rather than individual foundries sourcing it. Foundries were then contracted to make the high-speed steel, while factories were organised to make the tools.

Machines provide the power for the tools and hold the steel shape in place during the operation. The Ministry of Munitions' Machine Tool Department checked that companies had enough of the right type of machines before they awarded a contract. The area office drew up lists of machines in its area and a central clearing house transferred idle ones to where they were needed. It also distributed spare tools and stopped any machines or tools being exported.

PART II

Organising Industry

Chapter 3

The Administration

The Minister of Munitions' Responsibilities[1]

Parliament introduced the Defence of the Realm Act 1914 and the Munitions of War Act 1915 to facilitate the making of large quantities of munitions. However, it was down to the Minister of Munitions to work out the details, while his departments issued the regulations. Lloyd George visited the munitions areas between 28 May and 15 June 1915. He explained how the Defence of the Realm Act could improve production and how union customs and practices were not applicable in wartime. He also told them how France made munitions for its armed forces. Eventually, the Ministry of Munitions would run all aspects of industry and working life; it also dealt with some aspects of life outside of the factories.

The Minister of Munitions had the powers to promote anything that increased munitions supply or suppress anything that could hinder it. The Ministry could also force companies to hand over details of their inventions or processes; it banned anyone from publishing information or holding exhibitions relating to munitions. It could fine a company for supplying substandard steel, while sabotage was a serious offence.

The Ministry of Munitions could ask the Secretary of State or the Office of Works to buy or lease the land it needed and they had the power to force owners to hand it over. It could also control what factories were built and in what order. The Ministry could control what a factory made through permits and licenses. It eventually took control of all raw materials, components and machinery related to munitions, even setting prices to stop speculation. It later took control of transport, repair facilities and even power sources.

The Munitions of War Act controlled wages, working hours and employment terms and conditions. The Ministry of Munitions issued war badges to prove who was on essential work and it could remove troublesome workers from a factory. It could also control the movement of workers, an unpopular responsibility that was abolished in October 1917.

The Ministry of Munitions was responsible for implementing safety rules and conducting investigations into industrial accidents. While it improved fire protection and introduced several health and safety schemes, it also had to insure against damage caused to third party buildings after December 1916.

The Ministry of Munitions even took control of refreshments, entertainment and recreation rooms in the larger factories. However, it also banned the sale of alcohol and entertainment events that might interfere with production. Eventually, it regulated workers' housing through the Billeting of Civilians Act 1917 and appointed the Central Billeting Board to deal with tenancy issues.

Finally, when the end of the war was in sight, the Ministry of Munitions planned how to bring the munitions industry to an end, stopping production the moment the Armistice was declared. It paid for surplus materials and came to agreements over the buildings and plants. It also gave companies assistance as they switched back to making domestic items and slowly sold off stocks to limit price rises. Furthermore, it sold off the large amount of machinery and property it had acquired.

The Ministry of Munitions' Organisation[2]

The Ministry of Munitions outlined the organisation of departments, branches and sections it was going to use in June 1915, when it had fewer than 700 staff. While it started out with a simple structure, the increase in demand for labour, plant and materials required it to expand into one of the largest employers in the country with 107,000 staff by the end of the war. It employed 70,000 inspection staff and 300,000 workers in over 200 National Factories. It also had many working with factories in the United States and Canada, as well as offices dealing with imports from Switzerland and exports to France, Russia and Italy.

What follows is a brief explanation of the organisation that Winston Churchill formed in the summer of 1917. He streamlined what had become a complicated arrangement by bringing together departments into groups with similar objectives to discuss problems.

The Secretariat

The Secretariat dealt with the Ministry of Munitions' administration and answered questions from Parliament. It looked at priorities, statistics and programming when demand started to outstrip supply during 1916 and 1917. During the final months of the war, it looked at demobilisation and reconstruction. It also employed staff to make a historical record of the Ministry of Munitions' work.

Group F

Group F covered the finance matters of the departments in the other groups. It looked at the costs of acquiring land and building factories. It also monitored what was being spent on materials, labour, machinery, stores and salvage.

Group L

Group L dealt with all aspects of labour. It issued and administered regulations with the help of a team of advisors. It also had the difficult task of balancing the labour supply between the factories and the armed services.

Group M

Group M organised the extraction and importation of non-ferrous materials, as well as the development of new mineral resources and rolling mills. The group also had to look at transport on railways, roads, canals and coastal shipping.

Group S

Group S dealt with all aspects of making iron and steel for munitions and shipping. It also produced bricks and steel for building, as well as supervising the construction of new factories and extensions.

Group D

Group D supervised the design and inspection of the full array of weapons, ammunition, transport, tanks and aircraft.

Group O

Group O covered all aspects of making ordnance, which included working with the area offices. It dealt with the Royal Ordnance Factories and the factories making artillery pieces and shells, as well as those that filled shells. It organised the manufacture of rifles, machine guns and small arms ammunition. It also had to deal with the supply of machines, tools, gauges and timber.

Group X

Group X covered the manufacture of explosives and chemicals, as well as the filling of gas cylinders and shells. The acquisition and distribution of mineral oils was another of its responsibilities.

Group W

Group W dealt with mechanical warfare, which included tanks, lorries and traction engines. It organised trench warfare weapons, which included grenades and mortars. It also had to deal with inventions and the power supply to factories.

Group A

Group A covered everything related to air warfare. It had branches that looked at aircraft supply, technical issues and inspections. It also dealt with the supply of ball bearings and the assembling of aircraft parts sent from the United States.

The Munitions of War Act 1915[3]

The government and the Ministry of Munitions held private discussions with the unions throughout May and June 1915, resulting in a series of laws designed to increase the production of munitions in wartime. The plan was to legalise the suggestions made by the Treasury Agreement to organise labour, stop restrictive union practices and avoid disputes through arbitration. They were given full support by all sides in Parliament and given Royal Assent on 2 July 1915 under the title, the Munitions of War Act 1915. The key points are given below:

Clause 1

The Board of Trade would use arbitration to settle disagreements under Clause 1 but it had to act promptly.

Clauses 2 and 16

These clauses explained that it was an offence for a company to lock its workers out of their factory to make them accept their terms. The workforce was not allowed to use strike action to force their employer to accept their terms either.

Clauses 4 and 5

Restrictive union customs and practices were suspended, while company profits were limited under Clauses 4 and 5. However, the Ministry of Munitions could take control of a factory if actions by either the management or the workforce were seen to be restricting production.

Clause 6

Those who signed up to be a munitions volunteer agreed to work at any controlled establishment under Clause 6.

Clause 7

This stopped workers changing jobs to get better wages without permission. Factories were also banned from poaching workers from other factories.

Clause 9

Clause 9 allowed the Ministry of Munitions to transfer workers and plant between factories to improve output.

Clause 10

Clause 10 gave the Minister of Munitions the power to ask an employer for any information about their factory.

Clauses 11 and 13

These clauses detailed the penalties for making false statements or giving false information. It also outlined the penalties a worker faced for incorrectly using a war service badge or work certificate.

Clause 14

Finally, Clause 14 explained how munitions tribunals would deal with breaches of the Act.

Chapter 4

The Ministers

The Right Honourable David Lloyd George MP
(25 May 1915 to 9 July 1916)[1]

David Lloyd George had been Chancellor of the Exchequer for over six years when war broke out. He removed the responsibility for financial restrictions from the War Office, following a call for volunteers for the armed services from Secretary of State for War, Field Marshal Herbert Kitchener, so that British industry could expand to arm them.

Lloyd George and First Lord of the Admiralty Winston Churchill then spoke to contractors to find out what they could make, while the Board of Trade considered the labour situation. They also visited France to see what could be learnt from their factories and looked at placing orders with the United States and Canada.

The BEF was using far more ammunition than anticipated and the amount increased with the onset of trench warfare in September 1914. The factories were already finding it difficult to arm the Regular Army, while the Territorial Force and the New Armies were struggling to train due to shortages of everything.

On 28 February 1915, Lloyd George announced that the country was fighting an engineers' war and later said that the production of munitions would be 'a matter of life or death'. Prime Minister Herbert Asquith appointed Lloyd George as Chairman of the new Munitions of War Committee on 8 April 1915, so he could choose experienced businessmen or 'push and go' men to start organising the nation's engineering companies. His staff worked with the Armaments Output Committee to source labour, only to learn that thousands of skilled workers had already enlisted. Another of Lloyd George's decisions was rather less popular: he closed public houses near the munitions factories and reduced the opening hours of the rest.

Meanwhile, Commander-in-Chief of the BEF Field Marshal Sir John French was calling for 'an almost unlimited supply of ammunition' in March 1915. A recent offensive at Neuve Chapelle had severely depleted the BEF's ammunition supplies after just three days. A month later, a damning article by Lieutenant Colonel Charles à Court Repington in *The Times* newspaper reported on the disastrous attack near Aubers Ridge on 9 May 1915:

we had not sufficient high explosive to level the enemy's parapets to the ground, after the French practice. The infantry did splendidly, but the conditions were too hard. The want of an unlimited supply of high explosive was a fatal bar to our success.

The Ministry of Munitions was formed a week later and it received Royal Assent on 9 June 1915. Lloyd George was appointed as Minister of Munitions and he was told 'to ensure such supply of munitions for the present war as may be required by the Army Council or the Admiralty.' He immediately toured engineering districts, instructed businessmen to organise local resources and asked workers to sacrifice their individual liberties, the same as the men who had enlisted.

Lloyd George was supported by three secretaries:

- General Secretary, responsible for legislation, labour regulations and legal questions.
- Parliamentary Secretary, responsible for finance, explosives and trench warfare.
- Military Secretary, liaised with the War Office's requirements and oversaw the making of munitions and the release of skilled men from the armed services.

Lloyd George agreed to cooperate over materials, munitions and technology, when he met the French minister of munitions, Albert Thomas, in Boulogne in June 1915. He then announced,

ultimate victory or defeat in this war depends upon the supply of munitions which the rival countries can produce and with which they can equip their armies in the field. That is the cardinal [basic] fact of the military situation.

The Munitions of War Act banned workers from striking and managers from locking their workforce out. Trade unions suspended their restrictive customs and practices in the factories, while owners had their profits limited. The Ministry of Munitions aimed to meet the armed forces' demands, while Lord Kitchener promised the French that the BEF would soon be armed with more heavy artillery and far more shells.

Lloyd George may have appointed experienced businessmen with sound business principals but they also had strong personalities. Unfortunately, he rarely defined their duties, which led to arguments, work being duplicated and a chaotic expansion of the munitions industry. While the Central Advisory Committee met on 23 July 1915, it never met again because it was decided that it would slow down production. Lloyd George held a few meetings at the end of the year but they soon stopped because little was sorted out.

Lloyd George's staff were given responsibility for munitions expenditure in October 1915 and while they were concerned that Britain was spending too much on American munitions, it continued to help France, Russia and Italy. It was just one of a mountain of problems that the Ministry of Munitions had to deal with. There were material shortages, new factory owners needed help and inexperienced inspectors required guidance. It dealt with modifications to existing munitions and found labour, plants and materials for new ones. It had to contend with problems with American and Canadian imports. Finally, it had to overcome resistance to dilution, the employment of unskilled men and women. Nevertheless, it did eventually find complete or partial solutions to all these problems.

The Right Honourable Edwin Montagu MP
(9 July 1916 to 10 December 1916)[2]

Lloyd George was appointed the Secretary of State for War, following the death of Lord Kitchener at sea on 5 June 1916. Financial Secretary to the Treasury Edwin Montagu replaced him on 12 July 1916. The Somme campaign had just started in France and the non-stop demand for munitions would be a constant challenge for him.

Controls were implemented over raw materials and metals, while the railways had to be organised to move large amounts of materials and munitions. The Ministry of Munitions faced a constant struggle to find labour, while the BEF demanded replacements for the huge losses on the Somme. Factories to make tanks and aircraft also had to be found.

Overall, the Ministry of Munitions oversaw continuous growth and improved quality in all areas. However, financial pressures were starting to show after the unlimited expenditure of the early days. Investigations soon discovered £39 million of unpaid bills that needed to be recovered, while new financing and auditing procedures were implemented to tighten up spending.

Montagu started two initiatives that improved communications in October 1916. The first was to meet his department heads every fortnight to discuss new problems and find solutions. He also appointed the Advisory Committee, which discussed questions he or the parliamentary secretaries wanted answers to, with the relevant department heads.

Montagu was appointed Vice Chairman of the Committee of the Cabinet on Reconstruction when Lloyd George replaced Herbert Asquith as Prime Minister on 9 December 1916. He had continued Lloyd George's good work and shell production was finally meeting the BEF's requirements. The National Shell Factories were starting to work economically, which helped to moderate competition between the private factories, lower prices and reduce the reliance on imports.

The Right Honourable Dr Christopher Addison MP
(10 December 1916 to July 1917)[3]

Montagu was replaced by Christopher Addison who had been the Parliamentary Secretary to the Ministry of Munitions since it formed. Labour problems continued throughout 1917, so Neville Chamberlain was appointed as Director General of National Service to find more men for the army without disrupting the factories. The Trade Card Scheme was introduced to stop skilled men being called up. However, it was dropped in May 1917 because it did not protect key non-union workers. A Schedule of Protected Occupations was drawn up instead but the German submarine campaign meant that shipyard workers were exempt, putting the burden on the munitions factories.

Addison faced many problems because the country was short of raw materials, steel, munitions and food due to the large numbers of ships being sunk. It meant cutbacks had to be made, while the most had to be made of home supplies and recycling. He also had to deal with several large stoppages, caused by the rising cost of living, dilution and enlistment. In each case rapid action and a conciliatory approach was required to stop them spreading.

Important changes also took place outside Britain. The BEF's burden on the Western Front increased, after the French army suffered a serious setback in April 1917. The United States entered the war the same month and while it promised to send troops to Europe, it also restricted imports to Britain.

The Ministry of Munitions had grown so large that Addison delegated many decisions to parliamentary secretaries. Even so, he continued to meet his department heads every two weeks. Addison left the Ministry of Munitions to take charge of the Ministry of Reconstruction in July 1917 to look at issues the nation would have to face once the war was over.

The Right Honourable Winston Churchill MP
(17 July 1917 to 10 January 1919)[4]

Winston Churchill was the First Lord of the Admiralty at the outbreak of the war. He was appointed as Chancellor of the Duchy of Lancaster when Prime Minister Herbert Asquith formed a coalition government in May 1915. However, many held him personally responsible for the failure to capture the Gallipoli peninsula and clear the Dardanelles Strait in Turkey, so he resigned in November 1915 and went on active service in France and Flanders. After spending several months commanding an infantry battalion on the Western Front, he was given permission to return to Parliament in May 1916.

Churchill was appointed as Minister of Munitions on 17 July 1917 when the Allied situation was in dire straits. The BEF was about to launch the Third Ypres offensive on the Western Front, while the Russian army was in a state of collapse, having been driven back 150 miles following its disastrous Kerensky offensive in Austria-Hungary. Churchill took over seventy departments who were arguing over the limited amounts of labour and materials. It was proving impossible to prioritise their activities, so Churchill organised them into eleven groups with similar objectives.

The head of each group coordinated the activities of the departments under their control, while civil servants made sure they followed the correct procedures. Both the Munitions Council and the group heads appointed committees to deal with specific issues and the number of meetings reduced as problems were ironed out.

Churchill immediately stopped the Admiralty making priority claims on labour and material, while the War Priorities Committee rationed supplies. Labour departments from the Admiralty and the Ministry of Munitions were transferred to the Ministry of National Service in November 1917, to coordinate their efforts. The Joint Priority Board eventually started dealing with all government departments in October 1918.

Britain had always made munitions for its Allies and while the Russians dropped out of the war, the submarine campaign meant there were shortages of everything in 1917. Everyone was short of food, so imported munitions had to be reduced. Italy also needed munitions because the Germans had recently captured its coal producing areas.

The Russian Revolution meant that Germany had transferred large numbers of troops to the Western Front over the winter of 1917-18. Its offensives in the spring of 1918 resulted in the Inter-Allied Munitions Council being formed on 4 June to share information, raw materials, steel and transport. However, it only met three times and nothing went beyond the planning stage.

Churchill also had to deal with the potential for unofficial stoppages because workers were tired of the monotony of work and unsettled by conscription. Rather than deal with individual wages demands, Churchill awarded bonuses across the board over the winter of 1917-18 and while they cost millions of pounds, they also averted stoppages.

By the summer of 1918, Churchill told the press that skilled men 'hurried from place to place to bathe their hands in the golden fountain', as factories increased their wages to entice workers to join them. He also threatened conscription with the phrase, 'work or fight', following a stoppage in Coventry in July 1918.

One of Churchill's main problems was manpower. It was difficult to provide enough men for the army, while keeping sufficient men in industry to arm it. Repeated efforts had been made to comb unskilled men out of industry but a 'clean cut' of all 19 and 20 year olds had to be made after the spring 1918 offensives. It resulted in a coal shortage, after 75,000 miners were called up.

Despite the shortages, munitions production reached its peak during Churchill's time as Minister of Munitions. New furnaces and recycling had increased steel production, manufacturing issues had been ironed out and everyone had enough experience to deal with problems. Female workers had been trained, while dilution had been implemented as far as it could.

On 1 November 1918, Churchill said 'the foundation of the munitions budget is tonnage; the ground floor is steel; and the limiting factor in the construction is labour.' Just ten days later, the Armistice came into effect.

Chapter 5

Financing the Munitions Industry

Uncontrolled Spending, 1914 to 1916

During peacetime, Parliament agreed a military budget for the Treasury to manage.[1] The War Office's financial officers then monitored expenditure, while the Financial Secretary checked the accounts. When Britain went to war, it was impossible to estimate how much money the War Office would need, so the House of Commons immediately issued a Vote of Credit for £100 million (£5.9 billion today), expecting to grant more when it was required.

The Treasury wanted estimates of costs to support requests for further Votes of Credit. However, the War Office was soon placing contracts without them, believing that Chancellor of the Exchequer David Lloyd George wanted to get munitions as quickly as possible.[2]

The War Office had a finance member on the Army Council, a contracts director and an assistant financial secretary. The buying process involved three departments:

- Supply described the goods and advised on quantities.
- Contracts fixed the prices and terms.
- Finance checked estimates, sanctioned contracts and asked for Treasury approval.

Between them, they balanced the armed forces' demands according to what industry could make or what could be imported, while keeping the costs down.

The Treasury opened an account called Munitions Supply with £5 million credit (£300 million today) to run alongside a deposit account, which the supply departments drew cash from. However, expenditure was soon charged to a Munitions Vote, which had to be approved by the Treasury and Parliament.

General Headquarters (GHQ) told the War Office what it required. Contracts were arranged to fulfil the requests, as best they could, often without setting prices or quantities. While additional financial checks would have saved money, they would also have required negotiations, which would have delayed production. The objective was to meet the armed forces' demands and hope that the Ministry of Munitions' financial officers were doing their best to minimise prices.

The Ministry of Munitions took over the organisation of munitions production in June 1915. It started with supply departments for explosives, munitions and trench warfare. Goods were divided into List A items, which the contracts department could easily order. List B items were still being sourced by the supply departments and they were transferred to List A when suppliers were found.

The War Office ran the finances until it handed them over to the Ministry of Munitions' Finance Department in October 1915. Financial Secretary Hardman Lever was a chartered accountant who insisted on an account being submitted for every factory making munitions. He also stopped grants, while the Treasury had to approve any loan over £10,000; the maximum a company could borrow was £50,000.

The revised munitions kept Hardman's staff busy setting up contracts and establishing accounting systems. So busy, in fact, that the accountancy side of the Finance Department was neglected.

Movements of materials or goods were also being made without paperwork, so they were not recorded until they had been paid for. Eventually, the balance of outstanding advances topped £50 million (£2.9 billion today) and in one case, 250,000 tons of imported steel were acquired without invoices. It all meant that Chancellor The Right Honourable Reginald McKenna MP had little idea how much building the National Factories or making the munitions for the 1916 Somme campaign would cost, leaving Herbert Asquith's coalition Cabinet in the dark about the Ministry of Munitions' finances.

Taking Control of Finances, 1917 to 1918[3]

David Lloyd George was appointed Prime Minister in December 1916 and he immediately asked his Chancellor Bonar Law MP to get a grip on the Ministry of Munitions' finances. Its Finance Department had expanded to 1,200 staff when John Mann took over and his Financial Advisory Committee recommended closer cooperation between the Finance, Contracts, Supply and Stores departments. He also set up an Internal Audit Section, which chased up invoices relating to over 20,000 contracts. The auditors also discovered that companies were stockpiling raw materials and components, so checks on deliveries, production and wastage had to be introduced.[4]

Mann appointed a Munitions Works Board to supervise all construction associated with munitions in January 1917. The need for more ships due to the German submarine campaign limited the amount of steel available to build factories, so the Board was added to the Steel Group in March 1918 to make sure it built factories in the right order.

Mann also wanted to know what property assets the Ministry owned, so he could report their value to the Treasury. A Special Committee for Land and Buildings eventually discovered that it owned 210 National Factories, 122 Controlled Factories and 142 stores and bond areas. Mann also started an inventory of machinery, lifting equipment, vehicles and railway sidings but it was still being compiled when the Armistice was declared.

The Treasury asked Mann for a full cost breakdown of the Ministry of Munitions' assets in October 1917 and it took six months to calculate.[5] Bonar Law was astonished to learn that it had a working capital of £538 million, owned buildings and plant worth £80 million and had £23 million of materials in stock. (The total is equivalent to £18.63 billion today.)

After allowing the War Office and the Ministry of Munitions to spend three quarters of the national budget for three years, Churchill decided more spending control was required when he was appointed Minister of Munitions in July 1917 by appointing a Select Committee of National Expenditure. It soon concluded that spending had gone unchecked since the beginning of the war. For example, it discovered that the cost of the explosive factories had risen from £2.5 million (£148 million today) to over £17.5 million (£1 billion today). Many basic questions soon started saving large amounts of money. For example, one into War Office demands resulted in 2.4 million fewer rifles and 170 million fewer bullets, saving £29 million (£842 million today).

Churchill also streamlined how the Ministry of Munitions ran, by grouping the seventy departments according to their type of work and bringing them under a new Munitions Council.[6] Between them, they tightened up how the Accounts Department was run, taking better control of the £620 million (£18 billion today) annual budget and £200 million (£5.8 billion today) working capital it spent.

A plan to check up on company profits was cancelled in case it upset the managers and interfered with production. Instead, the Gun and Shell Department was the first to take control of its own accounts; every department started accounting for its raw materials at the beginning of 1918. Each department was then allowed to reduce the number of outstanding bills and advice notes they had. Even so, it would take until the end of the war to catch up with the financial mess created during the chaotic early months.

Churchill also appointed 500 staff to clear up the outstanding paperwork and they discovered a faulty financial system that misled Parliament over spending to the tune of £150 million (£8.8 billion today). So, a double accounting entry system was introduced to balance the books correctly. The Finance Department had grown to 3,500 staff by now and many of them spent the final years of the war chasing up money dating back to the early days of the war. While the exercise took until April 1919 to complete, it eventually recovered £39 million (£2.3 billion today).

The Ministry of Munitions had loaned over £120 million (£7.1 billion today) in cash, including £44 million (£2.6 billion) to American companies by the start of 1918. It had also advanced £60 million (£3.5 billion) in materials, including £10 million (£590 million) to French and Italian companies. The number of outstanding bills and incoming bills left the Internal Audit Section overwhelmed.

While the Treasury held the Ministry of Munitions responsible for such a massive amount of expenditure, it could not be blamed. The War Department had put production before spending to make sure the armed forces were equipped to fight a war. The Ministry had then hit the ground running, setting in motion an expensive construction programme with little experience and with no limit on its budget. Neither Bonar Law, nor his predecessors, Reginald McKenna and David Lloyd George, dared to restrict spending and interfere with production.

Awarding the Contracts[7]

The Ministry of Munitions' Contracts Department was divided in the same way as the Supply Department and their sections aimed to pay contractors, cost plus profit. However, several sections were often looking for the same raw material, resulting in overlapping work, high prices and waste. The Ministry had the power to investigate a company's books or to set the maximum price for goods to get the best value for money. It could also direct what work a factory did, requisition goods to help it maintain production or even take possession of the premises.

The Ministry of Munitions used several types of contracts, according to what was being made and the circumstances.[8] The War Office was desperate for factories to start making munitions during the early months of the war. Many companies refused to accept loans to build extensions or buy plant but they would accept an advance, either getting money up front or when they produced an invoice. They were called Assisted Contracts and they helped kickstart the munitions industry. The Ministry also loaned money to power companies, so they could supply the enormous amounts of electricity required by factories.

The Munitions of War Act reduced taxes, so companies could invest in production. It also introduced a munitions levy under which a company could invest its own money or the Ministry's money to extend their factory. The government bought the property rights when the building was complete and the company could either buy it back or insure it and keep it in good order. The expense was then written down out of their profits.

Cost Plus Percentage Contracts

Cost Plus Percentage Contracts were used when there were considerable unknowns. For example, when a factory's management had no experience of making munitions, or when building had to start before the construction plans were complete.

Provisional Price Contracts

These were issued when work had to be completed urgently to compensate for high material costs, inefficient working and overtime costs.

Cooperative Contracts

These contracts shared the profit and loss, when an agreement on price could not be made.

Cost Plus Bonus Contracts

These were used for large or unusual items that were difficult to price and the contractor was paid the cost and a percentage of the saving below the maximum price.

Fixed Price Contracts

Most were Fixed Price Contracts that were based on estimated or actual costs. The exception to the above styles of contract was shipbuilding, when the cost plus a fixed amount of profit per unit made was paid.

Setting the Prices[9]

The War Office offered high prices during the early months of the war to encourage companies to take on munitions work. They had little experience of making the components, they had no idea what the market prices for materials would be and they might struggle to get the labour and plant to meet the delivery dates. All the War Office wanted was to receive the munitions on time.

Profits were reduced in March 1915, under an amendment to the Defence of the Realm Act. The Ministry was then given the powers to ask experts for advice, check a contractor's books, or look at how a company administered subcontracts.

Enough financial and production evidence had been supplied to the Ministry of Munitions by the National Factories by February 1916, so new contracts with lower rates were issued.[10] Some owners complained that it would leave their factories running at a loss because they had set up their factories in the patriotic rush in the early months of the war, leaving them working inefficiently. So, the Ministry set three prices, according to how their workshops were organised, so as not to prejudice factories with layouts which were not suited to the work;

- Well laid out factories were paid a little less.
- Poorly laid out factories were paid a little more.
- The Ministry also used a sliding scale of prices with smaller factories being paid more to cover their higher overheads.

All the companies refused to tell the Ministry of Munitions their costs, while Armstrong Whitworth's refused to discuss a reduction in price. The established firms said they deserved higher rates on the grounds that they produced high quality shells on time. While they asked for profit rates ranging from 10 to 20 per cent, they all wanted local price anomalies, such as district wage rates to be considered. Prices were finalised at 10 per cent above cost in December 1916, despite many complaints. Negotiations with the American and Canadian companies also reduced their prices by 15 per cent. Experienced companies were paid 80 per cent on delivery to improve their cash flow as compensation.

Eventually, the Ministry of Munitions was given powers to investigate accounts and while there were complaints about the intrusion, companies always cooperated. A further price reduction was introduced in June 1917 in response to the German submarine campaign. Even more money was saved when the Select Committee on National Expenditure recommended paying contractors a fixed 10 per cent profit on their costs in October 1917. It was estimated that the price revisions saved £43 million (£2.5 billion today) by the end of the war.

Adjusting the Prices[11]

Prices rose and fell according to market conditions in peacetime. However, war made prices unpredictable. Early claims against price increases were paid without question, so as not to put contractors out of business. The Treasury always covered wage rises after the Treasury Agreement was made in March 1915 because it had sanctioned them. However, it always investigated rises in material costs to make sure the company was paying the best price. It also covered costs associated with problems outside the factory's control, such as faulty materials, poor components, design changes or modifications. As time passed, contracts included cost variations clauses, which covered price rises caused by government action.

Many factors pushed up costs and contractors were anxious to make sure their prices rose at the same rate. Competition for raw materials and the rising cost of imports, pushed up prices. By the autumn of 1915, companies were made to promise they would buy the cheapest materials they could find and their prices were adjusted accordingly. However, the Ministry eventually had to take control of the production, the importing and the distribution of all materials, to get the best prices. In March 1916, the Departmental Contracts Committee recommended renewing all pre-war contracts and checking post-war ones to eliminate any price anomalies.

The rising cost of living was the workers' biggest concern because food prices alone had risen 33 per cent by July 1915, 60 per cent by July 1916 and 100 per cent by July 1917. Rental costs also increased, as demand for accommodation increased. Companies had to pay district wage rates after March 1916 and they could not change them without the Ministry of Munitions' permission. The Ministry started matching wage rises with a similar price rise on shell contracts after November 1916 and it extended the idea to all its contracts in July 1917.

The Ministry simplified the scheme by increasing prices to match wage rises because it was far easier to implement across the 50,000 contracts a year it was issuing. Finally, a more sophisticated, yet more accurate way of increasing prices was used after February

1918. Munitions were classified into twelve groups and the wages element of the price of each one was decided. The price rise was the wages element multiplied by the percentage wage rise.

For example, there was a wage rise of 10 per cent when the wage element equalled 50 per cent. So, the price increase was 10 per cent multiplied by 50 per cent resulting in a 5 per cent price rise.

The same principal was about to be implemented for raw materials, when the war ended.

The Efficiency Branch

The Ministry of Munitions' Efficiency Branch watched for unexpected high costs and would send an engineer to the factory to investigate them and recommend how to reduce them. The Efficiency Branch was eventually able to compare how the National Projectile Factories were doing with the national average to obtain their 'efficiency figure'. Problems would either be identified as 'excusable' or 'reprehensible' and they would be dealt with accordingly. It was difficult to compare between the National Shell Factories because they had been set up in existing buildings, giving each one their own challenges.

Most factories had adopted modern production methods by 1917, so the Efficiency Branch only sent an engineer if the management ignored their suggestions. They were given a second chance to remedy the problems but the Ministry had the power to take over the factory if they refused or failed to.

Limiting Profits

Companies had been subjected to a munitions levy that limited their profits in exchange for the trade unions relaxing their customs and practices, under the Munitions of War Act. The levy was set as the average of the profit made during the two years before the war, with 20 per cent added to compensate for the urgency of the munitions work. Any excess profit was paid to the Exchequer.

It soon became clear that the levy removed the incentive for companies to work harder, because they did not generate any extra profit if they improved their output. So, a 60 per cent duty was charged on all profits instead, starting in the summer of 1916. Controlled establishments paid the higher of the two duties. The amount was later raised to 80 per cent but payments could be paid in instalments to help cash flow. Alternatively, a company could take an advance to enable them to continue making munitions.

Chapter 6

Commercial Control

Taking Control of Supplies[1]

The government was reluctant to take control of materials at the beginning of the war, preferring the armaments companies to source them. However, the War Office and later the Ministry of Munitions, could use Section 115 of the Army (Supply of Food, Forage and Stores) Act 1914 and Regulation 7 of the Defence of the Realm Act to requisition anything it needed.

The War Office only placed short term contracts for small amounts during the first nine months of the war but the Ministry placed extended contracts to secure prices. In doing so, it was able to build up reserves of materials, avoiding shortages that upset the supply chain. Initially, each department secured enough for the factories they were working with, which resulted in arguments. So, the largest user was told to buy enough materials for all the departments.

The Ministry of Munitions had taken control of explosives, aluminium and optical munitions by the end of 1915. It introduced licenses, fixed prices, banned speculation and reduced waste to get the best use out of the nation's resources. It would eventually end up controlling the supply and distribution of all raw materials. As the Somme campaign intensified in the summer of 1916, it also took control of steel and non-ferrous metals, building materials and machine tools. By distributing them according to priorities, it forced companies to use materials economically, resulting in financial savings.

As the war stretched from months into years, prices of everything rose, so the Ministry centralised buying to limit competition between departments and between private contractors.[2] It also stopped price rises and speculative buying. As soon as the National Factories started working at full speed, the Ministry knew what their maximum output was, so it could fix prices and promote production at a reasonable cost. However, the rising cost of imports and transport meant that the government had to subsidise the price of some items, such as steel. More control was required when the German submarine campaign created shortages in 1917 and the Ministry was controlling virtually all goods by the end of the war.

Taking Control of Distribution[3]

The Ministry had set up the Priority Branch in August 1915, to decide what each factory needed and it classified each one according to the urgency of the goods they were making. Supply departments issued manufacturing permits, while the Priority Advisory Committee issued priority certificates:

- Class A covered direct war work.
- Class B covered indirect war work.
- Class C included all other work.

Companies were penalised under Circular L.33 if they did not give munitions top priority.

Initially, the Priority Branch (later the Priority Department) could only make estimates, which sometimes left factories short of materials. The Admiralty and the Ministry of Munitions agreed to coordinate their buying in 1916, regularly prioritising what should be made first. It gave the Ministry the power to tell companies what to make, rather than their managers deciding.

While experience simplified decisions, the Admiralty and the Army Council often argued over what was more important. Shortages of raw materials and steel caused by the German submarine campaign resulted in having to decide what was made first, with shipping, aircraft and tanks being given the highest priority at different times. However, food shortages were more important than munitions by the summer of 1917, so the Urgent Supplies Board was appointed to decide what would be imported.

Central purchasing had been discussed in May 1916 when there was a copper shortage.[4] However, the Joint Committee of Finance and Contracts had to deal with many more shortages during the German submarine campaign in the first half of 1917. The Select Committee on National Expenditure insisted on coordinated buying to get better value for money, while the War Cabinet Committee on Priorities decided where money would be spent.

The Mineral Resources Development Department[5] was set up in March 1917 to look at how to exploit sources of raw materials at home. It looked at digging iron ore at Hodbarrow on the Cumberland (now Cumbrian) coast and at Eskdale in Lancashire. Four companies refused to reopen their mines because they did not want to pay the Excess Profits' Duty, so the Ministry of Munitions bought them out. Pyrites were also mined in Flint, coprolites (phosphate of lime) in Cambridgeshire, wolfram and tin in Cornwall, and coal in the north of Ireland. The Ministry gave loans to sixteen other mining companies but they failed to extract much tin, lead, zinc, or wolfram.

Eventually, direct war work had to be divided into classes A1, A2, A3 and A4, with A1 having the highest priority. By the time the Industries Committee and the Cabinet's War Priorities Committee took over in October 1917, the staff of the Priority Branch had made over 200,000 decisions.

The new Contracts Committee discovered that departments were still buying independently as late as April 1918 to bypass shortages. While an Interdepartmental

Contracts Committee was appointed to stop the practice, it only produced two reports before the Armistice.

Meanwhile, the Ministry of Munitions became the largest buying organisation in the world, working out the agreements that centralised the purchasing by the Allies. At times, the Ministry of Munitions bought iron, steel and non-ferrous metals for France and the other allies, while using British credit to get better deals for Russia. It also worked with the Allied Maritime Transport Council and the Inter-Allied Munitions Council, coordinating the transport and distribution of goods in 1918.

Import and Export Restrictions[6]

On the outbreak of war, Britain had enough coal and steel. However, sources of other materials across the British Empire had not been developed yet. So, the nation had to look to its European allies, America and Canada for help; help that would be limited by finances and shipping.

Britain had to secure existing contracts for imports of raw materials, munitions and food, while looking for new sources for what it had previously bought from Germany or Austria-Hungary. The War Trade Department then had to deal with the movement of raw materials and it sometimes had to resolve diplomatic issues, so that ships could sail.

Britain stopped making unnecessary items to export, to conserve raw materials and economise shipping tonnage. Initially, the Board of Trade made sure materials were exported to the country, which benefited the most. It drew up two lists of items and while those on List A required a license, those on List B did not, if they were going to be exported to a British possession or an Allied country.

The Ministry of Munitions also issued licenses to avoid any conflicts of interests with the Foreign Office or the Ministry of Blockade. Sometimes, exports to neutrals were restricted to stop them selling them on to the Central Powers. On occasions, materials were bought at an inflated price and imported to stop a neutral country selling them to Germany or Austria-Hungary. A few overseas owned companies were placed on a Black List in 1916, until it was established that they were not trading with Germany. Many more restrictions were placed on imports and exports in 1917 due to shipping shortages caused by the German submarine campaign.

Overseas Transport[7]

Britain initially imported machinery and complete shells but it switched to raw materials, as soon as its own factories were producing them. Eventually, it was importing nearly 1 million tons of materials and goods linked to munitions per month; it also needed to import a similar amount of food. Altogether, it would import 46 million tons of munitions between 1915 and 1918 of which 26 million tons was iron ore from Spain and Scandinavia.

The Ministry of Munitions took control of imports in June 1915 but the Shipping Control Committee soon realised that departments were placing orders without considering how to ship it. The Overseas Transport Department was set up in January 1916 and it made sure ships made the shortest journeys. Soon a wide range of raw materials was being imported from around the world to make munitions. These were the main sources:

- Norway: iron ore, pyrites, spelter, ammonium nitrate, calcium nitrate, calcium carbide, nickel steel, ferro-silicon, ferro-chrome and aluminium.
- Sweden: glycerine, dynamite and iron ore (to stop sales to Germany).
- France: bauxite, aluminium, aircraft, fuses, glycerine, glass and wood.
- Spain: Iron ore and pyrites in exchange for British coal.
- Algeria: phosphate rock.
- Sicily: sulphur.
- Greece: magnesite.

A Shipping Controller started organising the best routes in December 1916, while a Shipping Priority Committee started looking at what could be moved, when unrestricted submarine warfare caused serious shipping shortages, early in 1917. An Allied Maritime Transport Council had to be set up after the United States entered the war because ships were required to move the American Expeditionary Force (AEF) to Europe. The added complication of supplying munitions to Italy had to be considered following its setbacks at the end of 1917.

What follows is a summary of the tonnages of the main imports to Britain:

- 5.4 million tons of iron ore from Spain and 660,000 tons from other countries.
- 650,000 tons of finished munitions and 500,000 tons of shell steel.
- 150,000 tons of construction steel from the United States and 100,000 tons of iron from Sweden.
- 550,000 tons of sodium nitrate and 820,000 tons of pyrites.
- 360,000 tons of manganese ore and 220,000 of copper.
- 300,000 tons of lubricating oil and 300,000 tons of phosphate rock.

Unrestricted Submarine Warfare

The German submarine campaign had sunk nearly 2.7 million tons of shipping by the time the Shipping Priority Committee was set up in June 1917. It was supported by the Transports, Shipping Controller and Tonnage Priority Committee as they tried to sort out what could be imported. Eventually insurance bounties had to be offered, so shipping companies from neutral countries would continue to trade with Britain. Meanwhile, all unnecessary imports were stopped while a company could only export goods if its ship brought essential imports back. Even so, there was never enough capacity, so all the supply departments had to cut back what they used by up to 30 per cent.

The Ministry of Munitions' biggest problem in 1918 was a steel shortage. The Allocation of Urgent Supplies Board rationed what companies (carrying out non-essential work) could have and many had to close. The Joint Priorities Board was set up to decide what would be shipped first but it did not start meeting until September 1918.

Work at the Ports[8]

Agents supervised the loading and unloading of ships at the ports and they also advised the Overseas Transport Department. Lunham and Moore were appointed the shipping agents in the United States in 1915 to sort out congestion at the factories and in New York harbour. They redirected goods and ships to ports as far north as Massachusetts and as far south as Texas on America's eastern coastline.

Meanwhile, the unloading of ships in Britain became organised as well. Men with relevant experience were enlisted into Dock Battalions or Transport Workers' Battalions to work at the ports and wharves. Eventually, 15,000 men were unloading nearly 1 million tons of munitions a month. The Port Forwarding Department facilitated the onward train journeys to the factories and stores.

A shipping convoy system was introduced as a defence against submarines in 1917. While it meant ships were safer, it resulted in ships arriving en mass and unloading had to be carefully organised. Even so, British ports could still turn round forty ships a week.

Storing Munitions[9]

Before the war, the British Army stored its artillery pieces at the Royal Arsenal and its shells on nearby Plumstead Marshes, while its small arms were kept at Weedon in Northamptonshire. The Ministry of Munitions found that the stores system was overwhelmed and working hand to mouth when it took over in June 1915. Every order was urgent and there was a lack of record keeping, so the Munitions Stores Department was set up to supervise a system of warrants, inspection notes and advice notes. While the paperwork ensured the safe movement of thousands of tons of munitions by rail, it took staff time to learn how to administer it properly.

A large storage area was opened in the Midland Railway Carriage Works in Birmingham to deal with deliveries from Scotland, the North of England and the Midlands. Another was opened in Teddington in west London, for deliveries from the capital and surrounding counties. Extra storage areas were added at Altrincham near

Manchester, Creedon Hill in Herefordshire and Bramley in Hampshire as the amount of munitions required to be held in reserve in Britain was increased to four weeks. Intermediate stores were also opened along the railways, where munitions from different factories could be organised into train loads. They could then be taken to bonding areas at the ports, where they were inspected before they were loaded onto ships.

When American shells started to arrive in large numbers, they were armed at factories in Horley in Surrey and Devonport in Devon. The Ministry of Munitions also opened stores in Walton near Liverpool, Birkenhead, St Helens and Manchester for munitions en route to Russia.

The Ministry set up the Central Munitions Stores to take over 120 stores and bonding areas in April 1917. Extra depots were opened at Hereford, Quedgeley, Lewes and Middlewich when the reserve to be held in Britain was increased to six weeks. Additional space was added at Banbury Filling Factory in case bad weather prevented sailing for a time. Centralisation made it possible to find out what was held across the country and steps were taken to avoid overfilling the stores and limit the amount of money tied up in munitions. By the spring of 1918, around 19 million shells were stored in Britain with a similar amount stockpiled in France at any one time.

The Central Munitions Stores set about decentralising the organisation of materials, components and completed items to make it easier to organise them. While the Central Invoicing Section took control of the paperwork, it took its staff until the end of the war to catch up with all the bills.

The Explosives Supply Department also became responsible for storing 20,000 tons of explosives, with the main storage areas at Weedon near Northampton, Woolwich and Purfleet, east of London. When they were full, they were stored in everything from obsolete forts and brick works to tunnels and caves.

Between them, the two departments eventually employed 10,900 women and 5,400 men who handled of up to 100,000 tons of explosives and munitions a month.

Chapter 7

Programming Munitions Output

Supply and Demand Under the War Office[1]

Three factors determined what munitions the BEF required. The size of the army, what weapons were required and the rate of consumption of ammunition in battle. While the first two could be determined precisely, the third was an estimate based on what had been used in the Second Boer War over ten years before. The Master General of the Ordnance decided how much of each type of munitions were required, so the Chief Superintendent of the Ordnance Factories could start work on them or the Contracts Department could contact private companies to make them.

Programming munitions was easy in peacetime because it rarely changed. The hard part for the British Army and the Admiralty in wartime was predicting what their future needs were. The Army Council had agreed what size the BEF would be, so it could work out what weapons and equipment it required. However, it discovered that its predictions were wrong, as soon as it went into action, so the War Office had to make a new programme to meet its demands. The onset of trench warfare required even more ammunition while experience showed that a higher ratio of high explosive to shrapnel shells was needed. The British Army was soon left with just 175,000 rifles, 29 million bullets and a small quantity of high explosives in its stores.

The Armaments Contracts Branch transferred to the Director of Artillery's department at the beginning of 1915, making it easier to coordinate their work. The Master General of the Ordnance issued a munitions programme in April 1915, based on the recent experience at Neuve Chapelle but the challenge was how to meet it. The Ordnance Factories and the armament companies could not cope, so they were offered money to extend their facilities. But that involved constructing new buildings, finding plant and training workers before anything could be made. The alternative was to import munitions but companies still had to be found, factories had to be reorganised and shipping had to be arranged. Whatever source was going to be used, it was going to take time to organise and the BEF could not afford to wait.

The BEF's demand for weapons and ammunition continued to grow rapidly. Meanwhile, many of the Territorial Force divisions deployed with obsolete weapons, while the New Armies had to wait for theirs before they could head to the war zones.

No one had experience of accurately forecasting demand while the large number of new contracts and the volume of imports made it difficult to estimate when everything would be delivered. Everyone was making promises and few would be able to meet them until they had everything they needed.

Supply and Demand under the Ministry of Munitions[2]

The ordnance factories and the armament companies were overwhelmed by the time the Ministry of Munitions took over in June 1915. Lloyd George appointed businessmen, called 'push and go' men, to help company owners overcome shortages of everything from labour, plant and materials to tools, components and gauges.

Lloyd George immediately faced the challenge of meeting a promise to France to send seventy divisions to the Western Front. The Ministry had to assess how many new factories were needed to arm them all and how long they would take to get up and running. It also had to work out where to source the raw materials from and how to transport huge amounts of them to the factories.

The Ministry of Munitions started to budget and programme when it took over in June 1915, using information gathered by the Munitions Requirements and Statistics Department. Before long, the Ministry's Supply Department turned the information into programmes that were monitored through weekly reports.[3]

As the New Armies started deploying overseas in large numbers during the winter of 1915-16; munitions stocks were built up by introducing night shifts. However, the week long barrage before the Battle of the Somme started on 1 July 1916 used nearly 2.4 million shells. Shortages of ammunition affected how future operations were planned because an average of 1 million shells were required every week until the campaign ended in November 1916.

Programmes became more accurate over time as factories gained experience and there was more data to work from. Staff reported what progress was being made and what was needed. The Priority Committee started sending materials to where they were needed most, while advising the Labour Supply Department where to send labour.

Stocks of ammunition were built up during the winter of 1916-17. A programme for repairing guns and howitzers was also introduced because of their excessive use during the Somme campaign. Meanwhile, the Requirements and Statistics Department had been busy analysing data on ammunition expenditure, repairs, spares and wastage, to help it produce balanced munitions programmes.

Eventually, the output of the filling factories would set the numbers because the quantities of cordite and TNT were the limiting factors. Output of shell casings remained the same all year round to keep the lathes busy. Filling increased during the summer campaigning months and decreased during the winter months because it was unwise to keep large amounts of filled shells stored for long periods of time.

Unrestricted submarine warfare caused new problems during the early months of 1917. It not only reduced the quantities of raw materials that could be imported but it also increased the need for more shipping. Both factors changed how the Ministry of Munitions organised production and weak links in the supply chain were addressed at a weekly Central Statistical Conference. There was a lot to consider because changing demands required factories to switch work to keep the programme balanced. Even so, the Ministry was able to deliver 3.2 million rounds a week during the Messines and Third Ypres campaigns in the summer and autumn of 1917.

Getting the best use out of the limited resources of labour, machinery and finance was considered during the final months of the war.[4] It included looking at getting the best outcome for an attack from the least resources. For example, it required a lot less labour, steel and transport to make a few dozen tanks than make thousands of tons of shells. Yet they were both capable of supporting the infantry. While suggestions were made, GHQ always had the final say over what it thought was the best way to break down the enemy's defences.

The procedure for programming was finalised by the Munitions Requirements and Statistics Department in May 1918. It monitored output to see if plans were being followed and it could speed up or slow down manufacturing accordingly.

The Inter-Allied Munitions Council was then formed to consider how to match the demands of the combined Allied armies. It decided that Britain and France would make the munitions required by the AEF, so it could ship its men to Europe faster. It also confirmed that Britain would continue to supply materials and weapons that France and Italy were short of. Despite the extra commitments, the nation's factories were still able to supply the 3.5 million rounds a week required for the final battles in the autumn of 1918. While the Munitions Requirements and Statistics Department had everything running smoothly by the summer of 1918, the sudden Armistice on 11 November 1918 resulted in huge stocks of munitions being left over both in Britain and behind the front lines.

Chapter 8

Research, Testing and Inspections

The Research and Experimental Establishments

Many research laboratories and experimental areas were set up around the country to test modifications and inventions. Explosives were tested at three London sites. Raw materials were checked at Chiswick and manufacturing processes were examined at Grays. Explosives and shell components were tested at the Royal Arsenal, while the assembled articles were fired (proofed) at Shoeburyness on the Essex coast.

Trench warfare stores were examined at three more London sites: Grosvenor Road, Clapham Common and Claremont Park. Meanwhile, trench mortars were trialled at Porton Down in Wiltshire. Rifles and machine guns were tested at Hythe in Kent, while cartridges were checked at Perivale National Filling Factory in west London.

Technical advances meant that the aircraft and tank industries had much to learn. Materials were tested at Gower Street in London, while new aircraft designs were tested at the Royal Aircraft Establishment in Farnborough, Hampshire. Meanwhile, tanks were tested at Dollis Hill in north-west London and at Oldbury in the West Midlands.

Small-scale gas experiments were trialled at Wembley in north London, while large scale experiments were carried out at Porton Down. Meanwhile, gas masks were tested at University College London.

The Testing Organisation

Soldiers, seamen and airmen needed to be confident that their weapons and ammunition were practical, effective and safe to use. Accurate drawings, detailed specifications, comprehensive tests and thorough inspections were required to avoid problems.

The Master General of the Ordnance supervised the testing and inspection of everything made in the War Office's manufacturing departments.[1] He controlled the Directorate of Artillery, which dealt with guns and ammunition. The Directorate of Fortifications and Works dealt with engineering items. Both the Director of Artillery and the Director of Naval Ordnance worked with four consultants:

- Superintendent of Research considered ballistics and chemical issues.
- Superintendent of Experiments arranged testing.

- Royal Arsenal's Chief Inspector carried out testing and looked at service conditions.
- Chief Superintendent of Ordnance Factories dealt with manufacturing.

The Chief Inspector of Small Arms tested personal weapons, while the Inspector of Royal Engineer Stores tested engineering items. The Naval Inspection Department checked Admiralty items made in the South of England, while an Inspector of Steel based in Sheffield inspected guns made across Scotland and the North of England. Some naval stores were also tested at the Royal Arsenal.

The Chief Inspector's Department at the Royal Arsenal advised on all aspects of munitions. He had 1,300 staff before the war and half worked for the Laboratory Stores Division. They were kept busy checking cartridge cases, fuses and other shell components before they were assembled. The rest sourced and tested raw materials and supervised the control of specifications, drawings and patterns. They also advised on the placing of contracts and inspected the factories during the manufacturing process. They then examined the finished products with gauges and gave support during the firing of the proofs. Shells that came from batches that had passed all the tests were then painted, packed and passed to the stores ready for shipping to the front.[2]

Small calibre guns and howitzers were inspected by the Royal Arsenal's Guns and Carriages Division, while anything larger than 6-inch calibre was inspected at the Royal Gun Factory. The carriages section checked the limbers and ammunition caissons as well as the mountings for static guns. Meanwhile, rifles and cartridges were inspected and then proof tested on the rifle range on Plumstead Marshes, before they too were packed and sent to the stores.

Ordnance officers also had to periodically examine and test everything held in the Royal Arsenal's stores to make sure nothing had deteriorated. Chemical officers were kept busy analysing everything from paint to explosives, in conjunction with the Royal Laboratory or the Chemical Laboratories at Waltham Abbey.

Finally, the Royal Arsenal's Equipment Branch had the unenviable task of keeping track of all the stores. It had to record when everything was delivered, see that it was stored correctly and report when it was issued.

The Ministry of Munitions Takes Over Production[3]

Many of the inspectors working at the Royal Arsenal were reservists or serving in the Territorial Force who had been called up during the early months of the war. While a training school was opened, the volume of munitions soon overwhelmed the staff and filled the stores to overflowing. So, shells had to be filled at new factories in Newcastle-upon-Tyne and Faversham in Kent. Meanwhile, rifle cartridges were checked at Park Royal in west London, where female inspectors were used for the first time.

Research, Testing and Inspections 51

While the Ministry took over inspections and modifications in June 1915, the War Office still controlled designs, specifications, research and experiments. By now, the Chief Inspector's Department had 9,000 staff, including some civilians because many military inspectors had been sent to the United States to sort out problems.

The Inspector of Steel continued to test the steel made in the Midlands and the North of England, while Board of Trade staff inspected what was made in South Wales. Gun inspectors were sent to Newcastle-upon-Tyne, Manchester, Sheffield and Coventry to relieve the Royal Arsenal of some of its work. Chemists from the universities in Liverpool, Leeds, Manchester and Birmingham tested explosives, while the Royal Arsenal transferred its test facilities to Eltham, away from the rest of the factory.

To begin with, a shortage of gauges forced each factory to work off a model gun, which meant parts were not interchangeable with those made at other factories. A shortage of space on the Shoeburyness firing range, also meant that contractors had to test artillery pieces on their own ranges. Vickers tested at Eskmeals and Armstrong Whitworth's tested at Silloth, both on the Cumberland coast. Armstrong Whitworth's also had an inland range at Ridsdale near their Newcastle factory; the Coventry Ordnance Works also had one near theirs. Other proof ranges were opened at Boston in Lincolnshire, Buxton in Derbyshire, Meanwood near Leeds, Bilberry Hill near Birmingham and in the Nottingham area.

The BEF's demand for extra howitzers meant that some designs were rushed, resulting in the gun crews asking for modifications as soon as they reached the battlefield. Problems were also flagged up as the inexperienced manufacturers and inspectors tried to speed up output. So, design and inspection were transferred to the Ministry of Munitions, while the Chief Inspectors at Woolwich and Enfield were placed under the Deputy Director General of Inspection in December 1915 to try and reduce the number of problems.

The Ministry takes over Inspections[4]

The Director General of Munitions Inspection became responsible for 19,000 inspection staff in March 1916. He divided them between the Weapons, Ammunition and Explosives departments and then organised them into administrative, organisational and technical roles. He also set up the Training Section and while most only needed to learn a few basic checks, a few specialists were shown how to carry out the sophisticated ones.

The number of inspectors increased to 30,000 by the end of 1916 and around half were women. Factories had taken steps to make inspections easier, even acquiring lifting equipment so they could check heavier items. The Director of Inspection of Gun Ammunition and Director of Inspection of Munitions Areas took over during the winter of 1916-17. Staff from the Dudley and Birmingham inspection areas then moved to Perivale and Wandsworth near London, so they could inspect small and large shell components respectively.

The Inspection Areas

Slight differences in the ways factories made rifles required two inspection areas setting up, one in Birmingham and another in Enfield Lock in north London. Another at Slade Green checked the Vickers machine guns made in Erith and Crayford in east London, while Hotchkiss machine guns were checked in Coventry; Lewis machine guns were checked in Birmingham and the magazines were checked in Nottingham.

New and repaired artillery pieces were inspected at the Royal Arsenal or one of the National Ordnance Factories in Leeds and Nottingham. Many time-served or disabled artillery officers were trained to check them and it took ten days to inspect a gun.

Inspecting chemical shells required a high level of secrecy and they were tested at Porton Down. However, the inspectors rarely had the correct technical knowledge nor the current specifications to carry out their work properly.

The supply officers were expected to inspect everything during the early days of tanks to keep them a secret. However, there were so many complaints that Tank Corps officers had to be drafted in to check the tanks before they left the factories. Even then, they were checked again in France. The new Tank Board eventually took control of inspections in August 1918.

The Inspection and Design departments were finally brought together in January 1918, while nineteen new Central Bond areas were opened, where the final inspection of munitions could be carried out. The inspectors eventually started advising the Supply Department and manufacturers on how to pass inspections, reducing the time required by up to a third.

Unfortunately, it was difficult to keep inspectors because making shells on piece work was far more lucrative. Even so, the number increased to 64,000 men and women, who carried out hundreds of thousands of checks every week. Their diligence and attention to detail meant that the soldiers continued to be supplied with weapons and ammunition that were both safe and effective.

Inspecting Imported Goods[5]

Shells imported from the United States and Canada were examined before they were loaded onto ships but they were inspected again on arrival in Britain. Shipments sometimes did not match orders, while there were differing views about specifications. Samples were also proofed on British ranges because there were concerns about possible sabotage. Large quantities of fuses ordered from the United States, France and Switzerland were inspected at Luton and Perivale before they were sent to the Royal Arsenal.

British inspectors were sent to help the Canadian Inspection Department when it was put under the control of the Ministry of Munitions in the summer of 1916. There were also problems with American goods when the dockside inspectors became overwhelmed. Again, British inspectors were sent to help and they were soon travelling around the factories to deal with issues.

Quality Problems[6]

A new munitions component required rigorous testing before it was put into mass production and it then needed a meticulous inspection regime to maintain acceptable high standards. However, the urgent demand for munitions called for fast production, which contradicted both the testing and inspection requirements. The dilemma was how to make huge numbers of flawless shells quickly. They were dangerous if they exploded prematurely and a waste of effort if they failed to explode at all. The target was set at only one premature explosion per 250,000 shells; any more was unacceptable.

The Ministry of Munitions simply refused to pay for any items that failed inspection when it took over quality control at the end of 1915. But it still took time to build up a working relationship between the factories and the inspectors, particularly as most had no previous experience. Over time, modifications to the munitions and design changes to the machinery made it possible to speed up production and easier to pass the inspections.

New Patterns and Drawings

Modifications were either suggested following experiences in the field or by the factories to improve or speed up manufacturing.[7] They required alterations to drawings and the Ministry of Munitions' information bureau produced copies of drawings on a printing press. Urgent changes had to be implemented immediately but non-urgent ones were added at six week intervals to reduce the number of revised drawings. Eventually, air raids against London resulted in copies of all drawings being sent to a safe storage area.

Improvements were encouraged but they usually required a long break in production. For example, replacing a long gaine with a short gaine to improve the reliability of high explosive shells required an eight week shutdown during the winter of 1915-16. It left the BEF short of 1 million 18-pounder shells.

New weapons could take up to twelve months to research and test but ammunition usually only needed three months. Extra production capacity then had to be found, either by getting a factory to switch production or by building new facilities. After the summer of 1916, new designs were tested and approved before the factories had to change their machines and retrain their workforce. While it reduced the length of shutdowns it resulted in stockpiles of obsolete shells that had to be broken up and recycled.

The tank is a good example of how long it took to get an idea into action. The idea was discussed and developed for twelve months before the War Office accepted it in February 1916. Foundries had to be found to make the body, while a suitable engine and tracks had to be designed and made. Factories then had to be located to assemble the tanks before they were shipped to France. The crews were given little time to check their new weapons of war before they went into action on the Somme on 15 September 1916 but the survivors immediately suggested modifications highlighted by their battlefield experiences.

Improving Production[8]

Lloyd George sometimes ordered more than the War Office asked for, looking to get ahead in the constant race between supply and demand. Occasionally, he ignored the War Office's advice, such as when he ordered large numbers of Stokes mortars after GHQ had rejected it in favour of existing models.

Soldiers initially submitted ideas to the Inventions Department but it was overwhelmed by June 1917. So, they were then initially evaluated by GHQ, ending the contact between the designers and the troops. It meant the only way evaluators could learn about the conditions at the front line was to speak to returning officers.

Each department had different experiences when it came to making modifications. For example, the chemists and gunners argued over the best way to design a chemical shell until their ideas were discussed by the Chemical Warfare Committee at the end of 1917. Meanwhile, both the designer and the manufacturers failed to ask the tank crews about their experiences, resulting in delays over development. However, the manufacturers and pilots always kept in close contact as they developed and tested new aircraft models.

Chapter 9

The Railways

Planning for War[1]

The War Railway Council had made plans in case of war but they focused on the mobilisation of troops and they ignored the need to move munitions. The Executive Committee also studied how to control the nation's railways as a combined network because the 21,500 miles of track and 4,000 stations across the country were owned by 130 companies.

The government initially took over the 500 miles of track and 1,800 trains it needed to move the BEF to the ports in August 1914. Everything went smoothly and nearly 100,000 troops and 120,000 horses embarked for France without a hitch in just five days.[2]

Operating railways involves locomotives, rolling stock and track, so the War Office and then the Ministry of Munitions had five elements to consider:

- The maintenance of Britain's locomotives and rolling stock.
- The maintenance of Britain's rail network.
- The movement of munitions across Britain.
- The export of standard gauge items to support the Allies and the BEF.
- The export of narrow gauge items to support the BEF.

The problem that soon emerged was that 100,000 out of 700,00 workers had enlisted during the first few months of the war.

Maintaining Britain's Rolling Stock[3]

Commercial train travel reduced on the outbreak of war, as did the demand for new locomotives and wagons, so the large railway companies were given munitions work instead. The Directorate of Transport and Movement started placing contracts with the small railway companies on behalf of the Ministry of Munitions, when the demand for rolling stock resumed. While they worked to their own designs for the bodies and engines, they were instructed to work to two standard wheel arrangements. They built 2-6-0 engines to move mixed goods and slow passenger traffic, while 2-8-0 locomotives were made to pull heavier mineral traffic. Several companies were also contracted to make shunting engines.

The Ministry set up the Railway Materials Branch in May 1916, to locate new contractors and coordinate the manufacture of railway goods.[4] It took over the supply of locomotives, wagons and rails in October 1916, including the resale of scrap locomotives and wagons, which were to be reused or recycled.

Britain's rolling stock started to suffer by 1917 because staff shortages had resulted in fewer repairs. Many locomotives had been sent to the war zones, so the ones left behind were being used more.

By November 1917, the Ministry of Munitions started a register of locomotives to make sure they were all being used efficiently. Pooling rolling stock was more complicated because different goods required different wagons, ranging from iron ore and steel to explosives and gas to tanks and planes.[5] The Ministry considered hiring them but it was advised it would be expensive, impractical and could even hinder the movement of munitions. The Coal Controller also warned it could interfere with the supply of coal to power stations and steel works, so the idea was abandoned. The Ministry instead compiled a nationwide wagon register and fixed hire rates, so that the 20,000 private wagons could be shared across the network.

Maintaining Britain's Rail Network

The established munitions factories already had rail connections but they had to be upgraded to cope with the increase in traffic. The new National Projectile Factories and National Filling Factories were located close to main lines but they still needed sidings, platforms, signal boxes and signals. The Ministry of Munitions appointed the Railways Priority Committee to decide which tracks to build first and they used second hand rails from abandoned lines, whenever possible. Eventually, 200 miles of track per month were being laid.

The Ministry stopped the sale of second hand rails and sleepers at the end of 1916 to make sure they were used where they were needed the most. Large amounts were sent to France to lay between the ports and the BEF's railheads. Steel shortages caused by the German submarine campaign resulted in the Ministry having to take control of all second hand railway materials in 1917.[6]

The German submarine threat had two serious effects on rail transport:

- More ships were directed to the western ports, such as Liverpool and Bristol, so their rail facilities had to be upgraded.
- New tracks also had to be laid and 4,400 extra wagons had to be found to move iron ore from the recently opened Cumberland iron ore mines across the North of England to the Middlesbrough steel works.

The increase in heavy traffic and the lack of maintenance resulted in the rail network deteriorating as the months passed. There was insufficient trained staff to repair all the faults, so speed restrictions had to be installed instead to prevent accidents. It resulted in Britain's network being close to breaking point by the time the war ended.

Exporting Rolling Stock

As the Western Front settled into trench warfare, GHQ started asking for rolling stock to move supplies from the ports to the BEF's railheads. Over time, it asked for both standard gauge and narrow gauge track to deliver munitions to the front line.

Following the Paris Economy Pact with the Allies on 4 June 1916, Britain promised to send locomotives and wagons to move goods on the French railways system. The Ministry of Munitions was concerned the transfer would interfere with the movement of munitions across Britain, so it took control of the nation's railways in the autumn of 1916.

An assessment of the rolling stock on the Western Front in September 1916 by the transport expert Sir Eric Geddes suggested that the BEF would need 1,000 locomotives and 2,800 wagons.[7] The wagons were ordered from British workshops and some of the locomotives would be made by the 7,200 employees of the North British Locomotive Company in Glasgow. However, the rest had to be ordered from the United States and Canada. GHQ also asked for 300 miles of extra standard gauge at the end of the year to double all the tracks in the BEF's sector. It then wanted to add new lines at a rate of 150 miles a month.

The Directorate of Transport and Movement also had to deal with demands from the French and Russian railways in 1916. While the French government put in an order for 330 engines and 6,375 wagons, it soon complained that the prices were too high. Russia also asked for huge amounts of rolling stock and track, so it could advance across Polish territory in the summer of 1916. The Ministry of Munitions placed orders in the United States and Canada, only for Russian agents to interfere and nothing had been delivered by the time of the Russian Revolution in the autumn of 1917.

GHQ made another request for 1,000 miles of track in May 1917 to increase the capacity of the French ports from 550,000 to 960,000 tons a month. The London and North Western Railway's foundry was kept busy making over 5,000 tons of rail a month to fulfil the order. Another 200 miles of rarely used track were also taken up across Britain and shipped to France.

Standard gauge and narrow gauge shunting engines were in great demand at the French ports and railheads. Dick, Kerr and Company of Kilmarnock as well as British Westinghouse, and Nasmyth, Gaskell and Company both of Manchester employed over 11,500 making standard gauge models. The Hunslet Engine Company of Leeds and Kerr Stuart of Stoke-on-Trent made them for narrow gauge, while Motor Rail of Bedford made them for 60-centimetre gauge tracks. Around 3,000 narrow gauge wagons were also made.

Bolckow, Vaughan and Company of Middlesbrough and the Dowlais Ironworks of Merthyr Tydfil recycled shell steel scrap into 1,000 miles of narrow gauge track. Another 300 miles of track were pulled up in Canada and sent to France to be reused. Eventually, the little engines were able to move approximately 730,000 tons of goods a month.

Over 700 standard gauge locomotives had been sent to France by December 1917. However, the German offensives in the spring of 1918 captured or destroyed large amounts of rolling stock. So, another 100 locomotives and many wagons were sent from Britain to replace them.

The Railway Centralising Committee started prioritising supplies in June 1918 as the Allies prepared for their summer offensive.[8] The BEF required huge amounts of rails and sleepers to sustain its advances in the summer and autumn because the Germans destroyed everything as they fell back. Around 1,580 miles of track had to be repaired, while another 2,000 miles were built across the battlefields.

By the end of the war, 1,400 locomotives, 70,000 wagons and many converted troop and ambulance trains were supporting the BEF's Advance to Victory. The Railway Materials Department had sent 2,500 main line locomotives, 1,000 shunting engines, 80,000 wagons and 7,000 miles of track to France during the war.

Moving Munitions[9]

After years of only being used on their own company's track, trains were permitted to be used anywhere around the country. The number of rail movements started to increase in the autumn of 1915, so the Ministry of Munitions set up the Forwarding and Delivery Branch to coordinate the work of the War Office, the Railway Executive Committee and the railway companies.

The Branch's staff supervised new rail facilities, sidings to factories and munitions stores. They divided goods into classes and issued certificates, which prioritised traffic movements:

- Top priority goods were Class 1.
- Urgent loads were Class 2.
- Normal loads linked to government factories were Class 3a.
- Goods linked to private firms were Class 3b.

Explosives required special attention and while large quantities travelled on goods trains with a Certificate X, small quantities were moved on passenger trains with a Certificate Y. Once munitions were completed, they were handed over to the War Office and the Royal Arsenal's store alone was eventually handing over 100,000 packages a month.

The Forwarding and Delivery Branch was renamed the Munitions Railway Transport Branch at the beginning of 1916 because it was also given responsibility for getting workers to their factories. Many of the passenger trains travelled on the same tracks to the factories, so their movements had to be coordinated with the munition trains. Its staff worked hard to see that wagons were used economically and were loaded and unloaded efficiently. They kept track of raw materials, components and munitions and kept contractors and the Supply Department informed about their movements across the network.

The Munitions Railway Transport Branch employed travelling inspectors who notified railway companies of urgencies, delays and problems. They worked out the best routes to use, with the help of transport officers who were based in the busy areas. Area transport officers, who were the link between the Area Office and the railway companies were added later.

The transport officers tried to make the best use of rolling stock but there were always shortages despite the thousands of wagons on the network. They also had to supervise the transfer of huge amounts of goods from ships to wagons at the docks, often with the help of mechanical grabs. For example, 1.3 million tons of iron ore were unloaded from 345 ships at Glasgow docks in one month alone.

The Munitions Railway Transport Branch also controlled the transport of munitions on roads, canals and coastal transport. When possible, it convinced companies to move their goods by barge or coastal shipping, rather than by train. One decision alone transferred 300,000 tons of goods from a railway to a canal. The Munitions Railway Transport Branch also tried to convince companies to move goods by motor vehicles over short distances, particularly around busy munition areas. The Railway Transport Branch ended up controlling 2,000 motor vehicles by the end of the war and they carried nearly 2 million tons over 4.5 million miles.

In October 1917, the Munitions Railway Transport Branch was renamed the Munitions Inland Transport Branch because of the amount of canal and road traffic it was dealing with. Just 200 staff also had dealt with 26,000 special trains by the end of the war.

Two Wartime Ports

The Inland Waterways Transport Department was formed in December 1914 to take control of barges. They were loaded with munitions in England, towed across the Channel and then piloted along the French canals. They did away with the loading and unloading at the ports, while their shallow drafts made them immune from torpedo attack. However, the barges were unwelcome in the busy port of Dover, so a new facility, capable of handling 90,000 tons of traffic per month, was opened at Richborough on the Kent coast in 1916. The facilities were camouflaged to keep them a secret and over 1.2 million tons had been moved through the port by the end of the war.

Richborough also became a base for a roll on and roll off train ferry service, as did Southampton.[10] The dock facilities allowed loaded trains to be shunted onto boats, so they could be taken across the Channel and towed onto the French rail network. They proved very useful for moving large items, such as howitzers, tanks and locomotives.

Another large rail depot required to help the Admiralty was built at Aberdeen.[11] It could deliver 8,000 tons of supplies a month to the quayside, so ships could transfer them to the Grand Fleet's anchorage in Scarpa Flow in the Orkney Islands. Grangemouth on the Firth of Forth was developed to export 2 million tons of Scottish coal; it also handled 100,000 tons of munitions and nearly 140,000 tons of oil.

PART III

The Raw Materials

Chapter 10

The Coal Industry

Dangerous Work Underground[1]

Over 1.1 million men worked in coal mining before the war, digging 290 million tons a year. The Scottish coalfield, near Glasgow and Edinburgh, employed 133,000, while the coalfield along England's north-east coast, employed another 244,000. Over 100,000 men worked around Manchester, while 144,000 were employed in Yorkshire's West Riding (now South Yorkshire). About 100,000 miners were employed across the English Midlands, while 233,000 worked in the South Wales coalfields. Another 100,000 worked in smaller coalfields, such as Cumberland and North Wales.

Coal mining was a dangerous job, with hundreds killed and thousands maimed every year. Miners had struggled for safer working conditions for many years and while legislation had been introduced, the penalties for companies breaking the law were always set too low. The Royal Commission on Mines worked to get mine owners and colliers to agree on health and safety measures, resulting in the Coal Mines Act of 1911. However, an explosion at Senghenydd colliery in Glamorgan in South Wales on 14 October 1913 claimed 439 lives. It was the worst coal mining accident in British mining history.[2]

The investigation proved that safety recommendations had not been followed but there was no chance of an appeal. Instead, the mine owner was fined less than £25 (£2,000 today) and the press reported that a miner's life was only worth 1 shilling, 1 pence and 1 farthing (less than £5 today).

However, the outbreak of war meant that many factories stopped making luxuries, so the demand for coal fell. Some miners were put on short time while others were laid off. Around 220,000 had enlisted by May 1915, leaving the country short of 1 million tons of coal a month. Mine owners wanted to suspend the Eight Hours Act, so they could catch up with orders. The government wanted the same, so the price of coal would fall, bringing inflation down.

Trouble in South Wales[3]

Two issues came to the fore in 1915, which separated the miners from the rest of the nation's workforce. Following recent issues with government interference in wage negotiations, the Miners' Federation of Great Britain refused to sign up to the Treasury Agreement in March 1915, because it required compulsory arbitration. It also refused to sign up to the Munitions of War Act because it opposed industrial conscription. It meant the nation's coal mines and its miners did not come under the jurisdiction of the Ministry of Munitions.

Miners also wanted the Eight Hours Act suspending because the price of living was rising at an alarming rate. Food costs had risen by 25 per cent in just ten months; as much as it had over the past twenty years. The Miners' Federation of Great Britain wanted a national agreement to strengthen its position, so it asked for 20 per cent, only for the coalfield owners to offer 10 per cent. The Mining Association refused to make an award, stating that wage rises were decided by district conciliation boards, which resulted in increases of between 15 and 18.5 per cent.

Back in March 1915, the South Wales branch of the Miners' Federation of Great Britain had announced that its wage agreement would end on 30 June 1915. The area had been the centre of a prolonged strike back in 1910 and 1911 and the government was anxious to avoid a reoccurrence. So, the miners were offered a 10 per cent war bonus and asked to continue with the existing agreement until the end of the war. They wanted 25 per cent and while the offer was raised to 17.5 per cent, the miners demanded a new agreement to protect themselves against the inevitable drop in coal prices after the war.

The miners refused to go to arbitration, so Lloyd George threatened to use the Munitions of War Act to fine them.[4] Around 200,000 coal miners went on strike on 15 July 1915, so Lloyd George headed to Cardiff, accompanied by President of the Board of Trade, Walter Runciman and Chairman of the Workmen's Representatives, Arthur Henderson. They agreed to nearly everything the miners wanted, ending the strike.

Wages in the coal industry had always been linked to the price of the goods they dug. While workers had often complained and even gone on strike due to falling demand in peacetime, prices rose as the munitions factories started working and so did the wages of over 1 million men. By 1915, the government had to fix the price of coal and introduced subsidies to stabilise it. The Miners' Federation of Great Britain then asked for a 12.5 per cent bonus to match the predicted rise in the selling price. It meant the government had to compensate the mine owners for the increases. The Ministry of Munitions also became responsible for the coking plants and other industries that linked coal and iron production, involving many more key workers.

The industry remained outside the Ministry of Munitions' authority but Lloyd George talked about state control when he was appointed Prime Minister in December 1916. While that suggested nationalisation, he only wanted control over coal output and distribution, so the munitions factories could meet their orders. It resulted in a Coal Controller being appointed to head a new department in the Board of Trade in February 1917. The deal was that coalfield owners were guaranteed a minimum profit while an excess profit tax curbed the maximum.

The government also took over the setting of wages under the new Minster of Munitions, the miners' old adversary, Winston Churchill.[5] From now on wages were settled nationally, to combat the rising cost of living. The Miners' Federation of Great Britain asked for a 25 per cent war bonus in July 1917, only for the Coal Controller to award the underground workers the same as everyone else. The War Cabinet Labour Committee then agreed to give above ground colliery workers a similar raise.

Rather than relying on tribunals to keep a check on discipline, like the rest of the industries, joint pit committees were set up at every colliery. Miners responded better to being judged by their colleagues when it came to dealing with issues over working conditions or misdemeanours.

The Miners' Federation of Great Britain demanded a 'war wage' for all its members in the summer of 1918, as a reward for supplying coal through the recent crisis caused by the German spring offensives. It was countered by a lower offer, forcing the Prime Minister to step in.

However, the main issue during the summer of 1918 was manpower, because conscription hit the industry hard, resulting in coal shortages. Once the war was over, the status quo between the Miners' Federation of Great Britain, the Mining Association and the government was restored. Meanwhile, miners returning from the armed forces were soon back at their old pit, looking for their jobs back.

Chapter 11

Iron and Steel

The Development of Supplies

Companies acquired their own raw materials in the early days of the war. Britain's pre-war smelting and refining capacity was small. On the outbreak of war, the Foreign Office asked foundries across the British Empire to stop selling to Germany and Austria-Hungary and promised them grants to increase production. The Defence of the Realm Act could fix prices across Britain but prices around the world had tripled by the summer of 1915.

The Ministry of Munitions worked with the London Metal Exchange to reduce the increases and introduced centralised buying to prevent competition.[1] It bought explosives, steel and other raw materials to help factories with their cash flow. It negotiated better prices by bulk buying, eliminated competition and ensured fair distribution to where it was needed most. However, there were always arguments over whether materials should be issued for free, on repayment terms or if the cost should be deducted from their bills.[2]

Demand had grown so much by the summer of 1916, that the supply of steel and non-ferrous materials was split between two departments at the Ministry of Munitions. The Export Prohibition Act stopped companies exporting them, while a Priority Order took control of shipping, once the German submarine campaign began, early in 1917. The Requirements and Statistics Department helped monitor production, while the two departments became part of Group M (Materials) in August 1917. Prices of imports had increased after the United States entered the war and the Allies eventually set up the Non-Ferrous Council in 1918 to coordinate buying and distribution.

Iron Ore[3]

Britain had large deposits of iron ore and it mined 16 million tons a year. However, the majority had a high sulphur or phosphorous content, which made brittle steel that was unsuitable for shells. So, another 8 million tons of hematite iron ore was imported a year, over half of it from north and east Spain. The country stopped exporting to other countries in 1915, so it could ship all its supplies to Britain.

Manganese ore was particularly sought after because it was used to make hardened steel, which was required to make tools. Around 50 per cent was imported from India, with the rest coming from Sweden, Russia, or Brazil. Monthly imports increased to 45,000 tons in 1916 because a lot was required to make helmets and tanks. However, German submarines made the shipping route through the Baltic Sea too dangerous to use. So, trains started taking it from the mines in northern Sweden to the Norwegian port of Narvik in 1916.

Unrestricted submarine warfare in 1917 made neutrals reluctant to deliver their goods to Britain, which left iron ore stacked up in Bilbao on Spain's north coast. So, British merchant ships started delivering coal to Bayonne in south-west France, allowing trains to take it to Italy. They returned with Spanish iron ore.

Britain's iron ore industry expanded following a chance discovery in December 1914, when the German navy bombarded Scarborough, Whitby, Hartlepool and West Hartlepool, along the north-east coast. An analysis of shell fragments proved that they had a higher percentage of sulphur and phosphorous than British shells. Once tests convinced the War Office to relax their restrictions in December 1916, work started on extracting iron ore deposits across Cumberland and Lancashire. The Admiralty refused to relax their standard. The new Home Ore Supply Committee arranged for workers from Cornish clay mines and prisoners of war to help at the mines.

Coke[4]

Coal is baked in kilns to make coke, which is then used to smelt iron ore into pig iron in blast furnaces. Around 90,000 tons of coke a month were being produced in 1914 but British demand fell during the early part of the war as construction reduced and the demand for high grade steel for munitions increased. However, plenty was still being exported to France and Italy.

Benzol and toluol are byproducts of baking coke in the correct type of ovens and they were both used by the explosives industry. The decision was taken to make more pig iron and smelt it with scrap, to increase the output of high quality steel and byproducts. So, investments were made in new ovens, which helped to increase coke production to 115,000 tons a month.

Operating the Blast Furnaces[5]

Limestone is added to blast furnaces, to remove the impurities from iron ore during the smelting process. It was quarried across the country and miners worked alongside 1,500 prisoners of war to extract 4.5 million tons during the war.

The blast furnaces that made iron ore had to be constantly lined with millions of refractory bricks. Meanwhile, the converters and acid steel furnaces, which made steel needed large amounts of silica bricks. Shortages meant that the high grade bricks were only used in the vital parts of the ovens while magnesite bricks and coke oven bricks had to be imported.

Steel Production[6]

Britain was making 15 per cent of the world's steel in 1913 and it was also the world's second largest exporter, sending 5 million tons overseas every year. The steel industry may have been outdated but the nation had plenty of coal, coke and refractory materials to make it. The foundries made 10.3 million tons of pig iron in 1913 and a third of it had been converted into forge and foundry iron. They also made 7.7 million tons of steel of which 4.6 million tons was high grade acid steel, made by smelting hematite ore and scrap steel.

The country was a world leader at inventing special steels but it had to import the magnesite, manganese ore and other raw materials required to make them. It made high speed steel for the machine tools, which were used on lathes, while new alloys were made for new munitions. The University of Sheffield's Metallurgy Department would be kept busy casting and testing them, with the help of the city's foundries.

Making enough types of certain shapes of steel was also a problem. For example, most oversized forgings (the initial castings) had been imported from Germany before the war. It meant Britain's foundries had to become proficient at casting them, so they could make large items like gun barrels for ships and carriages for howitzers.

The Inspector of Steel was based in Sheffield with an assistant at Newcastle-upon-Tyne and they divided their inspectors between three departments: guns, munitions and trench warfare.[7] The inspectors watched the rolling of the steel, tested every casting or forging, analysed samples and controlled test pieces.

While Britain had a healthy steel industry, Germany had seized 80 per cent of the France's iron ore resources near Metz in August 1914. Italy was also unable to make enough steel to support its armed forces, when it entered the conflict in May 1915. In both cases, Britain either sent its own steel or helped them buy it from the United States.

Everyone wanted more steel by the summer of 1915 and the Ministry of Munitions gave shipbuilding the priority after the Admiralty complained that munitions work was getting too much. Steel companies were happy to build extensions to their foundries with government money, until a tax on excess profits was proposed. Steel came under the control of the Ministry of Munitions in November 1915 because it was looking for an extra 190,000 tons a month to meet the 1916 munitions programme.

American and Canadian steel was expensive but Britain's manufacturers said they could only make 100,000 tons per month by the end of 1915.[8] It meant that the Ministry of Munitions had to import a similar amount to meet the revised munitions programmes of both Britain and France. However, it would take American foundries six months to master how to make high standard shell steel. Steel was also imported from Scandinavia.

Imported steel was inspected at the American and Canadian foundries, and again when it reached Britain's ports. The Ministry of Munitions had to send inspectors to Canada after the wrong specification was used to make shell steel, resulting in several premature explosions in the field.

Steel bars, known as billets, imported from the United States were unloaded at the National Steel Billet Breaking Factory at Trafford Park on the Manchester Ship Canal.[9] They were cut into shell sized pieces and 30,000 tons a month were taken to a store in Fazakerley near Liverpool en route to the shell factories. There were similar sized billet breaking yards in Glasgow, Lancaster, Ellesmere Port, Wolverhampton and Stratford.

The Ministry of Munitions offered money for foundries to build new furnaces but they were concerned that there would be a surplus of capacity after the war. So, it formed a Steel Section in the summer of 1916 to look at where to get all the steel that the new National Factories would need. Meanwhile, its Priority Branch decided where the rest would be used. The new Iron and Steel Department wanted each of the Ministry's regional areas to be self-contained for iron and steel to reduce the amount of transport required. A plan to build a national steel works was shelved because it would take too long to complete, so companies were again asked to build extensions because it would be cheaper than importing in the long run.

By the end of 1916, Britain's foundries had increased to making 460,000 tons of steel a month; 165,000 tons short of what was required. Munitions alone required 210,000 tons, while shipping needed 105,000 tons. Britain was also exporting 50,000 tons of steel a month to France until the United States joined the war in April 1917.

Production had increased by the start of 1917 but demand had also risen. Losses from unrestricted submarine attacks meant an extras 60,000 tons was required for merchant ships, reducing what was available for munitions. The only consolation was that France started buying shell steel direct from the United States when it entered the war. However, iron and steel exports to Italy had to increase following the disaster at the Battle of Caporetto, which ended in November 1917.

The construction industry was also left short of steel and all non-essential work was stopped. Only essential buildings could be repaired if they were damaged by fire or bombing, while firms were fined for building without a license. The Works Construction Sub Committee started prioritising building work for the Ministry of Munitions in 1917, while the Munitions Works Board checked designs, advised on site locations and supervised work.

In September 1917, the new Minister of Munitions, Winston Churchill, told foundry owners they had to work around the clock because the nation was 'fighting a steel war'. Steel demands continued to rise in 1918, with the munitions industry eventually asking for 320,000 tons a month. The Admiralty asked 245,000 tons to restore merchant shipping to a safe level but the amount had to be reduced because the shipyards were all working flat out.

A shortage of coal, due to the enlistment of miners into the New Armies, rationed the country to 3.5 million tons of industrial coal a month. It prompted the Restrictions of Imports Committee to recommend reducing imports of iron ore from Spain and a cap on the iron and steel programme. It reduced the amount of the steel the country could make down to 540,000 million tons of steel, resulting in cuts all round. The Ministry of Munitions also required all foundries across Britain to have a license to forge and sell iron, steel, or non-ferrous materials.

As feared by the steel companies, demand for steel dropped rapidly when the war ended because ships were not being sunk and shells were not being fired. It resulted in furnaces being shut down and many redundancies.

The Iron and Steel Companies[10]

The following companies were some of the largest foundries making iron and steel. The Carron Company employed 3,100 men in Falkirk and the Steel Company employed over 3,400 in Glasgow. Meanwhile, David Colville and Sons, Lanarkshire Steel Company, and the Glasgow Iron and Steel Company employed nearly 10,600 employees at Motherwell, south of Glasgow.

Bolckow, Vaughan and Company was the largest employer in Middlesbrough, with 18,800 employees. Another 13,300 worked at Dorman Long and Company, Bell Brothers, Cochrane and Company, and the Cargo Fleet Iron Company. They all increased capacity when iron ore started to be delivered from Cumberland and Lancashire in 1917.

Workington Iron and Steel Company employed 4,600 on the Cumberland coast, while the Wigan Coal and Iron Company employed 10,500 in Wigan. The Partington Steel and Iron Company employed 2,200 west of Manchester while John Summers and Sons employed 3,600 near Chester. Pearson and Knowles Coal and Iron Company employed 2,600 in Warrington while Shelton Iron and Steel Company, and Robert Heath and Sons employed 7,500 in Stoke-on-Trent. Frodingham Iron Company employed 2,400 in Scunthorpe.

Sheffield was a major iron and steel producing city, with eight large companies employing over 47,000 men and 10,000 women. They were Hadfields, Vickers, Cammell Laird's, Thomas Firth's, John Brown's, Samuel Fox's, and Newton, Chambers and Company. Another 28,000 men and 15,000 women worked in smaller factories. The Park Gate Iron and Steel Company in Rotherham also employed 2,000.

Four large companies in South Wales and along the Welsh border employed over 28,000 making castings and forgings:

- Ebbw Vale Steel, Iron and Coal Company in Ebbw Vale.
- Richard Thomas and Company in Abergavenny and Lydney.
- Port Talbot Steel Company in Port Talbot.
- Baldwins Limited in Swansea.

Chapter 12

Non-Ferrous Materials

The Control of Supplies[1]

The munitions industry required many types of non-ferrous materials imported from around the world, such as copper, spelter, zinc, brass, aluminium, lead and tin. Demand often outstripped supply, as the Ministry of Munitions struggled to keep the factories busy.

Aluminium was the first non-ferrous material to be controlled in December 1915. Statistics gathered early in 1916, gave the Ministry of Munitions a better idea about stocks and it put controls on copper in May 1916, followed by spelter and lead over the winter. Tin was the final non-ferrous material to come under control in April 1918.

Copper[2]

Copper was used to make the brass required for shell fuses and cartridges (the casing which held the cordite propellant). It was also used to make the driving bands that fitted around the base of shells. The bands gripped the spiralled rifling in the barrel, when a gun was fired, causing the projectile to spin, so it travelled with greater accuracy during flight.

American refineries doubled their output of copper to 6,700 tons a month during the early months of the war. The Raw Materials Department started distributing copper to factories when the Ministry of Munitions took over in June 1915 but an American cartel had tripled the price by early 1916. Britain and France were concerned that German supporters in the United States would try and push it higher, so the two countries combined their buying power, while the London Metal Exchange fixed the price.

Imports rose to 23,500 tons a month but there were concerns that factories could close, following the loss of the SS *Cymric* and its load of copper in May 1916. So, the Ministry took control of copper. Consumption was also reduced by switching to cast iron fuses and by using thinner driving bands. Over 100 companies had made 173 million copper bands by the end of the war.

Zinc and Spelter[3]

Britain had been importing 30 per cent of its zinc and spelter (a zinc-lead alloy) from Germany when war broke out. So, it switched to Norwegian and Canadian zinc, while spelter came from the United States and Norway. The British government introduced the Enemies Contracts Annulment Act 1915 to end German control of Australian zinc mines. It also invested in the country's mining industry, after agreeing to import large amounts of zinc and spelter for ten years after the war.

Britain was soon importing 17,000 tons a month and large amounts were used to galvanise food containers or make brass. Extra smelting facilities had to be built, while a change in specification reduced how much was needed. As prices quadrupled, Britain sold ores to the Netherlands in exchange for spelter to try and undermine the profiteers. The Ministry of Munitions then seized stocks of zinc and spelter from companies that refused to sell at a reasonable amount before fixing the price in April 1917. It eventually invested in four new zinc foundries and opened the National Spelter Company in Avonmouth near Bristol.

Brass[4]

Brass is made from 60 per cent copper and 40 per cent zinc. It was initially bought from the United States to make shell components, such as fuses and cartridges. Scrap brass was eventually collected from the battlefields and up to 5,000 tons a month was shipped back to the remelted. Plant was also bought from the United States to turn shavings (swarf) and old fuses into brass rod to make new fuses. By the end of 1917, 9,000 tons of brass a month were being made.

The Carron Company of Falkirk, Robert MacLaren and Company of Glasgow, and the Midland Railway Company of Derby were soon making several million fuse stampings a month, while more were bought from Switzerland. Any surplus was sent to France's shell industry. The Ministry of Munitions set up a section at the end of 1916 to control the distribution of brass and the collection of scrap. Many stampings were made at the new Government Rolling Mill built at Southampton; it was particularly busy following the German spring offensives.

Aluminium[5]

Aluminium was used in everything from water bottles to engines and electrical parts. It was imported from the United States, Canada and Norway; controls had to be put on the British Aluminium Company in the Scottish Highlands and the Aluminium Company in North Wales when the price rose. Using brass to make fuses instead of aluminium reduced the amounts imported from 1,800 tons down to 1,150 tons a month. Eventually, the bauxite rights (aluminium ore) in British Guiana in the British West Indies were handed over to the Aluminium Company of America to secure enough aluminium for Britain, France and Russia.

While the United States increased production of aluminium when it entered the war, it also raised the price, so the Ministry of Munitions had to take control of scrap aluminium. The huge increase in the number of planes wanted by the Air Ministry in 1918 tripled its demand to 1,500 tons a month. Unfortunately, it overestimated orders and large amounts were left over when the war ended.

Lead[6]

Lead was used to make shrapnel balls and the core of rifle bullets. By 1917, the shell and bullet factories required up to 18,000 tons of lead a month. Most was imported from Spain but the Ministry of Munitions had to take control of stocks in 1917 when imports from Australia were delayed. It also seized all the scrap lead across Britain, including 25,000 tons of old printers' metal, to make up the deficit. In fact, it did so well at collecting lead that 160,000 tons were left over when the war ended.

Tin[7]

Britain required over 2,500 tons of tin a month. However, many Cornish tin miners enlisted during the early months of the war, so imports from Malaysia, Bolivia and the Dutch East Indies had to be increased. A third of the amount was used by factories in South Wales to plate hundreds of thousands of mess tins and food containers. The Ministry of Munitions took control of home production and imports at the end of December 1916. There were shortages after the SS *Glenartney* and SS *Eumaeus* were sunk in February 1917, so alternative ways had to be found to store food safely.

Scrap[8]

Companies were too busy meeting their orders to be worried about recycling in 1914 and 1915. However, the Raw Materials Branch instructed them to collect scrap and swarf (metal shavings), which were turned into easy to handle briquettes. The Ministry of Munitions wanted to make better use of both materials, so it offered loans to build new furnaces. Open hearth furnaces melted down heavy scrap, while electric furnaces melted down light scrap, with huge jolts of electricity. The Ministry also started distributing iron ore in May 1916 and stopped speculators making money from scrap steel in July 1916.

The Steel Production Department took over and charged factories for the scrap they used, stopping dealers buying and selling any. Hundreds of tons of non-ferrous scrap, including copper, zinc, brass, aluminium, lead and tin, were also collected.

The new Iron and Steel Department took total control of scrap at the beginning of 1917. Huge amounts were collected from factories, dockyards, scrapyards and from the battlefields. While it piled up at the steel works, it required young and fit men to operate the furnaces. Unfortunately, they were also ideal candidates for conscription and their enlistment resulted in furnaces being shut down (known as blown out) or put on part time work (known as slack blast).

Salvage[9]

The BEF had always made a point of collecting broken and discarded items, and mending what it could. However, salvaging began in earnest when the Ministry's Salvage Section opened depots at the minor ports of Renfrew near Glasgow, Blyth in Northumberland, Immingham in Lincolnshire, Trafford Park near Manchester and Ridham Dock in Kent in August 1915. Items were sorted and sent to the factories that made them, either to be repaired or broken up for spare parts. Eventually over 20,000 tons of broken items a month were being shipped to Britain and 70 per cent were either being repaired or reused.

The Salvage and Stores departments ended up dealing with all kinds of items. Pre-war ammunition boxes had been a robust design, capable of withstanding long journeys around the British Empire. However, cheaper designs suitable for the short journey to France were soon being made by the National Box Factories. They made 350,000 new boxes a month from 7,700 tons of recycled or salvaged wood.

Small calibre shell cases and cartridge cases were collected, while copper bands were removed from shells to be melted down. They were shipped to England in damaged boxes, which were sent to the National Cartridge and Box Repair Factories at Dagenham and Newport. Over 3,320 women and 450 men repaired 3 million cartridge cases and 750,000 ammunition boxes every month. The National Box Repair Factory at Beddington in Croydon also repaired 450,000 mortar bomb and grenade boxes a month.

A National Fuse Rectification Factory started repairing broken fuses in Camden, London in May 1916. Meanwhile, the National Gun Carriage Repair Factory carried out simple repairs in Southampton, while serious repairs were either carried out at the Royal Arsenal or at the factory where they were made.

Oil and Petroleum[10]

Britain needed over 200,000 tons of oil products a month in 1914. Most was imported from the United States and the Dutch East Indies (now Indonesia). However, Standard Oil of New Jersey and Standard Oil of New York put up the prices of American oil, while Royal Dutch Shell did the same with Indonesian oil. The London based Anglo-Persian Oil Company (APOC) had only recently been founded by the Burmah Shell Company. While it had bought majority shares in the Persian (now Iranian) oilfields, the British government immediately bought a controlling interest in the company on the outbreak of war, to provide the Admiralty with supplies for its warships.

APOC soon set up the British Tanker Company and acquired the British Petroleum Company to take control from the German owned European Petroleum Company. Meanwhile, an Inter-Departmental Oil Committee looked for oil sources and locations to set up fuel depots across the British Empire.

Britain also required 28,300 tons of petroleum per month:

- 13,750 tons for the War Office and Admiralty.
- 10,800 tons for commercial purposes.
- 2,900 tons for the explosives industry.

The Petrol Control Committee was appointed to take a census of vehicles in April 1916, while a fuel excise duty halved private usage. A Regulation of Petroleum Supplies Committee also banned the use of kerosene as a fuel.

The Pool Board was appointed at the beginning of 1917 to start negotiating prices with the main importers of oil and petrol. However, the main problem was unrestricted submarine warfare, which sank four tankers in January 1917 alone, so Britain had to ask the United States for replacements.

The Inter-Departmental Petroleum Committee decided how to distribute fuel between the services, shipping companies and domestic users, while the Petroleum Supplies Department handed out supplies to the Ministry's departments. Further restrictions had to be put in place by the Board of Trade's Petrol Control Department in June 1917 and it had to revoke 70,000 private licenses. Meanwhile, arguments between the services and the Ministry of Munitions led to the formation of the Petroleum Executive at the end of 1917. A conference was also held in February 1918 to try and coordinate fuel supplies between the Allies.

The Petroleum Research Department experimented unsuccessfully with new fuel sources across Britain. It mixed petrol with a bituminous coal (known as Cannel coal) to produce a mineral oil, while a creosote fuel produced from coal tar was used by the Admiralty. Meanwhile, plans to drill for oil were delayed until it was too late to make a difference, while a scheme to use Scottish shale oil was cancelled. Some people used coal gas stored in bags on the roof of their vehicle as a fuel, until a Gas Restriction Order stopped them early in 1918.

Chapter 13

The Explosives Industry

Types of Explosives[1]

The armed forces relied on three types of explosives: propulsive explosives, detonators and high explosives.[2] A primer detonated the propulsive explosive in the breech, shooting the shell fast from the barrel. Cordite MD (modified) was the original propulsive explosive but it was replaced by cordite RDB (Research Department formula B), when ether alcohol mix was used as a replacement for acetone.

Fine grained tetryl was used as the igniter for the high explosive and it was initiated either when a shell hit the target or after a set time, determined by a fuse. It lit the gunpowder in the base of the shell, which was used as the bursting charge. The explosion scattered the bullets when it exploded in a shrapnel shell in a shotgun action. The gunpowder detonated either the picric acid or TNT, which created the blast of a high explosive shell.

The Royal Navy and the British Army were both using the picric acid made by the Royal Gunpowder Factory at Waltham Abbey, as their high explosive when war broke out. The Defence of the Realm Act put the explosives industry under state control.[3] So, the War Department immediately took over the synthetic products' TNT purification factory in Rainham, Essex and started building another at Oldbury in the West Midlands. The War Office also appointed the High Explosives Committee to secure supplies of raw materials, stopped exports and it even bought 450 tons from the United States at a high price.

British explosive companies initially refused to make TNT, believing no one would want to buy it after the war, so four contractors were given money to build new plant:

- Brotherton and Company built a factory in Leeds.
- John W. Leitch and Company built their factory in Huddersfield in West Yorkshire.
- Nobel's Explosive Company built a factory in Pembrey in South Wales.
- Bragley's built their factory in Hackney Wick in London.

A large stock of crude TNT was also purified at the Clayton Aniline Company factory in Manchester.

Exploiting Britain's coal reserves may have produced excess of tar products but the country had to import the rest of the raw materials it required to manufacture explosives:

- Sulphur came from Sicily.
- Pyrites came from Spain.
- Sodium nitrate from Chile.

The Explosives Supply Branch was set up in January 1915 to look for sources of toluene, acetone and fuming sulphuric acid (also known as oleum), and to buy nitric acid to make TNT.

Contracts to acquire phenol were secured, while Chance and Hunt Limited were making 200 tons of TNT in Oldbury. Another ten firms were also installing plant which used a three step nitration process to turn toluene into TNT.

High explosive production was increasing by the time the Ministry of Munitions took over in June 1915 but estimates of how much the armed forces would require were four times higher than anticipated.[4] So, the Ministry took over the buying and distribution of raw materials to get the best prices and maximum output. It also restricted the sale of products related to the explosives industry through permits and licenses. Large numbers of shell casings were also due from the United States and Canada, so plans to export surplus picric acid to France and Russia were cancelled.

The Ministry of Munitions took control of the whole explosives industry in 1916 but financial pressures made it increasingly difficult to buy enough of everything. Unrestricted submarine warfare the following year made it increasingly difficult to import enough raw materials.

So, the chemists were asked to find substitutes and chemical plants were soon producing benzol to make synthetic phenol. The Ministry of Munitions also secured stocks of alcohol and grain to make ether alcohol, which replaced imported acetone. Meanwhile, soap and candles were bought up to make glycerine for the cordite industry.

The Propellants[5]

Cordite was used to create the explosion in the breech of the gun or howitzer, sending the shell flying through the air. Nitric acid and sulphuric acid were used to turn cellulose into nitrocellulose. It was mixed with nitroglyccrin and a small amount of petroleum jelly (a 65/30/5 mix), which acted as a lubricant causing less wear to the gun barrels than basic cordite. The mixture was then soaked into cotton waste to make guncotton. Acetone made the guncotton pliable, so it could be rolled into thin cords (like uncooked spaghetti), which made it easier to insert into the cartridge part of the shells, hence the name cordite or to give it its full name, cordite MD (modified).

A shortage of imported American acetone, resulted in the Royal Arsenal's Research Department introducing cordite RDB (Research Department formula B) in May 1915. It used a homemade ether alcohol mix (known as collodion), nitroglycerin and a small amount of petroleum jelly (a 52/42/6 mix).

The Ministry of Munitions also took control of alcohol distilleries in May 1916, while the recovery of solvent was improved. The industry used over 90 million gallons of plain ethanol and methylated spirits, and 10 million gallons of alcohol was left over when the war ended.

The Ministry financed National Wood Distillation and Acetone Factories at Dundee in Scotland, Coleford in Gloucestershire, Bideford in Devon and Longparish in Hampshire and they were soon making 100 tons a month between them. Two more factories at Ludlow in Shropshire and Chichester in Sussex were going to supply the extended aircraft programme but they were never finished. The Synthetic Products Company of King's Lynn in Norfolk tried making acetone from potatoes, maize and horse chestnuts but the product was poor, so the factory closed in July 1918.

Glycerine, the main ingredient of the soap and candle industries, was used in nitroglycerin, so the Ministry of Munitions stopped exports and took control of stocks in August 1915, forcing other industries to use substitutes. It also imported glycerine, increasing the amount available to 1,800 tons a month.

The cordite factories required huge amounts of cotton waste to soak up the explosive liquids, creating the volatile material that would explode when ignited. While imports increased to 3,500 tons a month, the British and Foreign Supply Association contracted eight National Cotton Waste Mills across Lancashire and Yorkshire to collect and prepare 1,350 tons a month.

Guncotton was rolled into thin sticks of cordite that were bound together with an ignitor pad and placed inside a silk bag. Tens of thousands of silk bags were required but replacement fabrics had to be sourced across Britain because supplies from Japan and the Far East were erratic.

The Propellant Factories[6]

The Royal Gunpowder Factory in Waltham Abbey employed 900 making guncotton and cordite before the war. While the cramped grounds and the later threat of air raids made it unsafe to extend the factory, the workforce increased to 3,100 men and 2,600 women after the Ministry of Munitions took it over in August 1915. The tetryl plant burnt down in July 1916 but the factory still made the following during the war:

- 31,700 tons of cordite.
- 1,650 tons of gunpowder.

- 1,650 tons of tetryl.
- 2,425 tons of guncotton.

Seven companies were also making small amounts of explosives for the mining and quarrying industries, so the War Office offered them money to extend their factories. Nobel's Explosive Company built a guncotton factory near Ardeer, south-west of Glasgow and a cordite factory at Pembrey in South Wales. Kynoch built a plant at Kynochtown in Essex for the Admiralty, while work was started on a Royal Naval Cordite Factory in Wareham in Dorset. The Asiatic Petroleum Company planned to produce guncotton for the Admiralty at Queensferry in Cheshire. However, in June 1915 it decided to use the Royal Naval Cordite Factory, so Queensferry started making guncotton for the British Army in December 1915. It would eventually make 18,000 tons of guncotton and nitrocellulose.

Most of the guncotton would be sent to a large new factory at Gretna in Dumfries on the Scottish border. The location had been chosen because it was in a rural area and could obtain the 10 million gallons of water a day it needed from the River Esk. It was also out of reach of the German airships. Gretna started production in the summer of 1916, using the nitrocotton made by Queensferry. Production had increased to 3,400 tons a month by the summer of 1917 and it eventually made 56,900 tons of cordite (RDB).

The amount of cordite used by the British armed forces increased from 2,150 tons a month in 1915 to 17,000 in 1917. Altogether the Royal Navy and the British Army used over 450,000 tons of cordite during the war and half of it had been imported. Reductions in the 1918 munitions programme resulted in Gretna and Pembrey lowering their output to 3,000 tons and 1,000 tons a month respectively. Around 58,000 tons of cordite and other propulsive explosives were left over at the end of the war.

The Detonator Factories[7]

The Royal Gunpowder Factory in Waltham Abbey made all the tetryl during the first twelve months of the war. The Admiralty built their own facility at Poole in Dorset. It was used to detonate the gunpowder that in turn detonated the picric acid or TNT in a high explosive shell.

Nobel's Explosive Company sent their product to Waltham Abbey for purification but most of what the Explosives and Chemical Products Company made was rejected. A standby plant at Queensferry started producing tetryl after the facilities at Waltham Abbey were destroyed in July 1916 but the War Office soon stopped using it because it was expensive and hazardous to make.

Gunpowder contained a mix of potassium nitrate (saltpetre), charcoal and sulphur (a 75/15/10 mix). Small amounts of fine grain gunpowder were used as a bursting charge to scatter the lead balls in shrapnel shells over their target. A coarser grain was used to detonate the picric acid or TNT in high explosive shells, when they hit their target. High grade TNT was used as an exploder.

Potassium nitrate had been imported from Germany before the war, so an alternative source was found in India. The three gunpowder firms increased their monthly production to 640 tons, when Russia asked for some.

The High Explosives[8]

The manufacture of picric acid and TNT starts with the distillation of coal tar, which Britain's coalfields produced an excess of, to make toluene. Picric acid (also known as lyddite) was the bursting charge used in high explosive shells in the summer of 1914. It was made from phenol, which came from processing coal tar.

However, TNT was safer to handle than picric acid and the War Office approved its use in September 1914. It starts with toluene, a byproduct made when coal is converted to coke in a coke oven, to form coke. A three stage nitration process turns the toluene into mononitrotoluene (MNT), then dinitrotoluene (DNT) and finally the explosive TNT.

The export of coal tar, benzene and MNT were banned on the outbreak of war but there were soon shortages. So, the High Explosives Committee gave companies advances to install coke ovens, benzene recovery plant and gas scrubbers in November 1914.[9] The output of toluene had increased by 800 per cent by the time the Ministry of Munitions took over and formed an Explosives Supply Department in June 1915.

The Acid Factories[10]

The explosives industry also needed large amounts of sodium nitrate, sulphur and pyrites (sulphur ore) to make nitric acid and sulphuric acid. The Admiralty's Transport Department dealt with imports until the Munitions Overseas Transport Department took over. Pyrites from Spain and Sicily were roasted in kilns to produce sulphur and imports had peaked at 94,000 tons a month by 1916.

Around 40,000 tons a month of sodium nitrate was imported from Chile and it was treated with fuming sulphuric acid (oleum) to make nitric acid. Meanwhile, hydrochloric acid was made by mixing sulphuric acid with common salt. The German submarine campaign and rising shipping costs affected imports in 1917, so oil and coal were offered to Spain, Sicily and Chile, in exchange for their raw materials.

Britain also increased its refining capacity to make its own supply of acids. The Royal Gunpowder Factory, Chance and Hunt Limited in Oldbury, and Spencer Chapman and Messel Limited in Silvertown all started making nitric acid. It was also made by Nobel's Explosive Company, south-west of Glasgow, Clayton Aniline Company in Manchester and Kynoch Limited in Arklow, Ireland (now the Republic of Ireland). New plants were also built at the Royal Naval Factory in Poole and at HM Factory, Queensferry.

The demand for acids increased, so companies were encouraged to reduce waste and recover as much as possible. Building new plants was taking longer than expected, so the Ministry of Munitions took control of sulphuric acid production at the beginning of 1916, extracting it from nitre cake, a byproduct of the nitric acid process. Ammonia liquor was used instead of ammonium sulphate to reduce the amount of sulphuric acid required to make ammonium nitrate. At its peak, British industry was producing 13,000 tons of nitric acid, 24,000 tons of hydrochloric acid and 24,000 tons of oleum a month. Oleum was also being imported from United States, Canada and the Netherlands.

The Picric Acid and Synthetic Phenol Factories[11]

Only 135 tons a month of picric acid (lyddite) was being made before the war. The High Explosives Committee offered money, so British Dyes Limited in Huddersfield and the Low Moor Munitions Company in Bradford in West Yorkshire extended their works, while Robert Graesser Limited rebuilt its plant on the Welsh border. The production of picric acid was reduced due to the switch to TNT in the autumn of 1914. However, the introduction of homemade synthetic phenol, which was made from benzene, in the summer of 1916, revived the demand for it until the destruction of the Low Moor factory on 21 August 1916. Even so, the other two factories increased their output, until 540 tons a month were being made. While the production of picric acid for shells ended in January 1918 it was later used to make lethal gas.

Benzol was extracted from coal tar to make synthetic phenol, which in turn made picric acid, ending the need to import phenol. Read Holliday and Sons in Huddersfield, Brunner Mond and Company in Northwich, the South Metropolitan Gas Company in London and a government factory at Ellesmere Port near Chester, were all successful. However, Chemical Products Company in Sutton Oak near St Helens and H.N. Morris and Company at West Gorton near Manchester had to be taken over.

Four factories were altered to make picric acid and then convert it into making chloropicrin lethal gas in 1917. Lance Blythe Limited in Lytham, Lancashire and Sharp and Mallett Limited in Greetland, West Yorkshire, were soon producing 700 tons a month between them. However, L.B. Holliday and Company did not start work in Bradley, West Yorkshire until the final days of the war. The Explosives Supply Department also converted a picric acid factory in Avonmouth to start making mustard gas in August 1918.

The TNT Factories[12]

Rainham Chemical Works in Essex was taken over by the War Department under the Defence of the Realm Act in November 1914. Coley and Wilbraham Limited initially converted butyl alcohol into TNT before it turned to recovering TNT from waste amatol later in the war. The factory was producing over 250 tons a month when it was destroyed by an explosion on 13 February 1918.

Chance and Hunt's plant at Oldbury in the West Midlands started making TNT in May 1915. While it was soon making 560 tons a month, improvements to the chemical processes increased the yield to 2,400 tons by the end of 1917.

Ergite was building a plant at Penrhyndeudraeth in North Wales to make crude TNT when an explosion destroyed part of it on 8 June 1915. The Ministry of Munitions rebuilt it and production eventually peaked at 180 tons a month. Nobel's Explosive Company started making TNT at Pembrey in Carmarthenshire in July 1915 and production soon rose to 1,285 tons a month, which required 120 million of gallons of water. The factory employed 2,850 women and 1,915 men at its peak but it was closed in April 1917.

Another source of toluene was the petroleum imported by the Asiatic Petroleum Company, most of it from Shell, which had oilfields around the world. After nitration at Oldbury, it was distilled into toluene at Portishead, near Bristol, using equipment taken from company's refinery in Rotterdam.

The Asiatic Petroleum Company also distilled petroleum into MNT at Sandycroft in Cheshire, so it could be nitrated into TNT at its adjacent Queensferry site. Production started at the beginning of 1916 and it eventually made 55,700 tons. Hardman and Holden Limited started refining toluene at Trafford Park near Manchester in July 1916. Production had risen to 100,000 gallons a month by 1918 and the plant had made 3 million gallons by the end of the war. It also made 315,000 gallons of naphtha solvent, which was used to made toluene, as well as 530,000 gallons of benzene, which was used to make synthetic phenol. A backup distillery was installed at Barrow-in-Furness in Cumberland in case there was an accident.

Queensferry also started producing fuming sulphuric acid in September 1916 and it had been used to make over 100,000 tons of sulphur monoxide by the end of the war. The two factories employed over 7,300 women and 2,200 men, and most travelled to the site by train and bus.

Brunner Mond and Company started purifying TNT at Gadbrook near Northwich in February 1916. The Ministry of Munitions took it over and introduced a safer purification process, following an explosion at the Silvertown plant on 19 January 1917. The factory had made over 31,000 tons of TNT by the end of the war.

H.N. Morris and Company made slow progress building a factory in West Gorton near Manchester, so it was taken over in October 1915. It had made 1,225 tons of phenol and 2,900 tons of TNT by the time it closed in April 1917.

Lothian Chemical Company built a factory at Craigleith in Edinburgh but work had to stop in June 1916 because it was in a built up area. A new factory was built outside the city and it started producing TNT in November 1917.

Bagley's was building a plant at Hackney Wick in east London but slow progress meant the Ministry of Munitions had to take over. The factory was shut down in April

1917 because it was in a built up area but it was kept on standby in case of an emergency. Brotherton and Company were also slow to start production at their Litherland plant, north of Liverpool, so it too was taken over in the spring of 1916. The plant was closed in April 1918.

The Ammonium Nitrate Factories[13]

Shortages of high grade TNT led the High Explosives Committee to suggest mixing it with ammonium nitrate to make Amatol in 1917. Royal Navy warships could not use it because moisture made ammonium nitrate unstable. However, the War Office was prepared to try it out and a reserve was prepared in case picric acid or TNT stocks ran low. Initially, a 40 per cent TNT and 60 per cent ammonium nitrate (40/60) mixture was used. The formula was later changed to 20 per cent and 80 per cent after tests proved it was good enough. The shortages of TNT ended when chemists introduced a new refining process, which increased the yield five-fold in October 1917.

Ammonium nitrate required ammonia, so coking plants, gas works and shale oil companies were encouraged to collect their ammonia byproducts. Brunner Mond's in Northwich then concentrated them into ammonia liquor.

Ammonium nitrate also required calcium nitrate, which was originally imported from Norway. The Salt Union started producing ammonium nitrate at Lostock near Northwich in February 1916, using sodium nitrate and calcium chloride from the Cheshire Alkali Works. However, it was difficult to find enough labour, so soldiers were employed, until 1,000 men were brought from Sheffield. The Ministry of Munitions took over the refinery in October 1917 because the management arrangement was not working but the factory had still produced 120,000 tons of calcium nitrate by the end of the war.

Stratton Works was opened in Swindon in September 1917 to make extra supplies of ammonium nitrate. While it could produce 6,700 tons a month, a reduced ammunition programme meant it usually only made 2,000. By the end of the war, the plant had made 25,000 tons.

Roburite and Ammonal Limited built a plant in Watford to make ammonal, a mining explosive that is made from ammonium nitrate and aluminium powder. Some of it was used by the Trench Warfare Filling Factories, while more was used for mining operations on the Western Front. The surplus was sent to Russia. British Westfalite at Denaby and the Thames Ammunition Works increased output to 800 tons a month. Production switched to making amatol at the beginning of 1917 and powdered TNT at the beginning of 1918.

The Langwith Byproduct Company started producing ammonium perchlorate near Mansfield in June 1917, ending the country's reliance on Swedish imports. It was used as a water safe explosive in the H.2 floating mines required by the Admiralty.

The use of ammonium nitrates by the explosives industry, left the agricultural industry short of what it needed to make fertilisers. So, the Ministry of Munitions had to import phosphorite from Chile to make superphosphates to replace them. The Nitrogen Products Company was building a plant at Billingham near Middlesbrough to make more ammonium compounds when the Armistice was declared.

Importing Explosives

Britain's explosive industry was making just 900 tons and importing another 1,120 tons of cordite and nitrocellulose powder when the Ministry of Munitions took over in June 1915. The quantity had changed to 5,800 tons a month made at home and 1,800 tons of imports by 1916. Home production had increased further still to 7,750 tons a month by 1917 but the Ministry was still importing a little to keep up with the expanded ammunition programme. Altogether, J.P. Morgan's sourced 227,000 tons of cordite and nitrocellulose in America, a lot of it from DuPont de Nemours and Company in Delaware.

Imports ended when the United States entered the war in the spring of 1917, so Nobel's Explosive Company stopped building a national nitrocellulose powder factory at Henbury near Bristol. It also started reconditioning damaged nitrocellulose powder at a factory in Irvine in Ayrshire.

Canadian Explosives Limited continued to ship cordite to England, while Canadian-made shells were filled with American cordite. Over time the country developed its own explosives industry, until it was making over 2,000 tons of cordite and nitrocellulose powder a month. The amount reduced after the Trenton explosives factory in Ontario burned down in October 1918.

Standards[14]

The rapid expansion of the explosives industry, the use of new processes and the shortage of qualified staff meant production standards sometimes dropped. So, extra testing was introduced in 1916, which resulted in explosives being divided into grades:

- Naval shells required Grade 1 picric acid.
- Army shells used Grade 2 picric acid.
- Grade 3 picric acid was used to make lethal gas or dyes.
- Grade 1 TNT was used for the exploders in shells.
- Grade 2 TNT was used to fill the shells.
- Grade 3 TNT was mixed with ammonium nitrate to make amatol.

It was also several months before the TNT made by the Nobel's Explosive Company at Ardeer in Ayrshire was accepted but an explosion destroyed the factory on 30 July 1915.

The reduction in the use of lethal gas on the Somme, meant that the Special Brigade was able to send men back to help at the factories in the summer of 1916. Many were chemistry students who had been enlisted to supervise the gas attack at the Battle of Loos the previous September. They were joined by chemists who had travelled from Australia and Canada.

Members of the Institute of Chemistry and University Chemistry departments helped the Royal Arsenal's Research Department, while a new laboratory opened at Chiswick in west London in the summer of 1916. Once chemical reactions had been tested in the laboratory, large-scale tests were tried at an experimental plant in Grays in Essex. Only then would companies be given money to build new factories.

The demand for high explosives had increased to 2,100 tons a month for the Royal Navy and 5,900 tons for the War Office by the summer of 1916. British factories were only making 4,800 tons of picric acid and TNT a month but the use of 8,300 tons of ammonium nitrate in the amatol mix, more than compensated for the shortfall. The factories also became more efficient and wastage was reduced as they gained experience. Continual experimentation improved production, while substituting raw materials reduced shipping and import costs.

Accidents and Safety[15]

Explosive companies were working according to the Explosives Act 1875 when war broke out. A rapid expansion of the industry meant factories were often designed with poor layouts or built with unsuitable material. Many were run by inexperienced managers and manned by an unskilled workforce. A few had to be abandoned because they had been built in urban areas. It was also realised too late that building large explosives and filling factories put the munitions industry in danger. One accident disrupted production to such an extent that supplies were put in jeopardy. So, spare factory capacity had to be built, ready to take over if a factory was put out of action.

Explosions destroyed two factories at Ardeer, south-west of Glasgow and Penrhyndeudraeth in North Wales in the summer of 1915. So, a new safety committee introduced extra rules, such as prohibiting smoking and matches in explosives' areas. Subsequent inspections by the Home Office resulted in two factories being taken over, due to dangerous practices.

To make matters worse, little was known about the new explosive, TNT. It was exempt from the Explosives Act to begin with but it was soon clear that it was causing health problems for many and the deaths of a few. Again, new rules were introduced to reduce the hazards.

Safety officers were eventually appointed to all explosives factories but the accidents did not stop. The picric acid factory at Low Moor Bradford was destroyed on 21 August 1916. The manufacture of TNT was included under the Explosives Act following a huge explosion at Brunner Mond's factory in Silvertown in east London on 19 January 1917.

The destruction of the Hooley Hill factory in Manchester resulted in the closing of all TNT factories in urban areas in June 1917.

However, the accidents continued and Morecambe's National Filling Factory burnt down in October 1917, followed by another fire at the TNT purification plant at Rainham on the River Thames in February 1918. The final major incident was a huge explosion at Chilwell National Filling Factory near Nottingham on 1 July 1918, which killed and injured 384 workers. Fortunately, Hereford National Filling Factory was able to step in when first Morecombe and then Chilwell were seriously damaged.

Storage and Insurance

Storing large amounts of explosives safely soon became a problem. The magazines at Chislehurst in south-east London were full by September 1915, so three new large ones were built. Propellants were stored on the marshes near the Royal Arsenal, while TNT was stored near the Rainham factory in Essex. Other places included slate quarries in Wales, mines in Dudley and Northwich, caves in Reigate and obsolete forts across the country.

The number of accidents resulted in the Ministry of Munitions having to take out insurance for its explosives plants after the Faversham explosion in April 1916. However, workers and third party property owners struggled to get compensation until the Munitions (Liability for Explosions) Act was introduced in December 1916.

Quantities

The increasing demands for explosives required new factories. So, the Ministry of Munitions offered advances to build plants to refine the raw materials, while the chemists looked for methods to improve production rates and yields. There was a shortage of chemical engineers to operate the factories, so many had to be taught on the job. Dilution of the workforce became widespread and eventually over half of the 30,000 workers in the explosives industry were women.

Britain's production of high explosives was just 875 tons a month in 1915. While it peaked at 27,400 a month in 1917 it had reduced to 23,300 in 1918 as the demand shell fell. Thirty-six explosive related factories were built at a cost of £26 million (£1.5 billion today). The total amounts of the main types of explosives made for the British armed services were:

	High Explosives	Ammonium Nitrate	Cordite
Home	242,500 tons	317,625 tons	223,400 tons
Imported	33,800 tons	18,700 tons	227,100 tons

Chapter 14

The Chemical Industry

The Control of Chemical Warfare[1]

The Engineer Munitions Department started researching lethal gas but it was renamed the Trench Warfare Department when it was transferred to the Ministry of Munitions in June 1915. It worked closely with the Special Brigade, which was based in France, while chemical industry experts supported the Scientific Advisory Committee at the Imperial College London. Laboratories were set up at Wimbledon in west London, while tests were carried out on Clapham Common in south London.

Research and design of chemical weapons separated at the beginning of 1916, when the Trench Warfare Department was reorganised. Section TW1 dealt with grenades, TW2 dealt with gas cylinders and TW7 dealt with mortar shells.

The Chemical Warfare Department took over chemical production in November 1917 and it appointed the Chemical Advisory Committee and the Anti-Gas Department. While it urged cooperation amongst the scientists it failed to get them to speak to the gunners.

The Explosives Supply Department started supervising the charging (filling) of shells when some of the National Explosives Factories switched to making lethal gas in April 1918.[2] Meanwhile, the Gun Ammunition Filling Department started assembling the shells, while some of the National Filling Factories switched to making chemical shells.

The Chemicals and their Factories[3]

A laboratory had to make samples and trials had to be completed before a new gas was accepted. But that was only the start of the process because the chemical engineers had to work out how to safely scale up laboratory production so it would work in factories. It was not just a matter of multiplying the size of the process because larger vessels and complex reactions required careful consideration.

Construction began once the engineers had completed their calculations but progressive testing was required to make sure they were correct. This took time and the BEF's requirements often changed, so that some plants were abandoned before they were complete. What follows, is a list of the main gases used and where they were made:

Tear Gas[4]

The War Office started testing chloroacetone and benzyl chloride, two non-lethal gases (tear gas) in shells, but they failed to produce sufficiently dense clouds to cause irritation when they exploded. The Cassel Cyanide Company of Glasgow then started producing ethyl iodoacetate, another type of tear gas, in May 1915. It was named South Kensington, where the formula was created and codenamed SK. Around 18,000 grenades had been sent to France by August 1915. It was mixed with the lethal gas hydrogen cyanide (also known as hydrocyanic acid), codenamed AK, in October 1917 as production increased to 1,800 tons a month.

Chlorine Gas (Red Star)[5]

The War Office had not experimented with lethal substances because they were in breach of the 1899 Hague Convention. However, GHQ wanted to retaliate with chlorine gas following the German attacks at Ypres in April and May 1915. Tests were carried out by the Castner-Kellner Company in Runcorn and 140 tons of gas were discharged from 5,100 cylinders at Loos on 25 September and 13 October 1915. It had varied success due to the wind speed and direction.

Castner-Kellner expanded its facilities to make 675 tons per month, while the United Alkali Company in Widnes and the Electro-Bleach Company in Middlewich built new plants. The Ministry of Munitions took control of chlorine production in October and 3,500 tons was being produced a month by the time the BEF stopped using it in January 1917.

The factories started making chlorine again in the summer of 1918 because it was used to make mustard gas. The Explosives Supply Department took control of all gas production and started running the Electro-Bleach plant, which became known as HM Factory, Middlewich.

Phosgene Gas (Carbonyl Chloride)[6]

Phosgene (also known as carbonyl carbide), codenamed CG was more deadly and it had an inoffensive odour, which made it harder to detect. It was introduced because it could be made from bleaching powder (calcium hypochlorite), which could be made in large quantities, unlike liquid chlorine (see below).

United Alkali Company started making phosgene in Gateshead in January 1916. It was mixed with chlorine to make White Star gas at Ardol Limited's factory in Selby. A factory opened in Calais in March 1916 to fill cylinders, mortar shells and Livens projectors with French supplies. Phosgene was also mixed with arsenious chloride imported from Australia to form CBR and it was used in some of the first gas shells in the autumn of 1916.

Chloropicrin Gas and NC[7]

Castner-Kellner, West Riding Chemical Company in Wakefield, West Yorkshire and Sneyd Bycars Limited in Stoke-on-Trent, started making chloropicrin after successful experiments on Porton Down in April 1916. United Alkali Company and the Electro-Bleach Company also started making it. The gas was codenamed PS after Port Sunlight on the Wirral, where it had first been made from large amounts of bleaching powder, a byproduct of other processes.

Castner-Kellner also made stannic chloride, codenamed KJ, so that all three factories could mix it with chloropicrin, to make NC, which was better at penetrating gas masks, in the spring of 1917. Chloropicrin was mixed with phosgene to create a mixture codenamed PG after September 1917.

Chloropicrin had also been mixed with chlorine to make Yellow Star gas and hydrogen sulphide to make Green Star gas before production halted in November 1917. Hydrogen sulphide was also mixed with carbon disulphide at Chance and Hunt's plant in Oldbury to make Two Red Star gas.[8]

Prussic Acid and Arsenic Compounds

The Admiralty started making Jellite gas, codenamed JL, which was based on prussic acid, in Stratford in July 1916.[9] Some was mixed with arsenious trichloride to make a gas codenamed JBR for the BEF. It was also mixed with sodium cyanide to make Vincennite, codenamed VN, until production of Jellite ended in December 1917. VN was used in some of the first gas shells in the autumn of 1916.

Work started on three arsenic compounds, codenamed TD, TA and DM, at Rainham, HM Factory, Queensferry and the HM Explosive Factories at Sutton Oak and Ellesmere Port in the autumn of 1918.[10] The filling was carried out at the HM National Filling Factory, Morecambe but only 118 tons had been made by the end of the war.

Mustard Gas[11]

The Germans used dichlorodiethyl sulphide or mustard gas, codenamed HS for Hun Stuff, on 12 July 1917. The fine mist of liquid droplets causes life threatening blisters in the lungs and painful ones on moist areas of skin. The University of St Andrew's eventually worked out how to make it in bulk and production started in the summer of 1918.

Mustard gas was made at Avonmouth near Bristol, while Albright and Wilson made the carbon tetrachloride used to dilute it, at HM Factory, Langley in Oldbury. Trains started hauling wagons of mustard gas to the Nobel's Explosive Company factory at nearby Chittening, where 6-inch shells were made, while small calibre shells were made at Banbury, Hayes and Hereford.

Although both the HS liquid and its vapour were dangerous, the urgent demands for gas shells meant safety came second. Only 400 tons were made because the Avonmouth factory had to close twice when the workforce were incapacitated due to poor ventilation.

Bleach[12]

In 1915, chlorine gas was manufactured through the electrolysis of brine, extracted from Cheshire's salt fields. Lime then absorbed the gas to manufacture bleaching powder (calcium hypochlorite), a common disinfectant. However, the chlorine required on the battlefield needed to be pressurised into cylinders. It would then spray out under pressure, so that the wind could push the gas across no man's land.

The only company capable of liquifying chlorine gas was Castner-Kellner in Runcorn and it was only manufacturing 45 tons of liquid chlorine in the summer of 1915. So, the Ministry of Munitions sourced new suppliers of bleaching powder to relieve Castner-Kellner of its trade obligations, allowing it to increase its output of liquid chlorine, so it could produce 140 tons of pressurised liquid chlorine in time for the Loos offensive. A shortage of liquid chlorine meant that deliveries to the trenches were suspended at the end of 1915, while United Alkali installed plant in Widnes refinery. Electro-Bleach Company installed plant in Middlewich but it was taken over and renamed HM Factory, Middlewich in August 1918.

An alternative called chloropicrin (trichloronitromethane), was made from picric acid and sodium hypochlorite (commonly known as bleach), in April 1916. But bleach shortages in October 1916 meant the Ministry of Munitions had to reduce exports, until the companies had installed extra plant to increase their output. They eventually produced 18,000 tons a month.

Delivery Methods[13]

The Germans used liquid chlorine released from pressurised cylinders near Ypres in April and May 1915. Tests were held at the Castner-Kellner factory in Runcorn on 4 June 1915 and 140 tons of chlorine gas were released from 5,100 pressurised cylinders at Loos on 25 September and 13 October 1915.

After trials on Clapham Common, phosgene was being tested at Porton Down. However, the Germans used it first at Ypres in December 1915. Fortunately, improved smoke helmets had already been issued, while adequate protective measures were in place. Phosgene was later mixed with stannic chloride, which added smoke to the gas cloud. It was also mixed with liquid chlorine to make White Star after January 1916 and it became the main gas used during the Somme campaign.

Improved gas cylinders were designed by the Ordnance Committee and approved by the Director General of Munitions Design. After the autumn of 1916, they were emptied at Langwith near Mansfield and refilled at Bucknall sawmills in Stoke-on-Trent. While chloropicrin and sulphuretted hydrogen were used to make Green Star gas, the mixture corroded the cylinders, so the idea was dropped.

The introduction of chemical shells and the Livens, projector ended the use of cylinders in the spring of 1917 after the female workforce had handled 360,000 cylinders. However, another 130,000 cylinders would be ordered for the 1918 campaign season.

Charging, Filling and Assembling Shells[14]

Early trials with chlorine filled shells were abandoned in August 1915 because the bursting charge dispersed the gas. Tear gas shells were more successful and 10,000 shells were delivered in April 1916. Tests with phosgene and Jellite worked and 160,000 shells had been delivered by the end of the year.

Shells were filled with gas by the firm that made the gas. They were then fitted with the bursting charge, which was done at the Royal Arsenal until gas leaks affected the rest of the works.

Baird and Tatlock Limited's factory in Walthamstow was taken over before it switched to making tear gas shells in February 1916 and then Livens projectors in the summer of 1918. Watford No. 1 filled mortar shells while Watford No. 2 filled artillery shells. HM Filling Factory, Greenford in east London, started making chemical shells in January 1917 but it found it difficult to get the 1,000 workers it needed because of the dangers. Other companies that filled shells were Ardol in Selby, Sneyd Bycars near Stoke-on-Trent and the West Riding Chemical Company in Wakefield.

The fuses and propellant charges were then fitted to the shell. The projectiles were finally marked with coloured rings to identify their contents, which often gave the gases their codename. Demand grew from 225,000 chemical projectiles per month in the summer of 1916 to 1.44 million per month by the summer of 1918. It meant that one in three shells fired during the final months of the war were filled with gas. Between them, the factories filled over 4 million gas and smoke shells.

Lethal Gas Summary[15]

Only 880 tons of chlorine gas were made in 1915 and 140 tons were discharged near Loos on 25 September. During the war, 70 plants made 92,000 tons of chemicals that were used in cylinders, shells, Livens projectors and grenades:

- 21,000 tons were liquid chlorine.
- 7,500 tons were phosgene.
- 8,000 tons were chloropicrin.

The industry also made over 50,000 tons of intermediate products, most of it the bleaching powder used to make chloropicrin (10 tons of bleaching powder made just 1 ton of chloropicrin). While some of the chloropicrin was used for offensive purposes, the rest was used as a disinfectant to prevent the spread of disease in the trenches.

The demand for gas kept increasing until the control of chemical supplies was handed to the Explosives Supply Department when the Trench Warfare Supply Department was disbanded in April 1918. Several explosive factories were then converted to chemical plants. An Inter-Allied Commission for Chemical Warfare Supply was set up at the same time to discuss how to share lethal gas supplies.

Anti-Gas Research and Gas Masks

The British Army's Medical Department dealt with the first gas masks, which were introduced in the summer of 1915.[16] The Royal Army Medical College at Millbank in London carried out the experimental work and it was soon renamed the Anti-Gas Department. During 1915, 2.5 million Hypo helmets and 9 million improved P (phenate) helmets were made to protect men from chlorine gas.

A gas mask was a complicated item, made by sewing fabric together with eye pieces, nose clips and elastic. James Spicer and Sons organised over thirty small factories across London to make and assemble the parts.[17] The National Gas Mask Factory and the Granule Factory were eventually opened.[18] In 1916, 14 million PH (phenate hexamine) helmets, which gave protection from phosgene and 1.7 million PHG helmets, which also gave protection from tear gas, were made.

The use of mustard gas by the Germans in the summer of 1917 changed how gas was used on the battlefield. The Porton Down laboratories looked at how to make it but it took a year to perfect the process and build the Avonmouth and Chittening factories near Bristol.

Around 200,000 large box respirators had been issued before the improved small box respirator appeared and while 13.5 million were made, 2 million were repaired.

PART IV

The Factories

Chapter 15

The Royal Arsenal

The Original Armaments Factory[1]

The Chief Superintendent of Ordnance Factories ran the Royal Arsenal, Woolwich in east London and it was split into three departments:

- The Royal Gun Factory and Royal Carriage Department made gun mechanisms, carriages, limbers and wagons.
- The Mechanical Engineer's Department dealt with engineering requirements.
- The Building Works Department dealt with construction.

Over 10,850 men worked at the Royal Factories before the war but many were reservists who were called up. Getting enough labour was difficult but overtime and night shifts increased production ten-fold, as workers completed up to 100 hours a week. Older men, women and boys replaced the reservists and the workforce peaked at 41,000 men, 25,700 women and 6,000 boys, who were organised into shifts to get the most out of the machinery.

The Royal Arsenal's core staff were experienced, so they could easily switch production and both the War Office and the Ministry of Munitions relied on it to deal with experimental items, or help if a private factory had a problem. During the early days of the war, many observers from private firms and National Factories were sent to the Royal Arsenal, to learn how it worked.

The Royal Arsenal filled all the British Army's shells until the end of 1915. It also filled half the Admiralty's shells; the rest were filled at the Naval Ordnance Depots. It would go on to make 5.8 million empty shells, 19.9 filled shells and over 60 million fuses. It also made or repaired over 10,000 gun mechanisms and 30,000 carriages. The workers also made 46 million cartridges, 1.7 billion bullets and 350,000 mortar bombs.

The Royal Laboratory made and filled ammunition for every type of weapon and had made nearly 300 million items by the end of the war. It was split into three departments in March 1916:

- Small arms ammunition
- Other ammunition
- Explosives

They designed new components and looked at problems reported by GHQ. They also dealt with new weapons and suggested modifications. Initially, they were thoroughly tested, to iron out any issues, before asking companies to tender for them. However, it slowed down the design process, so new items were given to the factories and they had to resolve any production issues.

Chapter 16

The Ministry Steps In

Area Offices and the Department of Area Organisation[1]

The Ministry of Munitions divided Britain and Ireland into eleven areas to report on progress in the private factories.

- Area 1 was the North West of England, covering the Tyne, Wear and Tees areas.
- Area 2 covered North West of England, which included the Lancashire cotton town and Manchester; it also covered North Wales.
- Area 3 included Yorkshire's three Ridings and Lincolnshire.
- Area 4 covered the Midlands, including Derby, Nottingham and Birmingham. Area 5 covered South Wales, including Swansea, Cardiff and the Valleys.
- Area 6 covered south-west England, including Bristol and Southampton.
- Area 7 covered London, the Home Counties and south-east England.
- Areas 8 and 9 split Scotland into west and east.
- Areas 10 and 11 covered south and north of Ireland.

The Ministry of Munitions used the Department of Area Organisation, under James Stevenson, to liaise between the Area Offices and the Boards of Management.[2] They dealt with problems ranging from materials shortages and defective materials to programme changes. The Area Offices did the same with the National Factories later. Lloyd George told the heads of the twenty-eight Boards of Management and the Area Engineers to use their local knowledge, when he visited them.

Stevenson appointed the Shell and Components Manufacture Executive Committee in January 1917 to deal with the shell factories. The Department of Area Organisation took over from it, when it joined Group O (Ordnance) in September 1917.

Building the National Factories[3]

Private building stopped when at the start of the war, so many unemployed labourers enlisted or found work in a munitions factory. It meant there was a labour shortage in the building industry, when the Ministry of Munitions decided it need a lot of new factories. The cost of building them was difficult to estimate but getting them up and running was far more important.

HM Office of Works purchased land, stating that the factories were for temporary military purposes. It supervised construction until the Munitions Works Board took over after the Defence of the Realm (Acquisition of Land) Act was passed at the end of 1916. They were built quickly, often before plans were finalised, which resulted in uneconomical construction and poor layouts. The positive feature of such a rapid building programme, was that the extra costs were soon recovered because the shells they made were much cheaper than American and Canadian imports.

Once steel became scarce, extensions were built using surplus materials. A few were built using prefabricated units made at two National Concrete Factories in Gotham in Nottinghamshire and Yate near Bristol.[4] Occasionally, labour was so short that soldiers were drafted in to help.

The Boards of Management had to work to a tight time scale, so they set up the National Shell Factories in existing buildings, often resulting in inefficient working environments. They also had tight budgets, so a lot of machines were second hand and soon had to be replaced. Experienced firms bought the equipment for the National Projectile Factories, while the Ministry of Munitions provided the plant for the Filling Factories.

Managing the National Factories[5]

Experienced companies supervised the building and running of the National Projectile Factories. However, some had bad habits, forcing Ministry staff to step in to stop them. The ones at Cardonald in Glasgow, Templeborough near Sheffield and Hackney Marshes in London had to be reorganised in the summer of 1916, while the one at Dudley in the West Midlands was so bad, it had been nicknamed the National Scrap Factory before it was reorganised.

Problems with the Boards of Management also had to be resolved. Members of the Birmingham Board had to be changed and the city's National Shell Factory had to be reorganised in May 1916. All the Boards of Management were then told to stop using inefficient companies in October 1916 and transfer their machines and tools to better performing factories. A stricter control of finances was also expected, starting in 1917 and the Metropolitan Munitions Committee was taken over by the Ministry of Munitions in May 1918, after it ran up unacceptable costs across London.

Other issues could cause the Ministry to change a company's management; for example, if they refused to take advice, resisted dilution, or objected to employing women. They could even prosecute or imprison anyone accused of manufacturing defective munitions.

Working in the National Factories[6]

Most of the National Factories were up and running by the end of 1916. However, it was difficult to run an efficient and safe factory with inexperienced staff. It did not help that the factories had been built without the foresight of what would happen if there was an accident. Many buildings were made from wood, while some were too close together. Danger building officers were kept busy making sure regulations were followed but fireproofing material and protective clothing were always in short supply.

Filling shells and fuses was dangerous work and its repetitive nature increased the risk. While every factory had targets to meet, the workers had to work slowly and carefully. They were paid piece rates but fast work led to careless work, so output was limited to prevent mistakes. Some were put on bonus schemes, which were only paid if the components passed their inspection.

While the workers were classed as unskilled, they had to be patient and conscientious. There was no time for horseplay nor disobedience but it was recognised that overstrict discipline hindered recruitment and caused unrest. The smallest error could result in problems at the front line, like shells prematurely exploding or not at all. Carelessness by the management or the workforce could also result in large quantities of munitions being rejected or even a catastrophic accident.

Over 70,000 men and women would end up working in the National Projectile Factories and National Filling Factories. The work was dangerous, unpleasant and repetitive, while news about explosions in other factories made everyone nervous. While some handed in their notice, most stuck to their work. Health problems through handling TNT also resulted in some leaving their jobs.

Over time conditions improved, experience was gained and problems were ironed out. But the overseers and their workers soon started to trust each other, while the inspectors learnt what to watch out for on the production line.

Improving Production[7]

The Ministry of Munitions' control of the munitions industry increased as the war dragged on. To begin with the emphasis was on maximum output at whatever cost. By 1917, the priority was to make as much as possible at the minimum cost before every department was told to economise on materials.

Each area had a superintendent engineer, who advised the National Shell Factories and contractors on how to get the best out their materials at the lowest price. The National Projectile Factories Executive Committee was set up in May 1916 to deal with teething troubles, while resident engineers recorded problems and suggested solutions at each factory. Over time, centralised control ended rivalries between factories and managers shared experiences of good working practices at conferences. The recording and analysing of records of machining and handling times started to circulate in August 1916. It meant that every factory could get their production line working efficiently. Factories were also encouraged to set up designated areas where defective shells could be rectified and to issue every worker with a spare set of tools, so there were no holdups.

Chapter 17

The National Shell Factories and the Cooperative Schemes

The Boards of Management[1]

The Munitions Committees started organising small firms into cooperatives. After visiting the Royal Arsenal, the Leeds Munitions Committee decided to put their spare plant under one roof and sent their workers to an ammunition factory for training. The idea was approved at the beginning of May 1915 and it was called a National Shell Factory. Six Boards of Management were operating by the time the Ministry of Munitions took over in June 1915 and another forty formed over the summer.

Each Board had four local engineers who reported to the Director of Area Organisation (DAO). They formed cooperatives of local contractors and provided them with forgings to make components. They also set up National Shell Factories to assemble shells in all sorts of buildings, from weaving sheds and fish curing sheds to tram depots and drill halls.[2] The assembled shells were then sent to a National Filling Factory to be armed with explosives.

In July 1915, each National Shell Factory was affiliated to a local armaments firm, which gave advice and trained workers. The Boards of Management eventually became responsible for issuing war badges, controlling dilution and dealing with transport.

Prices were initially set high to encourage subcontractors, so they would keep making components and because they were still cheaper than American imports. However, unsatisfactory companies were laid off in the autumn of 1916, while prices were reduced. While the Boards of Management started with small calibre shells, some switched to larger calibre shells, repairing guns, or making parts for tanks and aircraft when the munitions programme changed in 1917.

The National Shell Factories had produced 4.15 million shells by the end of 1916. The workforce peaked at 12,000 women and 6,400 men as production rose to 7.69 million in 1917 and 8.01 million in 1918. By the end of the war, they had made over 20 million shells, including the following:

- 11.3 million 18-pounder shells.
- 5.5 million 4.5-inch shells.

- 608,000 60-pounder shells.
- 1.7 million 6-inch calibre shells.

Area 1 Office: North East England[3]

The office controlled four Boards of Management from Newcastle-upon-Tyne. Most men living in the city either worked in the shipyards or for Armstrong Whitworth's, so the Lord Mayor formed the Tyne and Wear Board of Management in September 1915 to cover Northumberland and Durham. Its National Shell Factory in West Hartlepool's Central Marine Engine Works had made 81,000 8-inch shells by the time it was handed over to the Admiralty in December 1917; 6 other contractors had made another 424,000 4.5-inch shells by the end of the war.

The North-East Coast Armaments Committee had wanted to send labour to armaments firms in Newcastle but Middlesbrough's firms preferred to make their own shells. While the Cleveland Ironmasters' Association organised companies to make tools, the Teesside Board of Management supervised seven companies which made 814,000 18-pounder shells.

Eight Hull engineering firms formed a cooperative scheme and refused to work for the Leeds Board of Management. The city formed its own Board of Management and while it was January 1916 before inspection gauges could be found, they made 909,000 4.5-inch shells.

Grimsby's Board of Management opened a National Shell Factory in a herring curing factory in May 1915. While it made 335,000 6-inch shells another cooperative group in the town shut down after turning down a contract from the Ministry of Munitions.

Area 2 Office: North West England and North Wales[4]

The office supervised ten Boards of Management across North West England and North Wales from Manchester. Women had always worked in Lancashire's mill towns, so there were few objections to dilution.

A Munitions Committee was set up in Carlisle, even though the area's factories were on the coast. It resulted in two Boards of Management being appointed and they refused to work together. The East Cumberland Board set up two National Shell Factories in Carlisle's Rifle Drill Hall and Territorial Force Hall and they made 307,000 18-pounder shells. They also remade 50,000 shells recovered from the firing ranges on the coast. Meanwhile, the West Cumberland Board set up a National Shell Factory at the Milburn Hawkshead Foundry in Workington, which made 359,000 18-pounder shells.

The North and North-East Lancashire Munitions Committee appointed Blackburn's Board of Management in the spring of 1915. It supervised eighty contracts across seventeen towns and assembled over 3.5 million shells in places such as Blackburn's Electricity Works and Blackpool's Tram sheds. A Munitions Committee was set up in Rossendale Valley in September 1915 and 2 small National Shell Factories had made 157,000 4.5-inch shells before they started rectifying shells in the spring of 1918.

The Manchester and District Armaments Output Committee appointed Manchester's Board of Management after Lloyd George visited the city. While it set up a National Shell Factory in the Hyde Road Tramways Depot, it switched to making parts for planes and tank after only making 90,000 4.5-inch shells. Most of the work across the rest of the Manchester area was done by cooperative groups and they had made 9.67 million shells by the end of the war.

Bury's Board of Management was appointed in August 1915 and it organised 14 contractors to make components for 143,000 4.5-inch shells, which were assembled in the Central Tramways Depot. Cooperative groups across the area made another 533,000 shells. Rochdale's Board of Management was appointed in October 1915 and it made 90,000 6-inch shells in a National Shell Factory, which was in a tram shed. Cooperative groups made another 233,000 shells.

Liverpool's Munitions Committee formed the Liverpool Board of Management after Lloyd George visited the city. It opened six National Shell Factories and ran a large cooperative scheme, which brought together components made across the city. Approximately 2,100 women and 600 men assembled 3.18 million shells in the Agricultural Hall in Haymarket and at Cunard's Gladstone Docks on Primrose Road.

Cooperative groups made components for another 1.2 million shells, which were assembled in the Lambeth Road tramway depot. Tons of steel billets imported from the United States were cut into 1.8 million shell forgings at the Edge Lane Factory. The Board of Management also managed two small factories at Hoylake and West Kirby on the Wirral. A workshop in Bootle made gauges for the local factories.

Wrexham's Board of Management set up a National Shell Factory in a brewery, which made 895,000 shells 18-pounder shells. North Wales Board of Management set up three small National Shell Factories at Caernarfon, Porthmadog and Flint and they sent 1.4 million shells to Wrexham to be finished.

Area 3 Office: Yorkshire and Lincolnshire[5]

Area 3 supervised nine Boards of Management from its office in Leeds. Again, women had always worked in the mill towns, so there were few objections to dilution.

Keighley's Board of Management opened two factories at Price, Smith and Sons and Hall and Steels, which made 793,000 18-pounder shells. Bradford's Board of Management opened a National Shell Factory in the Valley Dye Works in November 1915. While it made 678,000 4.5-inch shells during the war, other factories across the city made 5.2 million components.

Leeds' Munitions Committee visited Armstrong Whitworth's factory in Newcastle before sending men to train there. It then formed the country's first Board of Management on 13 May 1915. The first shell factory opened at the Leeds Forge Company on Armley Road, while large calibre shells were made at the Schoen Wheel Locomotive Works in Newlay; a third factory opened in Hunslet. They employed over 10,600 between them and had made 1.5 million shells when they switched to re-lining and making artillery pieces in September 1917. They were then renamed No. 1, No. 2 and No. 3 National Ordnance Factories. Leeds Fuse Factory was based across three sites and 1,250 women and 220 men were making 100,000 fuses a week before they were renamed No. 4, No. 5 and No. 6 National Ordnance Factories.

Halifax's Board of Management coordinated the efforts of ten companies to make 1.3 million shells. Another twelve companies made machine tools. Huddersfield's Board of Management opened a National Shell Factory and while a lack of tools delayed deliveries until November 1915, it still made 470,000 18-pounder shells. The Board of Management also helped set up cooperatives in Dewsbury and Brighouse. Wakefield's Board of Management organised fifteen firms to start production but deliveries were delayed by a lack of gauges until October 1915. They still made 1.2 million shells during the war.

Rotherham's Board of Management opened two National Shell Factories in John Baker and Bessemer Limited's Brinsworth Ironworks and Owen and Dyson Limited's Rother Ironworks and they made 425,000 4.5-inch shells. Barnsley's Board of Management opened two more in the Dominion Works and the Hope Works, which made 305,000 more shells.

Sheffield was the stronghold of the major armament firms of Vickers, Thomas Firth's, Hadfields, Cammell Laird's, John Brown's and Steel, Peech and Tozer. The Munitions Committee contacted small companies to discover that many skilled men had joined the armed forces. So, plant was installed at the university to train replacement workers; its workshops also made gauges. The Board of Management formed cooperatives, which made 405,000 shells as well as tens of thousands of hand grenades and mortar bombs. The cutlery and silver trades also made over 2 million components and nearly 1 million helmets.

Area 4 Office: The English Midlands[6]

Area 4 supervised seven Boards of Management from its office in Birmingham.

Managers of eleven Lincolnshire companies refused to hand over their skilled workers to Vickers, preferring to make their own shells after visiting Armstrong Whitworth's factory. However, the largest company had a direct contract by the time the Board of Management received its first contract, so the rest could only make 8,000 Stokes mortar bombs.

Derbyshire's Board of Management set up the National Shell Factory at R. Russell and Sons Peel Foundry and it made 550,000 4.5-inch shells before switching to making aeroengine parts. Cooperative groups across the county made another 433,000 shells, some of them supervised by a sub-committee in Chesterfield.

Nottingham was a centre of the textile and lace trades, so it had many factories equipped with lightweight machinery and a female workforce looking for employment. Its Board of Management opened a National Shell Factory where 1.51 million 18-pounder shells were made. Cooperative groups assembled another 335,000 shells.

Some Birmingham companies were engaged in munitions work from the early days of the war. They objected to putting their workers into a labour battalion and formed a Board of Management. They opened a National Shell Factory in the Midland Railway Company Wagon Works, which employed 1,600 women and 800 men at its peak and made over 1.84 million 4.5-inch shells. The Board of Management ended up coordinating the work of over 360 companies across the city, while Stoke-on-Trent, Walsall, Kidderminster, Burton-on-Trent and West Bromwich all formed affiliated committees.

Coventry was home to a thriving motorcar and motorcycle industry and the Board of Management coordinated their work. The city's population had nearly doubled by 1917, as thousands of munitions workers flooded into the town. After making over 650,000 shells, the factories switched to making aircraft parts in 1917.

Leicester's Labour Exchange asked the local Association of Engineering Employers to send 30,000 skilled men to the armament firms in Sheffield and Coventry in January 1915. However, Robert Dumas of the British Thomas-Houston Company, from nearby Rugby, explained how he had seen French factories cooperate to make munitions. The War Office doubted it could be done in Leicester and it left the Association of Engineering Employers to sort out its own labour, materials and supervision.[7]

A committee arranged finances to buy forgings, while local firms moved their spare plant to a tram depot. Leicester District Armaments Group appointed Leicester Board of Management to run the factory and the first shells were delivered in September 1915. The area eventually made over 1 million shells and its success inspired other towns and cities to do the same.

Meanwhile, arguments between Banbury and Brackley delayed the forming of a committee until the Birmingham Area Office formed three in October 1915. However, most factories had contracts by then, so the Banbury and Brackley committees stood down while the Oxford Board of Management helped four companies make Stokes mortar bombs.

Area 5 Office: South Wales[8]

Most of the workforce in South Wales was busy in the coalfields, foundries, shipyards, copper smelting and tinplate industries. Area 5's office in Cardiff divided its area into the Eastern, Western and Central districts, only for them to argue over the limited labour and plant in the area.

The Western Division appointed the Swansea Board of Management, which opened a factory in the Port Talbot Steel Company; it made 635,000 18-pounder and 4.5-inch shells. Swansea Board of Management also supervised a cooperative group that made components and shells. Meanwhile, Llanelli set up its own Board of Management in September 1915, after refusing to hand over its machinery to Swansea. Its National Shell Factory made nearly 1.2 million 18-pounder and 6-inch shells in a toy factory.

The Central Division set up Cardiff Board of Management and while it was unable to organise a cooperative group it did set up a National Shell Factory, which made 500,000 18-pounder shells in a rope factory. The Eastern Division's Board of Management set up a National Shell Factory on the Ebbw Vale Iron and Steel Company's premises. However, a lack of labour, a refusal to employ women and a poor railway connection meant it closed in July 1916, after making only 89,000 18-pounder shells. Meanwhile, two Newport factories in the Great Western Railway Company's engine sheds and the Tyne Engineering Works made 600,000 60-pounder shells. A factory in the Uskside Engineering Works made gauges for the whole of South Wales.

Area 6 Office: South West England[9]

The Engineering Employers Federation elected a committee to organise ten firms with the help of Area 6's office in Bristol. Other towns coordinated another sixty firms making components, which were assembled at the National Shell Factory in the Castle Ironworks in Bristol. By the end of the war, it had made 3.2 million 18-pounder shells and rectified another 167,000. The War Office had wanted Cornwall to be run by the West of England Board of Management but the county insisted on setting up its own. It made nearly 1 million shells in a Camborne foundry.

Area 7A and 7B Offices: London and Surrounding Areas[10]

The south-east of England was organised by Area 7, with Area 7A office covering London and Area 7B covering the nearby counties. The Metropolitan Munitions Committee initially wanted London's lighting and power companies to make munitions in their factories. However, many other companies offered their services.

London's Board of Management divided the capital into ten divisions. It also formed three cooperative groups: the Gas Light and Coke Company, the Metropolitan Water Board and the London colleges. Altogether, 470 firms were given contracts. The London County Council's Tramways and Education departments, the Metropolitan Water Works and other public bodies made gauges for the rest of the factories, while a shell filling factory was opened in Perivale.

The number of companies involved had fallen to 100 by the beginning of 1918, as the shell programme reduced. Eventually, the work was all transferred to the Ministry of

Munitions and London Board of Management was closed in May 1918, having overseen the making of 6.9 million shells.

Three more Boards of Management organised the firms in the counties surrounding London. The South East Midland Board of Management dealt with seventeen firms across Bedfordshire, Buckinghamshire, Hertfordshire, Cambridgeshire and Huntingdonshire. They made 1.2 million shells and 1.3 million components between them.

East Anglia's Board of Management organised over forty firms across Norfolk, Suffolk and Essex, so 2 million 18-pounder shells and 4.7 million fuses could be assembled by Ransomes and Rapier Limited in Ipswich. Another 2.45 million shells were made by other companies. The Sussex Board of Management organised companies along the south-east coast and they had made 500,000 shell components and trench mortar bombs by the time they switched to aircraft work in the autumn of 1916.

Areas 8 and 9 Offices: West and East Scotland[11]

An Armaments Output Committee was formed in Glasgow but it was disbanded in June 1915, after making little progress. Instead, William Weir was appointed the Supervising Engineer for Scotland and he split the country into Area 8, which covered the west from Glasgow and Area 9, which covered the east from Edinburgh. Weir was made the Director of Munitions for the whole of Scotland in August 1915 and he created a smaller version of the Ministry of Munitions. While he was based in Glasgow, his staff dealt with all issues north of the border.

Most men along the River Clyde worked in the shipyards and supporting industries. So, Weir organised Glasgow's small factories to make components to assemble in nine National Shell Factories called Liège, Marne, ANZAC, Flanders, Mons, Argonne, La Bassée, Bethune and Lille. He also arranged for Babcock and Wilcox and G. and J. Weir's (his own company) to set up three National Projectile Factories, called Aisne, Ypres and Albert to make large calibre shells.

However, it took until May 1916 to agree how to organise the factories and October 1916 before they were producing. The North British Locomotive Company then shut its two factories, called Mons and Marne, in the spring of 1917 because it refused to accept a price reduction. Even so, Glasgow's factories had made over 4.5 million shells by the end of the war.

There were two other big factories in the Clydebank area. Singer Manufacturing Company employed 9,800 women and 4,200 men making fuses at its Combles factory (a village on the Somme). The Edith Cavell Projectile Factory (named after the nurse executed by the Germans) made trench mortar bombs.

The Area 9 office formed a Board of Management to supervise the factories in Edinburgh, Aberdeen and Dundee, while committees organised factories in Falkirk, Leith and Dunfermline. Edinburgh was short of labour but its cooperatives still made

549,000 shells. Aberdeen Board of Management opened a National Shell Factory in the William McKinnon Limited's factory but it had to be taken over after the manager was convicted of altering shells. It still made 100,000 6-inch shells, while cooperatives across the town made another 264,000. Meanwhile, Dundee's Board of Management opened a National Shell Factory in J. and A.D. Grimond Limited's jute mills, using machines confiscated from a ship sailing to Germany. They were used to make over 565,000 18-pounder shells, while cooperatives across the town made another 263,000.

The reduction in the shell programme in 1918, resulted in all three areas changing their production. While Aberdeen switched to artillery pieces and Dundee changed to chemical shell, Edinburgh started making grenades, bombs and aircraft parts. All three areas made mortar shells.

Areas 10 and 11 Offices: The South and North of Ireland[12]

Ireland was left to set up factories and contract companies, while the Ministry of Munitions was busy organising England, Wales and Scotland. The lack of progress led to workmen heading to English and Scottish factories, while the Irish press complained that the country wanted the opportunity to make munitions. Added to that the political situation over Home Rule required different forms of administration in the north and south.

Dublin's Board of Management was formed in the south of Ireland (now the Republic of Ireland) in July 1915. A committee coordinated firms across the city, while subcommittees set up factories in Galway, Limerick, Cork and Waterford but a lack of skilled labour, plant and transport made progress difficult.

Dublin's National Shell Factory was opened in a margarine factory on the north bank of the Liffey in March 1916, only for the building to come under fire a few weeks later, during the Easter Uprising. It still made 544,000 18-pounder shells and 300,000 fuses. Cork's committee was annoyed that many of its machines were sent to Dublin, leaving it able to only make 32,000 4.5-inch shells in St Peter's Market. Galway was only able to make 34,000 18-pounder shells in a marble works but nearly 250,000 cartridge cases were made in the Great Southern and Western Railway's sheds in Waterford.

While many Belfast men worked for the shipyards, such as Harland and Wolff Limited, the city's women were busy working in the linen industry. The Board of Management brought together a cooperative group which made 750,000 shells, while other companies made another 200,000 shells on direct contracts.

Chapter 18

The National Projectile Factories

Making Large Calibre Shells[1]

The BEF was demanding large calibre shells and heavy artillery when the Ministry of Munitions took over in June 1915. The armaments firms told Lloyd George that they were unable to extend their factories but they agreed to build and run new ones with money provided by the Ministry.

The firms started building eight new National Projectile Factories in the autumn and all but one were new structures; three more were added later. The factories were given priority when it came to labour and materials and they had made 2.5 million shells by the end of 1916: half of them in the final three months of the year.

All the factories were up and running by the beginning of 1917, so the National Projectile Factories Executive Committee merged with the Shell and Components Manufacture Executive Committee. While some of the factories switched to other tasks in 1917, the number of shells had trebled to 7.5 million. The Munitions Council took over running them at the end of the year.

The factories in Lancaster, Sheffield and Nottingham had employed women from the start, because those areas had employed them before the war. However, some managers resisted employing them because they believed the work was too heavy. Even so, half of the 40,000 strong workforce were women by the end of the war.

Initially the production costs of the National Projectile Factories were similar to those charged by private contractors. However, the price reduced as they gained experience and shared ideas. The savings more than offset the £7.4 million (£437 million today) it had cost to build the factories; their shells were also much cheaper than American and Canadian imports.

By the end of the war, the National Projectile Factories had made over 20 million shells:

- 1.61 million 18-pounder shells.
- 1.38 million 4.5-inch shells.
- 5.65 million 60-pounder shells.
- 7.92 million 6-inch shells.
- 2.06 million 8-inch shells.

- 1.44 million 9.2-inch shells.
- 13,000 12-inch shells.
- 7,000 15-inch shells.

Location of the National Projectile Factories

A brief history of each factory and where they were located follows:

Area 1: North East England

Armstrong Whitworth's was building a shell factory at Birtley, south of Gateshead when 1,000 skilled men were released from the Belgian army. They were housed in a community called Elisabethville by the time work started in July 1916. The number rose to over 3,800 men and they made 2.8 million large calibre shells. Many were repatriated when the war ended.

Armstrong Whitworth's had also been making 18-pounder shells in a factory owned by the North Eastern Railway Company since the summer of 1915. The Ministry of Munitions took it over in July 1916 and while it was known as the National Shell Factory after the summer of 1918, it was run as a National Projectile Factory. Around 800 women and 180 men made 1.2 million 18-pounder shells.

Area 2: North West England

Lancaster National Projectile Factory was run by Vickers but the Ministry of Munitions made the company replace its manager in December 1915. Production began in May 1916 and 4,590 men and 4,070 women made 2 million 60-pounder, 6-inch and 9.2-inch shells. The factory also made mortars and repaired guns, starting in 1917. Some of the workforce helped clear up Morecambe Filling Factory, following a fire in October 1917.

Area 3: Yorkshire

Thomas Firth's was the first company to start making large calibre shells at its Templeborough National Projectile Factory near Rotherham in January 1916. Approximately 4,950 women and 740 men made 2.6 million 60-pounder and 4.5-inch shells. It often coordinated production with its own works and Hadfields National Projectile Factory, both in nearby Sheffield.

Hadfields started making 9.2-inch shells in Tinsley near Sheffield in March 1916. The workforce of 2,465 men had made 289,000 shells by the time it switched to repairing artillery pieces during the winter of 1917-18; it was renamed a National Ordnance Factory.

Area 4: The Midlands

Cammell Laird's started producing shells on the Meadows in Nottingham in March 1916. The 3,150 women and 2,680 men had made 6-inch when until some switched to repairing artillery pieces at the beginning of 1917 and it was renamed a National Ordnance Factory in October 1916. They had made 894,000 shells by the time the factory closed and the machinery was sent to Lancaster in June 1918.

A. Harper, Sons and Bean started making 60-pounder shells in Dudley, West Midlands in May 1916. The factory also made 6-inch chemical shells, repaired guns and howitzers and built aeroengines. Labour shortages meant that soldiers had to be employed at times but the 3,175 men and 2,600 women still made 2.5 million shells.

Area 7: London and South East

Dick, Kerr and Company opened its factory on Hackney Marshes, north-east London in February 1916 but labour was short because other factories paid more, while the management did not want to employ women. It was affected by the shop stewards' stoppage in May 1917 and then the Ministry of Munitions took over control in August. Air raids damaged the factory at the end of the year but the 3,040 men and 1,430 women still made 1.4 million 6-inch shells.

The Ministry of Munitions took over Rees Roturbo Manufacturing Company's factory at Ponders End, north London in 1917. While it was not strictly a National Projectile Factory it made 600,000 6-inch and 8-inch shells before it switched to repairing artillery pieces.

Area 8: West Scotland

Beardmore's opened a new factory in Cardonald, south-west of Glasgow in March 1916 and the 2,215 women and 1,300 men had made over 500,000 6-inch and 8-inch shells by the time they switched to repairing guns and howitzers early in 1917. A second factory was opened in a cotton mill at Mile End in June 1916, where 1,600 women and 1,300 men made a further 2 million 18-pounder, 60-pounder and 6-inch shells.

Work started at G. and J. Weir Limited in Cathcart, south of Glasgow in June 1916 and the 620 women and 425 men had made 94,000 8-inch shells before they switched to making aircraft parts in May 1917. Babcock and Wilcox started work at two factories in Renfrew, west of Glasgow in the summer of 1916. Up to 1,690 women and 420 men made 646,000 60-pounder shells at the Aisne Factory while 70,000 9-inch and 12-inch shells were made at the smaller Ypres Factory.

Chapter 19

The National Filling Factories

Meeting the Demand[1]

To begin with, the Royal Ordnance Factories filled shells for the War Department. The Ministry of Munitions formed the Cartridge, Fuse and Shell Filling and Assembling Department when it took over in June 1915. The increase in the production of shells by the National Shell Factories and National Projectile Factories required extra capacity to fill them with high explosive. The first two National Filling Factories started production in the spring of 1916 in Leeds and Coventry. Another four were built near the ports of Glasgow, Liverpool, Gloucester and Plymouth to fill shell cases imported from the United States and Canada; a fifth was built at Horley, south of London.

A huge factory was built at Chilwell near Nottingham to fill large calibre shells made across the north and centre of England, while smaller filling factories were opened at Morecombe and Banbury. Work on two more at Otley near Leeds and Newburn near Newcastle-upon-Tyne were abandoned. Hereford was added and Morecombe was extended in case there was an accident at one of the others.

Seven factories for filling shell components were also built. Cardonald served the factories across Glasgow, while Coventry covered the north and centre of England. The Ministry of Munitions opened a large central store in Birmingham, capable of handling 1 million tons of shells a year, to free up space at the two factories. The remaining five factories were built in London, where there was plenty of labour.

Ten National Factories dedicated to filling shells and seven dedicated to filling fuses and other components, were all working by the summer of 1916. They employed 66,500 women and 15,500 men at their peak. They were operated by private companies or Boards of Management to begin with but the Ministry of Munitions had the powers to direct how they were run. It eventually took over from three of the five Boards of Management after they failed to meet their targets.

Filling the Shells

Shells and explosives were sent from their respective factories to the filling factories. The filling process required every component to be made correctly and delivered on time, otherwise output would be interrupted. Even the simple 18-pounder high explosive shell had eighty parts and a problem with any one of them would halt the assembly line.

Shrapnel shells were already assembled and only the powder burster in the base of the shell needed to be filled. The fuse would ignite the powder in the tube down the centre of the shell, called a gaine, which detonated the burster, scattering the shrapnel balls like a shotgun. Meanwhile, high explosive shells needed to be filled with their bursting charge, which would rip the shell casing into shards of steel when it exploded. The Cartridge, Fuse and Shell Filling and Assembling Department also took over the filling of grenades, mortar shells, aircraft bombs and chemical shells in the spring of 1918. It also set up factories to break up obsolete ammunition, so the parts could be melted down and recycled.

Small calibre shells, known as quick firing (QF) shells, were assembled in a filling factory. The cartridge case was filled with cordite and secured on the shell with a safety clip. A service primer replaced the dummy primer in the cartridge, while the fuse and gaine were screwed into the shell. The shell was then checked and boxed up, ready for despatch.

Larger calibre shells, known as breech loading (BL) shells were filled with explosive and plugged, while the fuses were filled and assembled. Cartridges were filled with cordite and then placed in a bag, which had an igniter sewn into it. The assembly of the shell was completed in the field.

The casing of a high explosive shell had to be filled with picric acid or TNT. Initially, they were heated up and slowly poured into the shell casing. The shells were later filled with amatol, a mixture of ammonium nitrate and TNT, to reduce the amount of TNT required.

The Explosives Loading Company of Faversham and Curtis's and Harvey of Medway made blocks of amatol which were hammered into the shell casings. A hot, loose mix was being poured into large calibre shells by the end of 1916. Mechanical devices which filled shells using a screw device were introduced in the summer of 1917. By the beginning of 1918, the shell programme had been reduced, so some factories switched to filling mortar bombs, aerial bombs and chemical shells.

The Location of the National Filling Factories

A brief history of each factory and their location follows:

Area 2: North West England

Vickers built No. 13 Filling Factory at Morecombe and it began filling the shells made at Lancaster National Projectile Factory in July 1916. The workforce of 1,650 men and 2,950 women had filled 2.89 million 6-inch shells when a fire broke out on 1 October

Rt Hon. David Lloyd George MP.

Rt Hon. Edwin Montagu MP.

Rt Hon. Dr Christopher Addison MP.

Rt Hon. Winston Churchill MP.

Above: Soldiers deploy to support the police during a strike.

Left: Kitchener encouraging men to enlist and fight for their country in August 1914.

Around 1 million miners dug 290 million tons of coal a year.

The munitions and shipbuilding industries needed 6 million tons of steel a year.

Mixing guncotton and ether alcohol to make cordite.

Making and testing gas masks.

Women worked long hours in dirty and cramped conditions in the shell factories.

Using gauges to check the dimension of 9.2-inch-high explosive shells.

Above: Sorting filled shells, ready for despatch, at Chilwell Filling Factory near Nottingham.

Right: Dug coal, forged steel, built ships, made shells, manufactured machine guns, assembled tanks.

Above left: Tens of thousands of women answered the call to take men's places in the munitions industry.

Above right: The Ministry of Munitions encouraged men to stay in their work in December 1916.

Women and children protest against rising rents in Glasgow.

Munitionettes head to their workplace after donning their safety clothing.

A factory full of machinery making the intricate parts for Lee-Enfield rifles.

Once a machine was set up, a task could be repeated many times with limited supervision.

Assembling gun turrets in Armstrong Whitworth's factory.

Assembling tanks in the Metropolitan Carriage Wagon and Finance Company factory.

Assembling Sopwith Triplanes in the Sopwith Aviation Company factory.

1917. Several days of explosions destroyed the factory, killing ten workers and seriously injuring others.

No. 2 Filling Factory was opened at Sefton, north of Liverpool, mainly to fill shells imported from the United States, starting in July 1916. At its peak 10,340 women and 500 men were employed and they filled 17.34 million 18-pounder and 6-inch shells. They also filled 180 million exploder bags and containers, as well as 30 million cartridges and components. There was only one serious accident, which killed three employees on 23 July 1918.

Area 3: Yorkshire

No. 1 Filling Factory, at Barnbow east of Leeds was the first to start filling in April 1916. At its peak, it employed 12,150 women and 1,150 men and they filled 24.57 million 18-pounder and 4.5-inch shells, as well as 36 million cartridges and millions more components. An explosion on 5 December 1916 killed thirty-five women and injured many more; two smaller explosions in March 1917 and May 1918 killed another five workers.

Area 4: The Midlands

Chilwell was chosen for the site of No. 6 Filling Factory to make use of the unemployed women from Nottingham's lace industry. Vickers ran the works and it began delivering in February 1916, completing most of the large calibre shells for the Somme campaign. At its peak, 5,720 women and 1,730 men were using 1,500 tons of amatol a week. However, a huge explosion on 1 July 1918 killed 134 workers and injured many more. Rebuilding started immediately and the factory had filled 19.34 million shells by the end of the war.

No. 9 Filling Factory in Banbury started filling shells in April 1916. At its peak it employed nearly 1,000 men and 550 women and they filled nearly 3.87 million explosive shells. They also filled 730,000 chemical shells and 20,000 mines for the Admiralty during the final months of the war.

The Ministry of Munitions decided to build a spare filling factory at Hereford in the summer of 1916, in case there was a problem at one of the other factories. No. 14 Filling Factory started delivering in November 1916, employing 1,900 men and 3,850 women. While the factory closed in April 1918, it reopened following the explosion at Chilwell on 1 July 1918. By the end of the war, it had filled 4.17 million 6-inch and 8-inch shells.

Area 5: South Wales

The Explosives Loading Company opened a filling factory next to Nobel's TNT factory in Pembrey, west of Swansea in July 1915 and the workforce of 1,000 women and 440 men travelled by train from Swansea and Carmarthen. It was called No. 18 Filling Factory when the Ministry of Munitions took over them both in January 1917. They had filled 1.1 million shells by the time the factory switched to taking apart 1.7 million defective rounds and 3 million fuses for recycling in May 1917.

Area 6: South West England

No. 5 Filling Factory started work in Gloucester in March 1916. Over 5,600 women and 720 men were employed at its peak and they filled 10.30 million 18-pounder shells, including 1.35 million American imported casings delivered to Bristol docks. They also filled 30 million exploder bags and components.

Area 7: London

Production began at No. 7 Filling Factory in Hayes in west London in October 1915. An extension was added and the factory employed 8,780 women and 1,850 men at its peak. They filled 12.38 million 18-pounder and 4.5-inch shells, including 4.04 million imported ones; they also filled over 20 million exploder bags and components.

Area 8: West Scotland

No. 4 Filling Factory in Georgetown had two factories that began production in March 1916. Many of the 12,000 women and 800 men travelled from Glasgow by train and they filled 19.29 million 18-pounder, 4.5-inch and 6-inch shells. They had also filled over 59 million cartridges and components by the end of the war. Forty-one minor accidents at the factories resulted in five deaths and many injuries.

Other Filling Factories

The Royal Laboratory at the Royal Arsenal filled and assembled shells for the War Office, while Woolwich, Chatham, Portsmouth and Plymouth did the same for the Admiralty before the war. Armstrong Whitworth's had experience dating back to the war in South Africa, while a handful of companies had filled shells for export before the war. Filling continued at Woolwich and it filled 43.3 million shells out of 196 million shells made during the war.

A few private companies started filling shells on the outbreak of war. While Vickers assembled 18-pounder shells in a new factory in Dartford, Armstrong Whitworth's filled large calibre and small calibre shells at nearby Lemington Point and Derwenthaugh respectively. Nobel's Explosive Company extended its factory at Pembrey in South Wales, while the Kings Norton Metal Company did the same at Abbey Wood in south-east London.

By the end of the war, private factories had filled 26.6 million rounds, while the National Filling Factories had filled 126 million shells. The breakdown of shells by calibre was:

- 59.95 million 18-pounder shells.
- 23.90 million 4.5-inch shells.
- 6.86 million 60-pounder shells.
- 26.29 million 6-inch shells.
- 3.03 million 9.2-inch shells.
- 218,000 12-inch shells.
- 12,000 15-inch shells.

Fuse Filling Factories

Shell fuses were armed with a small amount of tetryl. It detonated on impact in a high explosive shell, setting off the TNT or picric acid. It detonated after the set time (or on impact) in a shrapnel shell, setting off the exploder, which scattered the balls like a shotgun. Nobel's Explosives Company started filling shell components at No. 12 Filling Factory in Cardonald in Glasgow in January 1916. It had filled 73 million components by the end of the war.

White and Poppe Limited started fitting fuses to shells at Filling Factory No. 10 in Coventry in March 1916 and the workforce grew to 3,350 women and 500 men. During the winter of 1916-17 it was discovered that bad practice had resulted in shells exploding prematurely. The workers were retrained and it was renumbered No. 21 Filling Factory because F10 ammunition was seen to be dangerous. Around 214 million fuses were fitted at the factory.

No. 22 Filling Factory in Gainsborough started work in February 1918 and it made 8,000 floating mines for the Admiralty. George Kent Limited built a National Fuse Filling Factory next to his fuse making factory in Luton and while it started production in the spring of 1917, some buildings had to be rebuilt following an explosion on 1 March 1918.

No. 8 Filling Factory opened in Southwark, central London in October 1915 and the workforce had filled 8.9 million fuses by the time they switched to checking anti-gas equipment in the spring of 1918.

No. 3 Fuse Filling Factory in Perivale started production in December 1915 and the 4,850 women and 400 men had filled 28 million components by the end of the war. It also opened an experimental unit in August 1917, to test new production techniques.

Kings Norton Metal Company began work at No. 11 Filling Factory in Abbey Wood in south-east London in January 1916. At its peak, the factory employed nearly 1,625 women and 200 men and they had filled over 39 million components by the time of the Armistice.

The State Factories' Contribution[2]

The National Factories made huge amounts of munitions and it could be said that they saved the nation by making so much. By investing heavily in them, the Ministry of Munitions was able to prevent monopolies from controlling the supply of materials, plant and labour. The introduction of large scale production, meant that standardisation and scientific management could be used, while shared ideas resulted in increased output, lower prices and safer working conditions. While the State factories were costly to build, they saved money in the long run, by reducing the quantity of expensive imports required.

The National Factories made a huge contribution to the most important ammunition used by the armed forces:

- 86 per cent of filled shells.
- 50 per cent of rifles.
- 26 per cent of bullets.
- 99 per cent of mortar rounds.

Chapter 20

Tools of the Trade

Machines, Tools and Lifting Equipment[1]

Manufacturing processes were divided into many simple stages. Machines such as lathes, drills, grinders and boring equipment were set up by a skilled mechanic, so an unskilled operative could repeat a task hundreds of times a shift. Many managers failed to appreciate their mechanics, so over 20,000 (or half of them) had either enlisted or switched to higher paid work by the end of the war. The rest had to work hard to keep the machines going and around 5,000 women had to be trained to monitor and maintain machines.

There was huge demand for machines as factories expanded their premises, so factory inspectors started making lists of machines in March 1915, to discover that only half were busy on munitions work. The Machine Tool Advisory Committee then distributed new machines, including many imported from the United States, until the War Priorities Committee took over. The Machine Tool and Engineering Association dealt with any complaints, while the Central Clearing House rehoused idle or unwanted machines.

The country had enough machinery to equip every factory by early 1917, while regular servicing made sure they were well maintained. The Ministry of Munitions started a machinery survey in October 1916 but it would take until 1918 to complete. In the meantime, urgent orders were met with temporary night shifts or by transferring machines between factories. Whatever the emergency, the National Projectile Factories always had priority over the National Shell Factories.

Tools are the steel devices, such as the drills and blades, which do the actual boring and trimming. They are made from a tougher steel alloy called high speed steel. Originally, Swedish bar iron was used but the threat from German submarines soon limited imports. Fortunately, Professor Oliver Arnold of the University of Sheffield created a vanadium alloy, which was a suitable replacement and the city's foundries were soon making 20 tons a month.

Tools wore out or broke with repeated use, so factories required regular supplies to keep them busy. The demand for small tools increased until they were wearing out faster than they could be made, so the Machine Tool Department was set up. Nineteen tool making companies were given grants to extend their premises in the major munitions areas of Sheffield, Manchester and Birmingham, while other companies were encouraged to start making them.

Agents were sent to the United States to locate manufacturers but inspectors discovered that many tools were poor quality, when they arrived in Britain. Fortunately, there were few disasters such as the sinking of the SS *Cymric* in April 1916, which resulted in the loss of many machine tools. The United States' entry into the war meant that their factories required extra machines, resulting in a shortage across Britain. So, the Central Clearing House sourced enough spare machines to open National Tool Factories in Gateshead, Birmingham and Westminster in London. Even so, the Ministry of Munitions still had to control the use of small tools through permits and licenses. While most machines and tools were employed on steel work, the expansion of the aircraft industry in 1917 meant that similar controls had to be introduced on wood working tools.

Cranes and other lifting machines were important in factories making heavy items, such as guns and howitzers, ship and tank parts and large calibre shells. A register of equipment was started in March 1916 and the Ministry started to commandeer idle machinery in 1917.

Gauge Factories[2]

Every component had to be checked at every stage of the manufacturing process to make sure they were being made accurately. Steel gauges were more reliable for measuring than a ruler and they were the only way of checking some dimensions. However, the smallest component could require dozens of gauges, while the largest shell needed hundreds.

The Ordnance Factories made munitions gauges before the war and they were checked at the National Physical Laboratory in Bushey Park. The Ministry of Munitions allowed contractors to buy them from private contractors, following shortages in the autumn of 1915, while National Gauge Factories were opened in Woolwich and Croydon. Manufacturers always made sure parts fitted together in the factory, but they were not always interchangeable in the field. Shop gauges soon wore out, so inspectors had to regularly test them against check gauges. Eventually, gauges had to be sent to the United States and Canada to check imported goods before they were loaded onto ships.

The Gauge Department was set up to buy and distribute gauges at the end of 1915, to standardise measurements across every factory. It eventually contracted 150 firms to make gauges, while the Boards of Management set up gauge factories in the main munitions' centres. Production peaked at 50,000 a month and they were checked against master gauges, called Johansson gauges, at the Royal Arsenal or the National Physical Laboratory.

Power Supply[3]

Many British factories relied on steam power before the war but every factory owner soon wanted electricity. It required careful supervision to install it, because there was no national grid to transfer power across the country. So, the Ministry of Munitions appointed an electrical engineer to advise on existing power supplies and the requirements for new ones in July 1915. It financed loans to extend power stations, while some factories built their own. The new Electric Power Supply Department started controlling the nation's power supply through permits and priorities in June 1916.

New manufacturing processes required huge increases in electricity, such as the shipyards where compressors were installed to speed up work. The Royal Arsenal and Sheffield's steel works also required extra power to run electric arc furnaces, which used huge surges of electricity to melt scrap for recycling. The location of the National Factories was usually decided by its access to a suitable power source.

The nation's power supply had increased from 1.1 million kilowatts to 2.3 million kilowatts by the end of the war. There had been few difficulties getting enough coal until a shortage in 1918 resulted in the prioritising of power for the munitions factories, which lead to shortages for other industries. By the end of the war, the country had larger and more efficient power stations, while some ran off oil, waste heat and gas, reducing the power industry's reliance on coal.

Chapter 21

American Imports

The United States' Attitude to Imports

The Royal Navy's command of the High Seas meant that Britain could import raw materials and munitions, while stopping the Central Powers from doing so. Its only limit was how much could the nation afford, either as cash or credit. At times, it used gold to buy goods and on other occasions it sold British owned American securities, while loans also had to be raised.

American imports kept Britain supplied until its own National Factories were running at full production during the winter of 1916-17. Shipping then switched to importing raw materials but that was reduced by the German submarine campaign and again when the United States entered the war in April 1917. Britain then had to rely on Canadian imports, while the American munitions industry supplied its own expeditionary force. However, the German offensives in the spring of 1918 changed Washington DC's mind. In future, American troops would have to use French and British munitions, freeing up transatlantic shipping for manpower.

The J.P. Morgan and Company Agreement[1]

By the end of 1914, the War Office departments and their contractors were buying materials and munitions from the United States, resulting in competition. So, the Army Council appointed J.P. Morgan's, (a company underwriting war bonds for Britain and France) to negotiate on its behalf in January 1915. While the Admiralty was excluded from the agreement, J.P. Morgan's sometimes helped it out.

President of the Diamond Match Company, Edward R. Stettinius Sr., set up an office to deal with the exports. The Treasury transferred funds to New York when required but the Army Council's budget of £10 million soon ran out. Attempts to reduce J.P. Morgan's fees due to the increase in volume of exports was countered by the argument that its staff were also dealing with the shipping companies, inspecting goods and checking consignments. The Army Council relented because J.P. Morgan's was saving a considerable amount of money and they did not want it to withdraw from the arrangement. Some inspectors were eventually sent from the Royal Arsenal to help the American inspectors, either in the factories or on firing ranges.

J.P. Morgan's staff were instructed to get the best 'quality, price, delivery, discounts and rebates.' Its staff interviewed many American firms but few had any experience and they all wanted money up front for extensions and extra plant. Cartels of brokers started pushing prices up, so J.P. Morgan's started dealing with the wholesalers and manufacturers but they too raised their prices. It eventually had to make subtle enquiries to try and keep prices down.

Concerns that Canadian contractors working for the Canadian Minister of Militia had started to compete with British contracts resulted in a joint Allied purchasing scheme being organised in the spring of 1915. The French government also agreed to work via J.P. Morgan's but Russian buyers continued their own negotiations.

J.P. Morgan's had no transport experience, resulting in congestion on the railways and at the docks by the spring of 1915. So, the Admiralty paid Lunham and Moore, an experienced forwarding agent, to deal with transport, storage and loading.[2] Materials and munitions were still moved under J.P. Morgan's name to avoid publicity and for security reasons because some Americans were against supplying the Allies. J.P. Morgan's often had to check rumours about companies' German connections, including one about a plot to destroy the Remington Arms Company's factory in New York State in March 1915.

The American Munitions Industry[3]

After the Ministry of Munitions took over from the War Office, David Lloyd George asked David Thomas, an owner of Welsh and American coalfields to observe J.P. Morgan's work in July 1915. He soon learnt that its overworked staff had insufficient experience to check companies' credentials. So, Thomas appointed experienced advisors to the new British Munitions Board in September 1915. Ernest Moir, a civil engineer with American experience, took over from Thomas in December 1915 and 800 contracts were soon being run in his name, again for security reasons. However, Moir returned to England in May 1916 after upsetting J.P. Morgan's relationship with the Ministry of Munitions.

While many companies were given money to extend their factories, most had underestimated the difficulties of making munitions. Some argued over designs or specifications, while others delivered poor quality goods; a few even spent their advance and sent nothing.

The munitions contracts expanded so rapidly that it was impossible to inspect everything before it was shipped.[4] It meant that many goods were rejected when they reached Britain, so inspectors were sent to the United States to give advice. They started visiting factories in the spring of 1916, reducing the number of rejections to a fraction of what they had been.

Despite the difficulties, over 90,000 tons of freight was sailing from the United States every month by the beginning of 1916. Most of it was sailing from New York, creating a backlog, so a Traffic Department was formed to improve the loading. The Admiralty sent extra ships to help, while trains delivered goods to other ports along America's east coast.

The expansion of the ammunition programme in September 1916 increased orders to 300,000 tons a month. Worries about sabotage also increased, so factories and ports were given security guards, while sentries accompanied the munitions trains. American companies still struggled to deliver ammunition on time and orders were either cancelled or curtailed because Britain's National Factories were churning our cheaper shells.

The United States Enters the War[5]

Germany launched unrestricted submarine warfare in February 1917, to counter the Allied blockade. It sank 1 million tons of shipping in just two months, causing outrage in the United States because many of the ships were sailing under the Stars and Stripes. The publication of the Zimmerman Telegram, a secret offer from Germany to help Mexico regain territory, prompted President Woodrow Wilson to ask Congress to 'make the world safer for democracy.' It voted in favour for 'a war to end all wars' and the United States declared war on Germany on 6 April 1917.

The United States government wanted its factories to make munitions for the AEF, so J.P. Morgan's resigned on 24 May 1917, having dealt with £300 million (£12 billion today) of goods. It left the British and French governments having to buy materials and munitions through diplomatic channels.[6] Alfred Harmsworth, Viscount Northcliffe, set up the British War Mission to negotiate the future of imports, eventually agreeing that prices would remain the same. The Purchasing Department took over negotiations and contracts and while the American government bought raw materials, its agencies bought munitions.

British and French shell contracts ended in September 1917 and while over 30 million had been delivered, only 100,000 had been rejected after 1.4 million had been rectified. Instead, both countries offered to help equip the AEF with munitions, so its troops could be sent to Europe much faster. While both countries wanted to be paid in steel and timber, they were usually impossible to send because of shipping shortages.

The Inter-Allied Council for War Purchases and Finance started discussing how to buy imports in December 1917. The War Supplies Department headed by Sir Charles Gordon was also established in Washington DC in May 1918 to deal with 4,000 export licenses a month. The Munitions Council then began reporting the situation to the Inter-Allied Council.

By the end of the war, the quantities of the other main items imported from the United States included:

- 1.6 million tons of steel and pig iron.
- 1.1 million tons of non-ferrous metals.
- 117,000 tons of machine tools and 2 million tons of shell steel.
- 356,350 tons of explosives and 214,000 tons of propellants.
- 1.2 million rifles and 926 million bullets.
- 1,396 gun bodies and 1,134 gun carriages.
- 41,938 vehicles and 1,050 locomotives.
- 3,399 aircraft engines, as well as 866 aircraft and seaplanes.

Altogether, 16 per cent of the munitions used by the British armed forces had been imported from the United States. It had cost up to £150 million a year (£6 billion today).

Chapter 22

Canadian Imports

Establishing Canadian Imports

Canada only had five munition factories when war broke out and they were already struggling to supply the country's militia:

- Dominion Arsenal in Quebec.
- Ross Rifle Factory in Quebec.
- Dominion Cartridge Company in Quebec.
- Ottawa Car Company in Ontario.
- Canadian Explosives Company in Ontario.

The War Office asked Canada, a dominion of the British Empire, if it could supply 18-pounder shrapnel cases at the end of August 1914. Sam Hughes, the Canadian Minister of Militia and Defence, offered to source them in the United States, while new Canadian factories were built. He also set up the Shell Committee and gave it three objectives: 'Speed. Prices. Canada.'[1]

Britain was soon looking for complete rounds and Hughes offered to make 250,000 shells without fuses. Tests proved that basic steel was as good as the acid steel used for shells in Britain and the first shells were shipped to Britain at the beginning of 1915. While 120,000 Ross rifles were also supplied, it was discovered that it could not be used in the trenches because British made .303 bullets or mud jammed them. So, an order for more was cancelled.

The Ministry of Munitions took over in Britain in June 1915 and Lloyd George was soon hearing talk of political interference and corruption in Canada. He directed David Thomas to head north from the United States to investigate and while he learnt that the accusations were false, he discovered that the Canadian Shell Committee was overwhelmed with work. Sam Hughes refused to make any changes and while Thomas extended the shell contracts, the Shell Committee soon disbanded following critical reports in the press.

Lionel Hitchens of Cammell Laird's and The Honourable Robert Brand, Baron Brand, CMG, who had worked in South Africa, visited Canada in October 1917. They appointed senior businessmen to the Imperial Munitions Board, chaired by Joseph Flavelle, and made it directly responsible to the Ministry of Munitions.[2] Hughes was appointed its honorary president to get his cooperation. The Imperial Munitions Board had five departments:

- Purchasing
- Contracts
- Technical
- Inspections
- Finance

The Labour Department was added in September 1916 to help the factories find workers. The Aviation Department started training pilots in January 1917, while the Aeronautical Department started sourcing spruce to build aircraft in October 1917.

Importing Canadian Shells[3]

Canada shipped shell casings and then shells without fuses to begin with, buying them from the United States, France and Switzerland when its factories could not make enough. While it soon started sending completed shells, an error meant that half were sent without fuses. A shortage of inspectors in the early months of the war resulted in many items being rejected when they faced a second examination on arrival in Britain.[4] However, standards improved and by 1918 shells did not have to be re-examined.

Canadian factories were up to speed by the summer of 1916 but Britain did not make full use of them for three reasons:

- The Ministry preferred American factories because Canadian ones usually delivered late.
- The Treasury wanted to buy shells from the United States to keep Britain's credit up.
- The National Factories across Britain were getting to speed and their shells were much cheaper.

The Canadian factories tried switching to larger calibres but Britain was again making enough, so they cut back on production to save money. The large orders eventually began rolling in at the end of 1916.

While it had taken time to sort out the confusion left by the Shell Committee, the Imperial Munitions Board was supervising over 400 companies, employing 250,000 workers on contracts worth CAD $500 million, by the beginning of 1917. Eight National Factories had also been built to make forgings, explosives, chemicals, munitions and aircraft.[5] The Imperial Munitions Board introduced tighter financing, which saved a lot of money. It also started building ships with American steel in response to the German submarine campaign.

Canada decided do business with the United States after it entered the war in April 1917, only to see Britain and France offer munitions to the AEF, so it could deploy to Europe quicker. Despite the problems, Canada eventually sold 65 million shells and many components to the United States for CAD $900 million. Shipping shortages caused by the German submarine campaign resulted in supplies stacking up at the factories, on trains and at ports. It also meant that Britain needed to import foodstuffs rather than munitions from Canada by the spring of 1918. The total exports from Canada were as follows:

- 23,000 tons of steel.
- 25,000 tons of non-ferrous metals.
- 20,877 tons of high explosives.
- 45,880 tons of propellants.
- 11,230 tons other explosive materials.
- 16.52 million armed shells.
- 12.60 million assembled shells.
- 6.4 million forgings.
- 36.23 million shell casings.
- 37.88 million fuses and other shell components.

Canada also exported large amounts of timber for aircraft.

Combined Imports

The total amount of imports to Britain is given below. The majority came from the United States and Canada:

- 25.85 million tons of iron ore.
- 1.70 million tons of other ores.
- 4.52 million tons of ferrous metals.
- 3.83 million tons of non-ferrous metals.
- 7.29 million tons of explosives.
- 2.53 million tons of finished munitions.
- 237,000 tons of railway materials.
- 82,000 tons of mechanical goods.
- 118,000 tons of machine tools.
- 137,000 tons of agricultural machinery.

Chapter 23

Cooperation with the Allies

Exports to the Allies[1]

Britain sent munitions to the Belgian army because the country had lost all its factories during the early months of the war. France also lost its iron ore mining districts during the German advance into Lorraine in August 1914. It left its foundries unable to make enough iron and steel, so Britain started sending some until the amount topped 250,000 tons a month. The amount reduced when unrestricted submarine warfare began in 1917 and eventually stopped in the summer of 1918.

Britain sent its surplus of benzol, which came from coal tar products, to France, Russia, Belgium and Italy, so they could turn it into synthetic phenol to make picric acid. It also bought large amounts of explosive materials and propellants for France, Russia and Italy.

Once Britain's industry was running at full production, it was able to supply surplus weapons, ammunition and equipment to its Allies. France was happy to exchange aeroengines and optical munitions for British machine guns and bullets; it was also grateful for 1,200 Stokes mortars during the final months of the war. Large amounts of locomotives, rolling stock and railway track were also sent to France, to upgrade the railways between the Channel ports and the BEF's sector.

Lord Kitchener sent a representative to Grand Duke Nicholas and he returned with permission for Britain to buy munitions on Russia's behalf. Britain bought most items from the United States until its own factories were able to send everything from bullets to grenades and howitzers to aircraft parts. Factories also made the different calibre bullets required for the Japanese rifles bought by Russia; tons of obsolete weapons and ammunitions were also sent. The War Office Committee for the Purchase of Russian Supplies was appointed but Moscow complained about the deals being made in the United States and Canada, while its overseas staff argued over everything. Lord Kitchener was en route to Russia to sort out the situation when his ship, the HMS *Hampshire*, sank on 5 June 1916 and he drowned.

The War Office Committee was disbanded and the problem of Russian supplies was handed over to the Ministry of Munitions. While Moscow demanded huge amounts of everything, it was pointless sending them for several reasons. U-boats forced ships to sail to Russia's northern ports, which could only be reached in the summer months. Once there, poor logistics then meant that goods were either left in the open to rot or ended up stranded on the railways.

British exports changed significantly in 1917 for several reasons:

- America entered the war in April.
- Russia dropped out of the war in October.
- Italy suffered a huge setback in November.

Britain handed over the rifle making factories it had financed in the United States, so the country could make their own. It also sent many items to the AEF when it deployed to France in 1917 and 1918, ranging from helmets and bicycles to aircraft and artillery pieces.

Britain had always supplied small amounts of iron, steel and high explosives to Italy but it had to increase exports following the disaster at Caporetto, which ended in November 1917. It also started sending artillery pieces and Lewis guns, while 45 million bullets were diverted to it after Russia dropped out of the war. Total British exports to its Allies included:

- 5.5 million tons of iron and steel.
- 6 million tons of non-ferrous materials.
- 770,000 tons of explosives and chemicals.
- 304,000 tons of alloys.
- 1,340 artillery pieces and 15.33 million shells or casings.
- 51,400 machine guns, 1.39 million rifles and 2,800 million bullets.
- 2.83 million mortar shells, 3,700 mortars and 15 million grenades.
- 82,500 road vehicles and 120 tanks.
- 3,450 rail vehicles and 10,750 tons of railway materials.
- 860 complete aircraft and 825 aeroengines.

Cooperation with the Allies[2]

France and Britain set up the International Supply Commission (or *Commission Internationale de Ravitaillement*) on 18 August 1914. The object was to prevent their agents competing, however, jealousy and suspicion meant they continued to buy independently, driving the prices of raw materials and munitions up.

France started using J.P. Morgan's, Britain's commercial agent in the United States after May 1915. A conference in Boulogne in June 1915 resulted in Britain and France agreeing to share information and pool surpluses of materials and goods. Russia and Italy started to do the same at the end of the year. The Allies then met in Paris in the summer of 1916 to discuss exchanging labour or materials, while a further attempt was made to cooperate its buying in the United States and Canada. Eventually, Britain bought most things for Russia and Belgium, although Italy continued to do its own buying, causing problems.

The weak link in the Allied chain was Russia. While it was fighting across a massive front in Eastern Europe, it had little industrial capacity and no overseas credit. Both Britain and France had given £25 million credit to Russia in February 1915, while Britain offered to buy or make what Russia needed. However, Moscow insisted on sending their own agents to North America, where they caused problems by ordering 5 million shells.

Steel shortages brought the Allies closer together and the Inter-Allied Munitions Council was formed in Paris in September 1916. Decisions were guided by the Inter-Allied Bureau of Statistics after January 1917 because the German submarine campaign required better cooperation.[3]

The United States entered the war in April 1917, which meant it wanted to supply its own AEF for exporting goods. Britain and France supplied American units with munitions, so men could be sent to Europe quickly. Meanwhile, Russia's withdrawal from the war, resulted in the remaining Allies cooperating better.

The shipping shortage soon topped 10 million tons, which meant that the Allies had to decide what was the most urgent. The Allied Maritime Transport Council met for the first time in March 1918 and Britain declared it needed to import 31 million tons of supplies to survive, including 15 million tons of munitions and 13 million of food. The country was facing the same difficult situation when the Armistice was declared on 11 November 1918.

PART V

The Workforce

Chapter 24

Increasing the Workforce

The Rush to the Colours

Following the outbreak of war, recruitment posters appeared everywhere with the message, 'Your King and Country Needs You. Enlist Now.' Then on 5 September 1914, the famous image of Field Marshal Herbert Kitchener pointing out from the front page of the *London Opinion* magazine appeared. It was soon on posters across the country, giving a boost to recruitment.

It was the start of a free for all for manpower that lasted until the summer of 1915. Both the Admiralty and the War Office accepted any man who was willing and fit enough to fight. No one paid attention to what a recruit's job was because there were no shortages of munitions yet. The volunteers thought they were doing the best thing for their country, while the government and the factory owners believed that men who were too old to join up would take over their jobs.

Meanwhile, companies relied on advertisements and walk in applicants to fill up the vacancies left by those who had enlisted. Older men, the infirm and the unemployed were all looking to earn money while fulfilling a patriotic urge to help.

Around 1.19 million men had enlisted, at a rate of 237,200 a month, by the end of 1914. The armament factories started reporting a shortage of skilled workers but the recruiting officers still carried on enlisting anyone fit enough, despite being told not to. Companies were reporting a serious shortage of skilled labour by the summer of 1915, so they were told to stop doing private work and either employ unskilled workers or use overtime. They were also told to speak to the Labour Exchanges and even make lists of who they wanted releasing from the armed forces. The Labour Exchanges were also instructed to advise companies how to get the best out of their workforce and their machinery.

The War Service Badge[1]

The Admiralty and a few private companies started issuing war service badges to their key workers in December 1914, to stop their workers being called 'shirkers and slackers'. However, there was no register of issue, leaving the system open to abuse, so the War Office drew up four lists of important industries and jobs:

- List A contained the trades making munitions.
- List B named the firms making munitions.
- List C named the firms making warships.
- List D contained the trades engaged in Admiralty work.

It then started issuing numbered badges to key workers and gave matching certificates to their employers.

Badges had been issued to everyone working for the Royal Factories and the main armaments companies by July 1915. Those making shell components and tools came next, followed by men involved with shipbuilding, munitions transport and power supplies. Despite the possible advantages, war service badges were not issued to coal miners, dock labourers and railway workers. Probably because it was obvious they were doing key work.

Companies were asked to identify their key workers but each factory had different needs. For example, engineering companies relied on experienced mechanics to maintain its machines, while steel works required strong men to do the physically demanding work. Meanwhile, every company required trained clerks to run their offices.

The wearing of war badges was controlled by the Munitions of War Act and both employers and individuals could be fined for misusing them. Company managers were entrusted with distributing badges and while they sometimes made the wrong choices, they were eventually allowed to issue a badge to all their employees. It gave workers a collective pride in their work and encouraged loyalty to their factory.

War service badges turned the munition factories into no go areas for the recruiting officers. They also helped the Ministry of Munitions understand how the industry was shaping up. By the summer of 1916, 900,000 men had been badged, including the following:

- 105,000 in foundries and steel works.
- 62,000 making plant and machine tools.
- 150,000 in munitions factories.
- 150,000 in the shipyards.
- 87,000 in transport factories.
- 41,000 making explosives.

The Regulation of Labour[2]

The Munitions of War Act only applied to munitions related trades because the coal and cotton unions had refused to sign up to it. The Act prohibited employers from locking out their workers and banned employees from striking. Problems had to be reported to the Chief Industrial Commissioner and the Board of Trade then had twenty-one days to arrange an investigation by the Production Committee, an agreed arbitrator, or a court of arbitration.

The Ministry of Munitions could take control of any factory making munitions if it felt it needed to. It could then limit its profits, suspend union rules and impose certain standards of health and safety. The number of controlled factories had increased to over 2,400 by the end of 1915 and many owners had signed up because they preferred to pay the Munitions Levy rather than the Excess Profits Tax. Meanwhile, Lloyd George's plan was to make the Ministry the model employer; something that would take until the end of 1916 to achieve.

The rising cost of living, poor accommodation and over work unsettled the workforce, so they occasionally chose to stop work or refuse to do overtime. While the public condemned industrial action, the trade unions wanted to avoid stoppages because they could not authorise strike pay for them. One such stoppage occurred in the South Wales coalfield in July 1915, when 200,000 miners refused to work until a new wage agreement had been signed.

Discipline in the Factories[3]

Workers were obliged to follow the Munitions (Ordering of Work) Regulations, which called for good timekeeping and discipline in the workplace. Model Rules asked workers to obey instructions, work hard, refrain from disruptive behaviour and to be sober while at work. Some companies introduced factory specific rules with their own system of fines.

Each town and city had a Local Munitions Tribunal, while the General Munitions Tribunal dealt with more serious issues. Both employers and employees could be fined for committing offences under the Munitions of War Act and they could be imprisoned if they refused to pay a fine. Neither side was allowed access to a solicitor but a worker could be represented by a trade union official. The aim was to keep the charges informal, so the summons was posted rather than delivered by a police officer like a court summons.

Over 4,000 workers had appeared before a tribunal by the end of 1915 but only 2,750 had been convicted. Some were late for work due to poor transport links, while others were ill due to excessive overtime or old age. Companies were fined for trying to poach workers through advertising or offering higher wages. Meanwhile, workers were found guilty of changing company for a better wage, without their employer's consent. Persistent offenders were warned by a labour officer before they were prosecuted.

Factory managers had been called upon to impose discipline on the workforce, while workers' rights had been suspended. Patriotism and a desire to support the men in the trenches made most workers tolerant of their situation. Meanwhile, the Ministry of Munitions stepped in when it learnt that an employer was exploiting its workers. Between them, the Ministry, factory managers and workers cooperated to limit the number of days lost.

The Clyde Stoppages[4]

Trouble had been brewing in the shipyards and factories along the River Clyde since the beginning of 1915 because the Amalgamated Society of Engineers (ASE) needed a new wage agreement. The North Western Engineering Trades Employers' Association asked for a 24 per cent rise, only to be offered just 6 per cent. Meanwhile, other trade unions were asking for pay rises for their members to keep pace with the rising cost of living.

Matters came to a head when 2,000 men walked out at G. and J. Weir, on 16 February 1915, after learning that American workers at the Cathcart Foundry were getting paid a bonus. Another 8,000 men from nearby shipyards also stopped work, so the Admiralty asked the ASE to intervene. While everyone returned to work, there was an overtime ban until the Production Committee awarded a 12 per cent pay rise on 23 March 1915.

As one problem was solved, another one was being discussed. Shipyard workers were getting more overtime pay, so they were drinking more, to the point that it was affecting production. On 29 March 1915, the Shipbuilding Employers' Federation said it wanted to prohibit the sale of liquors near the shipyards. A month later, Chancellor David Lloyd George announced a control of the liquor trade and a higher tax on all alcohol sales.

The newspapers blamed Scottish workmen for the decision, stirring up resentment across the country. If the government and the press had investigated the situation properly, they would have discovered that production in Glasgow's shipyards and factories was suffering because so many skilled men had enlisted, while companies were struggling to get materials.

Talk about the Munitions of War Bill bringing factories under tighter government control to maximise munitions output was treated with suspicion by many. The fact that it included the suspension of trade union customs and practices made it unpopular in union strongholds, such as along the River Clyde. It was Glasgow's holiday week when the Munitions of War Act came into force in July 1915, resulting in lots of discussion and the spreading of rumours. Some even referred to it as the Slavery Act. Tensions continued to rise until the coppersmiths at Fairfield Shipbuilding and Engineering Company walked out on 27 July, after plumbers were instructed to help them catch up with their work. The coppersmiths lost their case because they had failed to ask for arbitration and they went back to work after their union paid the fines.

There was further trouble at the same shipyard on 26 August 1915, after a manager found a group of men shirking. While the company wanted to dismiss them, with the offer of a clean leaving certificate, their shop stewards put them in front of a tribunal. Most paid their fines but three were sent to prison after they refused. Again, their union paid the fines and they returned to work after the rest of the factory threatened to walk out.

An investigation into the stoppages revealed that employers were exploiting the Munitions of War Act for their own benefit, either by threatening workers with the sack or by withholding their leaving certificates. Foremen were also intimidating workers by putting them on harder work for less money or threatening to reduce their piece rates. News of lots of little problems like these soon spread and the trade unions were unable to protect their members any more.

Releasing Men from the Colours[5]

In January 1915, the Army Council was asked to locate skilled men who had signed up at the beginning of the war for a release scheme. Unit commanders had to tell their men to return to their factories to help fulfil munitions contracts because factory work was equal to serving in the field. A man who returned to their original employer was referred to as an 'individual release' while a man willing to work anywhere was referred to as a 'bulk release'.

Returning soldiers were given army pay and allowances and were allowed to wear their uniform while at work. However, some found it hard to readjust, so their employers threatened to send them back to the trenches if they complained. Before long, their uniforms were dirty and so they had to wear civilian clothes until they were eventually transferred to the Army Reserve and demobilised. The Armaments Output Committee had released 5,000 men by June 1915 and while the scheme had been helpful, a far bigger one was required.

The next attempt to get skilled men back into the factories involved asking factories for lists of their key men who had joined up. While 50,000 names were submitted, some were already overseas, some were busy in specialist units (known as barred units), while others could not be found. The problem was then convincing the men to leave their comrades in the trenches; only 5,000 would return to the factories.

A second attempt was made to retrieve men from the divisions still training across Britain in September 1915. Infantry battalions posted a list of key trades and while over 100,000 men said they had the appropriate skills, only some did; the rest had just had enough of army life. Another issue was that only a few had skills in the trades short of workers.

On top of everything, the release schemes were causing unrest in the factories. Stoppages were threatened at Armstrong Whitworth's in Newcastle and John I. Thornycroft and Company in Southampton because unskilled men had been sent to work there to replace skilled men who were still serving in the ranks. The schemes were also causing unrest in the training camps, where the soldiers were preparing to embark for France. So, the Ministry of Munitions had to accept that no more skilled men could be retrieved from the armed forces. While it had placed nearly 20,000 men in their original place of work, another 31,000 had been placed with other companies, with many being sent to the new National Factories.

War Munitions Volunteers[6]

Lloyd George implemented a new scheme to move skilled men to the factories that needed them most, when he was appointed Minister of Munitions in June 1915. Over 5,000 men had joined the North East Coast Armament's Committee trial project, so similar War Munition Volunteer projects were set up across the country. Lloyd George appealed to the workforce to show the same loyalty as the men in the trenches but many were reluctant to register at the Labour Exchanges because they were traditionally related to unemployment. So, the trade unions set up Munitions Work Bureaux, which did not have the same stigma.

The Munitions Workers' Enrolment Department was given a list of 450 companies that needed skilled labour. It was also given a list of companies it could not take volunteers from because they were already on munitions work. The department's staff soon discovered that many of the volunteers had no idea they were already doing war work.

Meanwhile, over 100,000 men volunteered over the next ten weeks. The Labour Exchanges were kept busy checking through the names, while the Ministry kept track of the transfers on four lists:

- Live: men available to be moved.
- Dead: incompetent or non-transferrable men.
- Placed: recently moved men.
- Adjudication: men waiting for their case to be heard.

The Munitions Workers' Enrolment Department took weeks to decide which companies needed skilled men. Meanwhile, it was inundated with protests from managers who did not want to let their skilled workers go. However, they were happy to let go of their badly behaved workers only for them to be rejected. So, managers were told to remove troublemakers and shirkers from their lists, resulting in 90 per cent of the names being removed from the Live Register.

The Labour Advisory Board intervened if a man objected to being transferred but the protests increased as volunteers tried to settle into their new job. Many did not like their new factories nor the crowded accommodation. All the Minister of Munitions could do was appeal to their patriotism and remind them of the hardships the soldiers faced.

Only 4,500 War Munitions Volunteers had been placed by the time the scheme was scrapped in August 1915. All it had done was waste time and create a mountain of paperwork for little return. The only positive effect of the War Munitions Volunteers Scheme was that it convinced many firms to switch from private work to government work, so they could hold onto their key staff.

Released soldiers had been sent to the firms on what was called the White List, while munition volunteers had been sent to those on what was called the Black List.

The Ministry of Munitions drew up a third list of companies that it supported. A new list of firms drawn up by the Priority Committee soon replaced the Black List. Meanwhile, the Ministry's list was divided into those known to be doing urgent work and those still to be investigated. It took the Ministry a year to complete their checks, by which time the Priority List was meaningless because every factory said their work was urgent.

The National Registration Act and the Derby Scheme[7]

On the outbreak of war, over 1.4 million men worked in the metal and chemical industries, which ended up making munitions. Another 1.1 million men worked in coal mining. Over 600,000 had enlisted by August 1915 and only 55,000 had been encouraged to return work by the autumn of 1915. It left both industries short of labour.

During the same period, over 570,000 men transferred to the key industries from trades hit hard by the war, such as construction and making luxury items. Around 260,000 women had also been employed and again, many came from depressed industries, such as textiles, lace and clothing. While the metal and chemical industries had increased to 2.1 million workers, many had never worked in them before.

One of the first things the Ministry of Munitions wanted to know was the size of the nation's workforce and what everyone was doing. So, the National Registration Act 1915 obliged every civilian man and woman aged between the ages of 15 and 65 to register in August 1915. They had to state what their job was, if they were on government work and if they were prepared to do similar work. While the scheme gave the Ministry the information it required, it was criticised because it had included men over the recruitment age and 13 million women, creating a lot of work for little return.

The results were of no use to the armed services, so a second register called the First Military Service Act (or the Derby Scheme after the Director-General of Recruiting, Edward Stanley, 17th Earl of Derby) was started. Every man of military age had to state if he was prepared to enlist immediately or if he wanted to wait until he was called for service; a declaration called attesting. Many went to the recruiting office to fill in the pink form, while those who did not had been visited at home by the end of 1915.

Men who had attested were given a khaki armband, to show they had registered. They were split into unmarried and married men and then divided again into twenty-three year groups, according to their age. The forty-six groups were called up in order, starting with the youngest unmarried men.

Essential occupations were known as starred jobs and they were arranged into four lists:

- List A covered munitions; the Ministry decided if an occupation was starred.
- List B covered coal mining; the Home Office decided which jobs were starred.

- List C covered agricultural, railway and other mining work; a tribunal decided if an occupation was starred.
- Any other important occupations were considered individually before they were put on List D.

Key workers had their pink forms marked with a black star. They were only allowed to enlist with their employer's permission. Around 10,000 men complained that their jobs should have been starred but only 112 had their cases proved. However, it would later transpire that some jobs essential to munitions had been missed off List A.

The Derby Scheme involved a lot of time and effort but it had been done for an important reason, which was close to the heart of working men back in 1915. They believed the working classes would bear the brunt of conscription, while volunteering for military service put the rich and the poor on an equal footing. Making sure the maximum effort to secure voluntary recruitment was used would hopefully avoid industrial unrest.

The Derby Scheme meant that employers could show the recruiting officers lists of their badged men. The surprise for the Ministry of Munitions was that it had thought there would be 750,000 starred men but there were twice as many.

The Munitions of War (Amendment) Act 1916[8]

The Munitions of War Act raised many new issues which were discussed in Parliament during the summer of 1915. The Permanent Secretary of the Board of Trade, Sir Hubert Llewellyn Smith, issued a redraft of the Bill in September 1915 resulting in the Munitions of War Act being amended in January 1916.

The revision precisely described munitions work and listed its supporting industries. It instructed managers to tell their workers who was and was not on munitions work. The revision also transferred control of all docks from the Admiralty to the Minister of Munitions.

Ministry inspectors were allowed to check any aspect of a munitions factory and the Minister of Munitions could declare an unsatisfactory one a controlled establishment. He could set wages, working hours and conditions for semi-skilled men, unskilled men and women. He could also appoint arbitration tribunals to deal with any differences, while managers had to employ non-union labour.

Munitions tribunals dealt with fines up to £5 but the accused could appeal to the High Court (the Court of Session in Scotland) and would be compensated if they had received an unfair hearing. However, they were liable to imprisonment or a large fine if they made false statements or used a certificate fraudulently. Company managers could also be imprisoned or fined if they used Ministry information without permission.

A company could only take on a worker if they had a leaving certificate or if they had been unemployed for six weeks. A manager had to give a worker at least a week's notice of dismissal but they could not dismiss anyone within six weeks of taking them on. They also had to issue a leaving certificate and were not allowed to add comments to them.

Priority Work and Reserved Occupations[9]

Around 2.25 million out of 5 million men of military age attested between August and December 1915, under a voluntary scheme known as the Derby Scheme. Another 275,000 men had enlisted while 429,000 had been rejected on medical grounds. After deducting starred and unfit men, it left only 343,000 single and 488,000 married unstarred men who could be called up. On top of that, it was believed that there were another 1 million unmarried men who had not attested. They were made liable for service under the January 1916 Military Service Act, before married men became liable under a second Military Service Act, in May 1916.

Workers were concerned that attested men might be employed on lower wages or be used as blacklegs if they called a stoppage. A third fear was that the threat of enlistment would be used if they did not do what their employers asked of them. So, the Bill was amended to avert these fears.

The Military Service Act became law on 27 January 1916. The Munitions Priority Committee spent the next four months prioritising work, putting it into the following five classes:

- Class I (a): work of national importance.
- Class I (b): shipbuilding and marine engineering.
- Class I (c): important contracts that needed verifying.
- Class II: unsupported claims for skilled labour.
- Class III: required skilled labour on unskilled or non-essential work.

The amended Munitions of War Act also listed the industries that supported munitions work. For example, those who extracted the raw materials, built and powered the factories or transported workers and goods. Munitions related work eventually included 80 per cent of industries and 80 per cent of the workforce.

Throughout January 1916, every worker was told to hand in their war service badge and work certificate in exchange for an exemption certificate. Managers then withdrew the exemption certificate from anyone who spent more than 25 per cent of their time on commercial work. It also withdrew them from anyone doing a job that could be done by a woman.

While the investigations found some recruits for the armed services, there were far more exemptions than anticipated. The Ministry's response was to appoint the Reserved Occupations Committee, which changed the exemption lists and raised the age limit, so that far more exemption certificates could be withdrawn. By September 1916, the

Badge Committee had withdrawn over 30,000 exemptions from 850,000 men working at nearly 9,500 companies. The Special Committee set up to investigate 'flagrant cases of men deliberately evading military services' had only proved 175 cases, proving that skiving and shirking was negligible.

While there was no visible sign that a man worked in a munitions factory any more, public vigilance would reduce the misuse of the new certificates to a minimum. Ironically, while the Ministry of Munitions had been withdrawing badges from the men, it had been issuing them to female munitions workers in recognition of their contribution to the war effort.

Chapter 25

Agreeing Wages and Hours

A Patriotic Truce and Early Wage Discussions[10]

Trade union leaders recommended a patriotic industrial truce on the outbreak of war and there were few disputes over the next six months. The government wanted to keep the industrial peace because it did not want employers locking their employees out, nor did it want workers walking out. However, Prime Minister Herbert Asquith admitted that the cost of living was increasing in February 1915 and it required quick decisions rather than lengthy discussions to negotiate new wage rates.

The Production Committee was appointed in February 1915 to look for ways to increase production. The shipyards suggested forming riveting squads, which was a break with union rules. Engineering companies suggested maintaining piece rates, suspending workplace demarcations and using female labour. The recommendations were agreed in the Shells and Fuses Agreement of 5 March 1915 on the proviso that they would all be reversed when the war ended.

The Production Committee also suggested granting temporary wage increases to appease shipyard and munition workers. However, employers preferred to use piece rates, bonuses and overtime to reward their workers, because advances ate into their profits.

Union leaders said there was enough skilled labour to go round during the Treasury Conferences in March 1915 but the Board of Trade disagreed. Many factories were reporting falling output because their skilled workers were enlisting or finding better paid jobs. Industry had to come up with a way to restrict the movement of labour or take control of wages, to make sure factories ran efficiently.

Most of the unions also agreed to suspend their right to strike and would instead rely on arbitration. The coal mining and cotton manufacturing unions refused but they did agree to settle disputes without stopping work.[11] These temporary solutions were put into what was called the Treasury Agreement.

The Effect of the Munitions of War Act 1915 on Wages[12]

The Treasury Agreement failed to work, so the Ministry of Munitions asked for new laws to help it maximise munitions production, when it took over in June 1915, resulting in the Munitions of War Act. The suspension of restrictive practices by trade unions was confirmed, while workers agreed to abide by factory rules. Profits would be limited, while companies were banned from transferring labour or plant between factories without permission. Employees could only leave their job with permission and they would then be issued leaving certificates, which they had to present to their new employer. They would be unemployable for six weeks without one.

The Ministry of Munitions had to rely on recommendations and diplomacy to settle wage disputes, because any change in a district's rates was followed by demands for rises from local factories. It reported issues to the Board of Trade, which passed them on either to the Production Committee, an arbitrator or to a special court. Workers could only go on strike and companies could only lock out their workforce if no action was taken for three weeks. Meanwhile, wages and hours had to be recognised by employers, trade societies and the Fair Wages Clause.

The Administration of Wages[13]

Wartime competition and shortages pushed material prices up, while the rising cost of living left workers asking for better wages. Both led to companies wanting more money for what they made, so the Ministry of Munitions had to add suitable clauses to their contracts. The Ministry avoided changing wages to prevent unrest in the workforce and to curb inflation. However, many questions needed to be resolved, such as the rising cost of living and the setting of district rates to match local prices. Piece workers wanted paying according to their output, while time workers wanted comparative wages. Unrest resulted if the questions remained unresolved.

The Labour Department used the 1911 Fair Wages Clause to determine what private companies paid their workers until district rates were established. Meanwhile, the Ministry of Munitions dealt with wages in the National Factories and controlled firms. In all cases, employers and trade union representatives were asked to air their complaints, while the Labour Department reported what other companies had done. It was always agreed that a new rate could not exceed the district rate nor contradict the department's policies.

Wages were set by local agreements but if one company awarded an increase, it triggered demands in the surrounding factories. If one industry agreed a wage rise, its work overlapped with other industries and if one union argued successfully for an increase, its members were soon telling others. The Munitions of War Act was used to set time rates in controlled factories in the summer of 1915. However, it was accepted that employers could award bonuses, called 'time and a bit', 'work on the corner' or 'hallelujah rates'. Awards were always published in the *Labour Gazette*. Circulars L.2 and L.3 set rates for semi-skilled and unskilled men and women after October 1915.

The Production Committee dealt with between 150 and 250 wage increase applications a month and while some were made by an area, others were made by an entire trade.[14] They all had to justify their claim and it was often down to the rising cost of living or because overtime had been cut. Employers either had to pay the union rate, the district rate or an amount scaled against the national rate. However, quite often a rate for a new trade had to be set, such as working on tanks or aircraft, by comparing it to a peacetime trade.

Sometimes workers became worried that the use of unskilled labour or dilution was keeping their wages down. At other times they complained that their companies were profiteering. Some London factories even believed that piece rates were too high as production rates increased. There was unrest when they cut their rates in the autumn of 1915 and the Minister of Munitions reinstated them before making it an offence to cut them without permission.

The Production Committee had approved over 3,750 awards by the start of 1917, but it was turning down more and more as the months passed. The trade unions suggested making national wage awards every four months to ease tensions. The first award was announced in April 1917 but it failed to match food prices, which had risen 90 per cent since the start of the war. Still the unions believed it was the best way to pacify the workers. By October 1917, forty-eight unions had signed up to the national wage agreements.

Equal Pay for Equal Work[15]

The Central Munitions Labour Supply Committee was appointed to promote the employment of unskilled men and women in September 1915. Skilled workers saw them as a threat to their wages, so Circular L.3 stated that skilled and unskilled men were paid the same for doing the same work. Circular L.2 stated that women were paid the same as men when doing work traditionally done by men before the war, such as munitions work.

The Minister of Munitions was only allowed to set the wages of semi-skilled and unskilled men in controlled factories. But more factories came under its control, when the amended Munitions of War Act changed what companies it covered in January 1916. However, the Minister of Munitions could still only recommend rates to privately owned factories.

The Admiralty started to regulate the wages of all its employees, including the 90,000 working in the Royal Dockyards after January 1916. Meanwhile, the Production Committee started refusing most applications for wage increases during the first half of 1916 to try and control inflation. It relaxed its approach in the summer of 1916.

By 1917, it was considered easier to judge the impact of a wage rise on profits, so district rates could be used to decide contract prices. The Lubbock Committee was appointed to deal with complaints made by those who refused to use them, referring to them as 'hard cases'. Firms could even be punished for paying their workers too much by the end of the year.

The Munitions of War (Amendment) Act 1917[16]

Churchill was appointed the Minister of Munitions in July 1917. He introduced a second amendment to the Munitions of War which was given Royal Assent on 21 August 1917. It allowed him to compare the wages of skilled time workers with those on piece work. It also allowed him to set the wages of female munitions workers, to appease the women's unions. While these two rulings were useful, they only applied in National Factories and controlled companies, which only covered 6,000 factories out of 30,000. Collective bargaining had to be relied on in the rest. Finally, the Act cancelled the provisions of the unpopular leaving certificate.

Payment by Results or Piece Work[17]

Piece work was used when a task was easy to measure and it involved paying workers by results. Approximately 60 per cent of shipworkers were on piece work but there were less in the engineering industry because the work was more varied. Some work was new and so rates had to be agreed. Wages also had to be revised if a component was modified or if a production method was changed. The potential for disputes over changing piece work rates was reduced when the Ministry of Munitions became responsible for them in September 1915.

Piece work spread across the munitions industry, with thousands of workers doing a single task on a production line. The potential to make money motivated people to work faster and made them easier to manage. It also meant their machinery did not have to be reset to carry out several tasks.

While the Ministry of Munitions favoured piece work, the employers and unions had to agree to use them because it was linked to dilution. If factories split complex jobs into simple tasks, unskilled workers could do what skilled and semi-skilled workers had done before.

The core issue with piece work was what to set wages at, so the Gun Ammunition Department carried out timing tests for making shells in the summer of 1915. However, the shipping unions were unenthusiastic in the spring of 1917, so the idea was dropped to prevent ongoing stoppages in the munitions factories spreading to the shipyards.

Aircraft manufacturers also objected because the industry involved many complex tasks, which required unique skills and new rates. Managers believed that piece work would encourage rushed work, which was unwise when making aircraft parts. Workers also rejected piece work because material shortages, poor management and inexperienced inspectors often held up their work. Instead, bonuses were paid to workers who were both efficient and diligent.

Time Work and Shift Work[18]

During the first twelve months of the war, piece workers were paid according to their output and many worked up to ninety hours a week making shells. They earned far more than the skilled men who set up their machines and taught them how to use them, causing resentment. It left many skilled workers wanting to transfer to piece work for better pay. So, the Ministry of Munitions authorised the Production Committee to give bonuses to the time workers to reflect the importance of their work. Of course, this upset the piece workers who felt the award was unfair.

The amended Munitions of War allowed the Minister of Munitions to award wage increases. So, Winston Churchill gave a 12.5 per cent rise to 200,000 skilled workers in October 1917, even though it would cost £5.5 million a year. It was followed by a demand by 300,000 engineers in every other industry across the country, which cost another £4.5 million. That triggered a payment to the 560,000 workers semi-skilled and unskilled workers on war work, costing another £6.5 million. Churchill ordered to 2,600 companies to pay the increase on 11 December 1917, to prevent further industrial unrest. They, in turn, revised their costs to recover the payments.

Setting Fair Wages for Women[19]

Men had relied on trade unions, arbitration and industrial action to set their wages before the war. The Trade Boards Act 1908 set wages for women working in industries such as textiles, but they now wanted to work in the munitions factories, both to earn money and to help the war effort.

Women came from many different backgrounds and few were members of trade unions, so companies wanted to know what to pay them. Meanwhile, trade unions were concerned that their members' jobs would be at risk if women were paid lower wages. Men's work was bound by the Treasury Agreement of March 1915 and while women's wages were an afterthought, both the government and the trade unions agreed there would be no low piece rates.

The Ministry of Munitions took over in June 1915 and it wanted wages to reflect a worker's skills and the type of work they did.[20] But it also maintained the principles of 'equal pay for equal work' and an entitlement to 'a living wage'. So, Lloyd George agreed to a demand for fair wages for women by Emmeline Pankhurst of the Women's Social and Political Union and Mary Macarthur of the National Federation of Women Workers.

The Central Munitions Labour Supply Committee[21] was appointed in September 1915 with instructions to settle women's wages. The Ministry of Munitions could set them in controlled factories and National Factories but it could only recommend them in privately owned factories. It took the Trade Boards several months to work out all the district wages for the many types of jobs but they were regulated after when the Munitions of War Act was amended in January 1916.

Circular L.2 stated that women would be paid £1 per week when they were doing work 'customarily done by men'. However, they would be paid the same as skilled men when they were doing the same work as them. Time rates were the same across districts and while factories were to set their own piece rates and bonuses, they waited until their women workers had experience before setting their rates.

Some companies argued over what work 'customarily done by men' meant and a few ignored Circular L.2 for as long as they could. The women working at Beardmore's eventually threatened to walk out when their manager refused to adopt its recommendations. Some companies reduced women's wages because their working week was shorter than men's, while others paid them less when they did overtime or night shifts. All companies deducted money for training, while most made a deduction because skilled men set up their machines. A few companies refused to employ any women for as long as possible.

Circular L.2 resulted in anomalies, such as some women being paid as doing men's work, while others were paid as doing women's work in the same factory. Some companies split a skilled man's job into many simple tasks and collectively paid women less to make the same item.

As women became involved in more jobs, it was often difficult to assess if they were doing was same work as men.[22] So, the Central Munitions Labour Supply Committee and Special Arbitration Tribunals addressed the anomalies and Order 447 set fixed rates for 111,000 women and girls in July 1916.

The rising cost of living was always an issue and while many men had union solidarity to rely on, few women did.[23] For example, the Production Committee started awarding men nationwide advances every four months in 1917.[24] However, women did not get them because the rise was considered extra to the basic rate, rather than an increase to it.

The situation left many women staying away from home and short of money but advances were eventually paid to encourage them to keep working. The rates of women engaged on 'especially laborious or responsible work or on work requiring special ability' were also given an increase in May 1918. The differences between the wages of the time and piece workers were eventually resolved but it had taken far too long. The women's only consolation was that working long, monotonous days at a lathe was the best way to get a good wage.

Working Hours[25]

Trade unions had been campaigning for a maximum eight hour working day for many years. The Factory and Workshop Act 1901 limited the working week for women, boys and girls to fifty-five hours per week in textiles and sixty hours in non-textile factories. It also banned them from Sunday and night work. However, emergency work for the Crown was exempted from the restrictions on the outbreak of war, so working long shifts, seven days a week was allowed.

Everyone was willing to do as much overtime as possible during the early months of the war, both for financial and patriotic reasons. Many worked between 70 and 100 hour weeks. However, some only had one day every fortnight off, or even one every month. Long commutes on overcrowded trains or trams left many workers with no free time, while the Ministry of Munitions even cancelled public holidays in the summer of 1915.

Excessive overtime may have resulted in good wages but it was also bad for workers' health. So much so that poor timekeeping became a problem as tired workers wanted more free time. The Admiralty stopped Sunday work in April 1915, while a report published by the Health of Munition Workers Committee in September suggested that overwork was responsible for mistakes, accidents and illness. Some employers thought excessive overtime reduced profits and while Circular L.18 suggested stopping Sunday work, few firms did. The Sunday Labour Committee (renamed the Hours of Labour Committee) followed it up with a reminder to adhere to the Factory Acts hours.

The Ministry of Munitions suggested working back to back shifts, to keep machinery working around the clock. However, factories did not have enough supervisors, while there was insufficient housing for so many workers. The one exception was the Gretna cordite factory, which had been designed for round the clock working.

The Health of Munition Workers Committee suggested tea breaks to divide shifts into manageable parts and wanted to stop putting women on night work. It also wanted those on heavy tasks to work shorter days and even suggested giving everyone one day a week off. While the recommendations were sensible, factory managers were concerned about completing orders if they cut back on hours. They were also worried their workers would look for other jobs if they cut their overtime. So, most did not start reducing their hours until the autumn of 1916.

A Home Office order issued back in July 1915 had limited men to sixty-seven hours and boys, women and girls to sixty-five hours a week.[26] In October 1916, the Joint Hours of Labour Committee reduced it to sixty-five hours and sixty hours respectively. The exception was ship repairs because of a shipping shortage, which became critical when unrestricted submarine warfare began early in 1917.

The Munitions Ordering of Work Regulations allowed workers to ask for Sundays off, however, 120,000 workers continued to work them. Many office workers and educated women joined volunteer groups in the munitions areas with the intention of covering weekend shifts. However, most employers refused to use them, believing that they could damage their machinery, so they soon disbanded.

Armstrong Whitworth, the largest employer in the North East of England, decided to shut their factory on Saturday afternoons and Sundays. Other factories followed suit after it reported an increase in output, fewer mistakes and less accidents. Eventually, the Hours of Labour Committee called for an end to Sunday work and the numbers of workers involved was reduced to the 40,000 workers engaged in urgent work or continuous processes, such as making explosives or steel.

Inspectors were tasked with monitoring the effects of long hours on the workforce. By October 1917, the Health of Munition Workers Committee reported that the strain of prolonged hard work was taking its toll on the older and disabled workers, as well as the women and youngsters.

The Workington National Shell Factory then reported it was able to make more shells for less cost after trying a fifty-hour week in February 1918. However, plans for a general reduction of the working week were shelved because the munitions lost during the German spring offensives had to be replaced. Workers started asking for a shorter working week for the same money once the crisis was over and the Hours of Labour Committee was considering implementing it when the war ended. The Home Office would revoke the 1916 exemption order for munitions works in March 1919 and each factory was once again allowed to set the length of its working week.

Timekeeping[27]

The Munitions of War Act stated that workers had a duty to 'attend regularly and work diligently', while factory rules addressed obedience, sobriety and suspended trade union restrictions. There were few problems during the early months of the war but poor timekeeping soon increased. Members of Parliament toured the munitions areas to make patriotic appeals and while most workers were 'doing splendidly', a minority ignored their pleas.

Some absenteeism was due to sickness and injuries, particularly amongst the older men or injured ex-soldiers who had been discharged. Other absences were due to overwork, bad workshop hygiene or poor transport. Medical referees were sometimes appointed to check health issues because doctors charged a fee to give a diagnosis. The Ministry of Munitions also had to issue sickness certificates to counter the number of fakes in circulation. However, a few absentees gave unacceptable explanations, such as the after effects of alcohol or wanting a holiday. Some simply said they had enough money and wanted more free time, particularly those on piece work.

A study reported that timekeeping in 80 per cent of controlled establishments was satisfactory but the rest were warned they would be cautioned if too many hours continued to be lost. Many firms stopped late comers entering their factory until the morning break in a procedure known as quartering. Shipyards were known to punish late comers by locking them out for their full shift.

Offenders were cautioned by the Labour Advisory Board, a trade union official or a Ministry of Munitions' officer. Persistent lateness resulted in a summons before a munitions tribunal and around 1,000 men a month were being fined up to £3 by 1917. (Women, boys, older men and men working over sixty hours a week were exempt.) While this was a deterrent to most, 'confirmed slackers' could be suspended for several days or even dismissed. After May 1917, the final resort was to withdraw a bad timekeeper's exemption from military service; something that happened to around twenty-five men a month.

Meanwhile, the coal mines relied on work committees to deal with absenteeism or bad timekeeping, rather than munition tribunals. Workers responded better to a committee of their colleagues and some munitions factories used them during the final months of the war.

Scientific studies of the shift patterns, welfare conditions, and health and safety, affected the attitude of employees to their work. Over time, it was recognised that reasonable hours, regular breaks, good management and a healthy factory environment resulted in a satisfied workforce, increased production and lower costs.

At the end of the war, discussions were held about giving a service award to munitions workers but there were inadequate timekeeping records to make one meaningful. So, only a few were awarded the Order of the British Empire for outstanding service to the munitions industry.

Wages Summary[28]

Setting the level of wages had always been decided between an employer and their employees, or their trade unions, before the war. However, the government had been forced to get involved in wage issues, to motivate a workforce facing a rising cost of living, because the nation could not afford a prolonged stoppage which would delay munitions or shipping production.

At the same time, the Ministry of Munitions had to adjust its prices, to placate companies. It also had to link women's wages to men's, to stop companies using them as cheap labour. It meant that the war had forced the government into taking control of wages, pitting the workforce against the state for the first time. Only time would tell what would happen when the status quo between the companies and the trade unions reasserted itself after the war.

Chapter 26

Dilution of the Workforce

Skills Terms[1]

The trade unions used three terms to determine jobs and set wages and they still referred to them after their customs and practices were suspended:

- Skilled
- Semi-skilled
- Unskilled

These referred to an operative's training rather than their abilities. This is how the three terms were used in engineering, the largest element of munitions work.

Skilled Workers

A skilled operative had completed an apprenticeship and was considered competent to set up machines, work to drawings and complete accurate work.

Semi-Skilled Workers

A semi-skilled worker had learnt the same tasks but through practice, rather than training. In some cases, semi-skilled workers were better than skilled workers because they had more experience.

Unskilled Workers

Unskilled operatives could only do a repetitive task on a machine that had been set up by someone else. They could be taught the task in a few days and while they could become as good as a skilled or semi-skilled operative with practice, it was only at that one task.

Dilution

An amendment to the Defence of the Realm Act in March 1915 only suggested dilution in private factories but the Munitions of War Act enforced dilution in the National

Factories in July 1915. Dilution involved dividing complicated tasks, which were done by skilled and semi-skilled workers, into many simple tasks. A machine could then be set up by an experienced operative, so an unskilled worker could make thousands of identical items with minimal supervision. The suspension of trade union customs and practices had allowed companies to reorganise their factories to achieve what was known as the dilution of the workforce.

Introducing Dilution[2]

Once it was clear that the War Munitions Volunteers Scheme and the Release From the Colours Scheme had failed, it was time to push forward with dilution. Lloyd George told the National Advisory Committee that private factories had to send their skilled men to the National Factories and replace them with unskilled workers.[3]

On 9 September 1915, Lloyd George told the Trade Union Congress that the country was fighting for its life and they had to make munitions to 'give our gallant fellows fair play in the field.' He thought unskilled labour could be trained to do what skilled and semi-skilled workers did. The danger was workers would think their jobs were being taken by cheaper labour and there would be no jobs to go back to when the war was over.

Lloyd George wanted equal pay for piece workers but Emmeline Pankhurst of the Women's Social and Political Union, also wanted equal pay for time workers. While it was agreed that women would start on lower probationary rates, their wages would match the men's as soon as they completed their training. The only exception was any work that was recognised as women's work before the war, such as textile work.

Lloyd George wanted to find out which companies were doing private work and get the Labour Exchanges to help them replace their skilled men with unskilled men. The skilled men would join the King's Munition Corps and either be placed with a local munitions factory or be transferred to one in another area by the National Clearing House.

The trade unions accepted Lloyd George's recommendations and they agreed to suspend their rules, practices and customs. They would cooperate with the reorganisation of factories and the transfer of surplus skilled labour between them. They also agreed to end overtime limitations and would allow piece work when necessary.

Implementing Dilution[4]

The Central Munitions Labour Supply Committee was appointed on 20 September 1915 to advise factory owners on the implementation of dilution, the movement of skilled labour and the settling of disputes. It issued Circular CE.1, which asked companies to list their skilled labour and machinery on Form Z.8. However, some results looked suspicious, so the Central Munitions Labour Supply Committee sent inspectors to check them.

The Local Advisory Boards and the trade unions then found out which men were on private work or were under employed. They discussed how to reorganise the factory and made sure that managers recorded any changes in workshop practices, so they could be restored after the war. Meanwhile, inspectors from the Labour Supply Department worked out how many women each factory could employ, while the Labour Advisory Board dealt with objections. Circular L.2 was sent out early in November 1915 and Lloyd George then toured the industrial areas to explain why dilution was so important and how it would be implemented.

It took time to convince companies that dilution would work and it required patience and tact to get the approval of the managers, the trade unions and the rest of the workforce. Employers were worried they would lose key operatives and there might be stoppages. Trade unions were worried that their customs and practices might not be restored.

There were still concerns that unskilled workers, particularly women, would be paid lower wages than their members. There had been protests when John Lang's announced it was planning to employ women in its machine tool factory in Johnstone, south-west of Glasgow in the autumn of 1915.[5] The ASE confirmed they would be paid the same rate as the men but shop stewards threatened to call a stoppage when women started work in December 1915. So, Lloyd George went to Glasgow to tell them how the Ministry of Munitions needed women to work in private factories, to replace the skilled workers who were needed to set up the National Factories. Unfortunately, it left the shop stewards thinking that the government wanted to take over every factory.

A socialist newspaper, called *Forward*, was closed under the Defence of the Realm Regulations after it published misleading information about the meeting. The Clyde Workers' Committee then published an article in *The Worker* newspaper titled 'Should Workers Arm? A Desperate Situation'. So, the police raided its offices, smashed its printing press and arrested the committee members for treason and undermining the war effort. Around 2,000 workers stopped work in protest until they realised what the three men had been arrested for. William Gallacher and John Muir were imprisoned for a year, while Walter Bell was locked up for three months. John Maclean, editor of a third newspaper called *Vanguard* was imprisoned for three years after pleading not guilty.

While these troubles were being settled, an amendment to the Munitions of War Act was being discussed. The plan was to define what munitions work was, so the Minister could declare which factories were controlled. It would also allow the Minister to set the wages and working conditions for women under Circular L.2.

While most of the trade unions agreed, representatives of the ASE asked Prime Minister Herbert Asquith and Minister David Lloyd George to include the semi-skilled and unskilled men working in controlled factories. They agreed and the amended Munitions of War Act was given Royal Assent on 27 January 1916.

After a difficult start, companies across Glasgow used consultation before employing unskilled workers into their factories. They submitted plans to the Clyde Dilution Committee, who discussed them with the union representatives and shop stewards. They in turn explained them to the workforce, in what turned out to be a successful approach. The Clyde Dilution Committee helped transfer 7,500 skilled men from 150 private factories to the National Factories.

There were a few more stoppages along the River Clyde, such as when women were barred from doing machine tool work at John Beardmore's. Another occurred at William Beardmore's on 17 March 1916, when 1,000 workers stopped making howitzers. The Clyde Workers' Commission convinced four more companies to halt production before the five ringleaders were arrested. The Federated Engineering and Shipbuilding Trades Union then voted against the stoppage and everyone returned to work after being threatened with fines or the sack.

Training Unskilled Workers[6]

The expansion of munitions factories required the employment of thousands of unskilled workers. While production processes could be divided into simple tasks, everyone needed some training, so more than fifty universities and technical colleges offered their premises as training areas. But there were shortages of machines and trainers because most were needed in the munitions factories.

Traditional courses covered every aspect of machining steel, so short courses were designed to only teach the munitions workers what they needed to know. Companies soon complained they required more machine setters, so new courses were designed to train them. Again, they were short and practical, only covering the make of machine the operator would work on. Despite the difficulties, 13,500 men and 9,000 women had been trained to work in the munitions factories by the summer of 1916.

Reaction to the 1916 Somme Campaign[7]

As the Somme campaign entered its second month in August 1916, the Ministry of Munitions was looking for extra men to meet the munitions programme. However, the BEF was also desperate for men to replace the casualties it was suffering. So, the Manpower Distribution Board was appointed to find men for the armed forces and the munitions industry. Chairman, Neville Chamberlain, stated that the Manpower Distribution Board would follow three policies:

- No skilled man should do work which could be performed by a lesser skilled man.
- No young or fit man should do work which could be done by an older or less fit man.
- No man should do work which could be done by a woman.

As the Somme campaign came to an end, GHQ increased the number of men it required for the BEF to 940,000.

While more dilution was required, it posed two potential problems. Firstly, taking skilled men from the armed forces for the factories would unsettle their comrades in the trenches. Secondly, taking skilled men from the factories for the BEF would upset the trade unions. Meanwhile, the War Committee was left considering whether it would have to introduce compulsory military and industrial service.

The Admiralty needed extra men to work in the dockyards by the end of 1916, so another release scheme was organised to help the shipbuilding industry. Over 1,000 skilled men were released from the BEF, so they could head back to the dockyards, having had experienced enough of trench life on the Somme. The scheme hit the battalions that had recruited from Glasgow, Belfast, Newcastle-upon-Tyne and Liverpool the hardest.

War Service Badge Problems[8]

Nothing could be done about the 250,000 men who had been rejected on medical grounds nor the 500,000 men who were exempted from military service for legitimate reasons. However, the Manpower Distribution Board soon discovered that 900,000 men of military age had been issued with a war service badge because companies had found it easier to issue them to all their employees. It meant that many semi-skilled and unskilled men were wearing them and some were anxious to avoid military service.

The Manpower Distribution Board wanted the tribunals to speed up the 1.1 million outstanding appeals. It also told companies to release young skilled men who were new to their trade and unskilled men, under the age of 30. In return, it offered older men to replace them. However, employers were anxious to keep their favourites and released their troublesome men, no matter what their skills were.

The Manpower Distribution Board recognised that an unbiased system was required, so it drew up a list of skilled occupations during the winter of 1916-17. The Ministry of Munitions said it needed 300,000 more munitions workers to meet the expanding munitions programme, while the BEF also needed another 300,000 men for its spring offensives.[9] Meanwhile, both the shipbuilding and engineering unions complained that recruiting officers were still hassling their members, so it wanted them to carry a trade card. They also said that thousands of their members were still serving in the BEF and they asked for them to be sent back to the factories. However, the Ministry suspended its investigation because trouble was brewing in Sheffield.

The Army Reserve Munition Workers' Substitution Scheme[10]

The Military Service Act of May 1916 had allowed soldiers with useful skills to be transferred to the Army Reserve. They were then allowed to work where they liked, which was of little use to the Ministry of Munitions. So, the Army Reserve Munitions Workers' Substitution Scheme was introduced, to allow the Ministry to place such men where it needed them.

A second feature of the scheme was that disabled soldiers, who had recovered from injuries, were allowed to substitute fit, unskilled men in the factories, once the British Army had discharged them. An exasperated War Office soon asked why very few of the 70,000 discharged disabled soldiers had been given munitions work. The Ministry of Munitions retorted that only a few were fit enough to work; the rest had done more than 'their bit' for their country.

The Manpower Board had also suggested de-certifying all de-badged men aged 26 and under, so they could be enrolled as War Munitions Volunteers. It could then reissue the badges without bias and with the unions' help. While the idea was a sensible one, the Board of Trade rejected it because trouble was brewing in Sheffield.

Tens of thousands had stopped work across Sheffield, following a meeting at the Vickers factory concerning the enlistment of skilled men on 16 November 1916. Motorcycle messengers spread the news, causing another 30,000 to walk out at the Vickers' shipyard in Barrow-in-Furness. While everyone returned to work after just a few days, it was clear there would be another stoppage if anyone else was victimised. The Ministry of Munitions, the Manpower Board and the Board of Trade all noted that they would have to proceed carefully to avoid further industrial trouble.

The medicals continued throughout November 1916, to see who could be called up. After six weeks, 42,000 unskilled men under 30 had been checked and while 30,000 men had been found to be unfit, only 7,000 had been released for military service.

The Trade Card Scheme, November 1916[11]

The Trade Card Scheme was introduced on 18 November 1916 and the ASE led the way, issuing cards to all its members. However, many unions refused to sign up because only some of their members were entitled to exemption cards, dividing their membership into have and have nots.

Another unpopular division of the workforce also emerged. Shortages of steel and a need to build more merchant ships, meant that workers in both industries were exempted. While the Trade Card Scheme had gone part way to resolving the BEF's manpower shortage, it had started a new debate across the nation's workforce.

The Clean Cut[12]

A change of government took place on 9 December 1916, with Lloyd George replacing Herbert Asquith as Prime Minister. Lloyd George's new War Cabinet appointed Neville

Chamberlain as Director General of National Service. The plan was to withdraw exemptions from all 18 to 21 year olds in what was called a 'clean cut'. There would be no exceptions but anyone serving an apprenticeship would initially join the Army Reserve to give their company time to replace them.

The companies complained that such a 'clean cut' would disrupt production. They wanted to keep those holding trade cards or doing an essential job identified on the White List. The suggestion attracted criticism in Parliament because only certain unions had signed up to the Trade Card Scheme. It did not help that trade union officials were offering trade cards a defence against the recruiting officer to boost membership.

Despite the complaints, the Ministry of Munitions withdrew badges and certificates from all unskilled and semi-skilled men in mid-December 1916. Dilution officers then discussed with each factory who could be released. Older and unfit men were enrolled as Army Reserve Munition Workers, ready to replace the younger ones. The scheme worked but it also unsettled the entire workforce, despite posters telling munitions workers that they 'may be serving your country better at your present job than in the trenches' and to 'stay at your work'.

The National Service Volunteers' Scheme, February 1917

On 6 February 1917, Neville Chamberlain announced the new National Service Volunteers' Scheme, calling for men of any age to volunteer to work in the munitions industry. Lloyd George warned that it was the last call for industrial volunteers and that compulsory work would have to follow. However, he soon withdrew the warning because of fears that it would be met 'with the sternest and bitterest opposition from the working classes.'

Instead, the War Cabinet announced that the Protected Occupations Schedule would replace the Trade Card Scheme and the White List at the end of March 1917. The plan was to compare the number of skilled men in each occupation with the number required by the munitions industry. Any surplus would be liable to enlistment.

Each man's occupation was detailed on his National Registration Card. Companies then submitted lists of their employees and gave exemption certificates to those with protected occupations and the unfit men. Anyone with a protected occupation doing commercial work was enrolled as a war munitions volunteer and had to be prepared to transfer to a munitions factory.

The dilution officer then chose which skilled men under 25 years old and semi-skilled and unskilled men under 32 years old would be given a medical. Meanwhile, the Labour Enlistment Complaints Committee dealt with anyone who disagreed with the decision. Those who passed the medical had two months to put their affairs in order before they were summoned to the enlistment office. Meanwhile, the dilution officer offered the factory a suitably skilled but older replacement worker.

The Lancashire Engineers' Stoppage, May 1917

By spring 1917, munitions workers were told they had to continue working hard because attacks by German submarines were threatening the country's supply lines. Around 500,000 tons of shipping had been sunk in February and March, while 880,000 tons had been lost in April.

Food shortages and the rising cost of living were putting the workers were on edge. They were living in poor accommodation with no social life, while the recent offensives near Arras in France reminded them that their loved ones were in danger. Many believed their union leaders were working hand in hand with the government, so they looked to their shop stewards to speak up for them. The only factor in their favour was that they knew the Ministry of Munitions could not afford to allow any stoppage drag on.

Meanwhile, trouble had been brewing in Lancashire since Tweedales and Smalley Limited, a textile company in Rochdale, sacked several men for refusing to help women do commercial work.[13] The factory manager was in the wrong but he refused to speak to either the Ministry of Munitions or the unions. The ASE had put in a complaint but 2,000 men walked out on 30 April 1917, before the Ministry could follow it up.

News of the stoppage was censored but word of mouth made sure another 60,000 stopped work across Lancashire, while motorcycle couriers spread the news across the rest of the country. There were further stoppages in Sheffield, Rotherham, Coventry and London but workers along the River Clyde, the River Tyne, in Barrow-in-Furness and across Birmingham refused to take part.

Government representatives met the union leaders and resorted to blaming them for the spreading stoppage, when the news finally appeared in the press. Meanwhile, the Shop Stewards' Committee told the union leaders to keep out of the industrial action, while union leaders retaliated by calling the committee 'an irresponsible and unauthorised body.'

Every factory was instructed to display posters stating that halting munitions work was an offence under the Defence of the Realm Regulations. The threat of prison meant that the majority were back to work by 12 May 1917, however, intermittent stoppages continued until the government arrested seven agitators. They were soon released on the grounds that the stoppage had been a mass walkout at several factories, rather than one organised by a few militants. But their example was enough to get everyone back to work by 19 May.

Altogether, 200,000 workers had stopped work, resulting in 1.5 million working days being lost; more than all the days lost since the war started. An investigation discovered that again, the rising cost of living, food shortages and a lack of confidence in Lloyd George's government were to blame.[14] New negotiations with trade unions and employers followed and they included the extension of wage awards and the protection of piece rates. They also looked at speeding up the arbitration process and cancelling leaving certificates. However, the ASE rejected the Bill by a large majority, which raised the question: was it worth expanding dilution?

Abolishing Leaving Certificates, August 1917[15]

The trade unions that had refused to sign up to the Trade Card Scheme continued to argue that it was unfair and divisive. However, the ASE refused to get involved because further dilution would affect its 200,000 members more than the others. It wanted every unskilled man called up before its members were, even if they were doing important jobs.

The government agreed, raising the enlistment age limit to 32 and ending the leaving certificate system, to get the ASE's cooperation. These changes left both the Ministry of Munitions and the BEF short of men, so Christopher Addison resigned on 18 July 1917.

Winston Churchill was appointed Minister of Munitions and he immediately met the trade unions' representatives. He agreed to drop the dilution of private work and amendments to the Munitions of War Act were granted Royal Assent on 21 August 1917. The amendment abolished leaving certificates and repealed the rule that stopped a worker starting a new job for six weeks. Both employers and employees could now just give a week's notice. The only counter to this was that any man who was out of work for more than fourteen days could be called up. It also stated that a worker could not be sacked for being a union member nor for taking part in a dispute, while the Ministry of Munitions would take steps to speed up the arbitration process.

The government and the Ministry of Munitions were both relieved to hear that there was no 'ugly rush' of labour transfers over the weeks that followed. There was, however, a rise in poor timekeeping because employers were afraid to discipline their workers in case they walked out of their job. Local unrest in Manchester and Birmingham occurred when employers collectively agreed not to employ anyone without a character reference, so the Ministry of Munitions reminded them that such action was not allowed. The worst effect of the amendment was a rise in wages as skilled men looked for better pay.

The Shop Stewards Stoppage, November 1917[16]

After omitting a law to force private companies to accept dilution, Churchill asked the Ministry of National Service to work out how to transfer workers from commercial work onto munitions work. It did so by prioritising reserved occupations, putting men through medicals and found replacements for those who were fit enough to enlist.

Dilution continued to increase and the Ministry of Munitions promoted it with exhibitions, educational films and training centres. While the number of women in the munitions industry had increased to over 200,000, the Labour Supply Department predicted that far more would be required. While the trade unions supported dilution, the men on the shop floor were less enthusiastic and there were concerns that they could stop work, if dilution was pushed too hard.

The rising cost of living and food shortages continued to upset many. The fact that a woman could earn more money doing piece work on a lathe than the man who set up the lathe was one issue. So, the Ministry of Munitions gave skilled workers a 12.5 per cent wage rise in October 1917 to stop them switching jobs. The award triggered stoppages amongst unskilled workers in Burnley, Manchester, Sheffield, Derby and Bedford, so they were awarded a 7.5 per cent pay rise to avert further trouble.

Another issue now came to the fore, as a power struggle in the trade unions threatened to cause industrial unrest. The leaders may have taken a step back from industrial action but the shop stewards had been organising unofficial stoppages. The Ministry of Munitions had encouraged companies to organise works committees to represent workers throughout 1917 instead of referring issues to the munition tribunals. The Trade Union Advisory Committee eventually approved them in September 1917 but the shop stewards had again, been involved in sorting out many issues.

Meanwhile, the National Administrative Council of shop stewards had been appointed back in June 1917 and while most of the members wanted the best for their members, a militant minority preferred to talk about a workers' revolution. The main problem was, many workers believed their union leaders were working with the government, rather than looking after their interests.

However, not everyone was happy with the shop stewards representing the workers. Companies in Coventry were against them playing a dominant role in their factories, until 50,000 aircraft workers stopped work on 26 November 1917. They returned to work a week later, after declaring shop stewards must represent them. While thirteen trade unions agreed to give them a role in their organisations, the rest, including the ASE, refused to do so.

Men for the Army or for Munitions, 1918[17]

Britain's manpower situation was critical by the winter of 1917-18, following the BEF's gruelling campaign around Ypres. The Ministry of National Service reported that the armed forces needed 690,000 men, while the number joining up had fallen to just 36,500 a month. So, it proposed three schemes to get 150,000 recruits from munitions and shipbuilding.

The first scheme involved enlisting all young men up to 23 years old, on the grounds that they had little work experience in what was referred to as a 'clean cut'. The second scheme was to raise the upper recruitment age to 50 years old. The third was to revise the Protected Occupations Schedule, ending the exemptions for many. The two month period of grace after withdrawing exemption certificates would also be abolished because many used the time to find a protected job to avoid military service.

However, the ASE said the Protected Occupations Schedule had been agreed with them and could only be changed with them. So, the Ministry of National Service proposed changing the Protected Occupations Schedule's terms, so it only covered workers over 24 years old. Protection would also be withdrawn from any job that could be done by an unfit man or by a woman. There was widespread resistance to the proposals and while some unions wanted the government to ask for a peace settlement, the Clyde Workers' Committee went as far as asking for an immediate Armistice.

The Germans started their spring offensives on 21 March 1918 and the Minister of National Service was instructed to prepare Military Service (No. 2) Act two days later. The BEF had stopped two huge attacks on the Somme and on the Lys by the time the Act was given Royal Assent on 20 April 1918. The National Administrative Council of Shop Stewards and Workers Committees recommended calling a national stoppage to show their opposition to it. The trade unions refused, fearing it would turn public opinion against their cause at such a sensitive time.

The End is in Sight[18]

British industry was going to struggle to find anywhere near enough spare men to replace the 250,000 casualties suffered during the German spring offensives. Even so, the L (for Labour) Committee started identifying which companies it could conscript men from. It also put a stop to volunteering because young men preferred the Royal Air Force (RAF) or technical units, rather than the infantry, where they were needed.

The L Committee banned eighty firms from employing skilled men because they had their full quota. However, the management at the Hotchkiss machine gun factory in Coventry failed to explain the reasons for the ban properly, leaving their workers thinking that they were not allowed to change jobs. The news was seen as 'the thin end of the wedge for industrial conscription' and they stopped work. News spread to the nearby Siddeley-Deasy and Triumph factories and 22,000 workers had stopped work by 24 July 1918. Again, motorcycle messengers spread news to other industrial centres, while there was talk of a nationwide stoppage at a conference being held in Leeds.

The situation led to the Ministry of Munitions suspending the ban, while it explained the situation. Churchill sternly suggested that any man not back at work on 29 July 1918 would be liable for military service. While an investigation into the stoppage heard the same old issues, it also reported that the workforce had had enough. While the German spring offensives had temporarily revived patriotism, it had quickly waned. The labour shortages and new rules left workers feeling that they were facing industrial conscription and a few militants started spreading unrest.

The L Committee also discovered that workers wanted no more changes because they believed the end of the war was near. They were anxious to know what would happen to their jobs once it was over. With the end in sight, it was time for their employers and their trade unions to start talking about the future.

Meanwhile, the War Office admitted that the German offensives had left the BEF was at its lowest manpower level.[19] It also said that it was prepared to accept a reduction in munitions, if it could have more men. So, the War Priorities Committee looked at reducing output and took men from where it could over the next two months. By September 1918, there was no one left to take, without leaving workshops dangerously short of supervisors or shutting down factories. The spring offensives had exhausted Britain's capacity to wage war, both on the front and at home.

Chapter 27

Welfare Arrangements

A New Welfare Policy[1]

Industry had been controlled by the Factory Acts since 1802. Aspects of working life had been subject to the Public Health Acts since 1848 and the Housing of the Working Classes Acts since 1885. Trade unions had also fought for better working conditions and workers' welfare in some industries for years, resulting in many industrial disputes before the war.

Ministry of Munitions' inspectors started reporting welfare issues to the Home Office in the summer of 1915, resulting from managers being focused on long working hours. Fatigue was increasing and discipline was declining, affecting both the quantity and quality of munitions being made. So, the Health of Munition Workers' Committee was formed in September 1915 to study working conditions and health issues. It made many sensible recommendations but they were difficult to implement in busy factories and while some companies ignored the suggestions, equipment shortages delayed them in others.

The Ministry of Munitions set up the Welfare Section in December 1915 and its aim was 'the payment of due consideration to the workers as individuals, securing consideration and absolute fairness of treatment for each worker.' So, it introduced the Health of Munition Workers' Committee's recommendations into the National Factories first, before introducing them into the controlled firms. It was hoped that the private factories would follow.

Welfare Inside the Factories[2]

Factory welfare required good management to achieve a satisfactory working environment. However, Home Office inspectors discovered that only one in three factories were satisfactory in 1916. While many of the National Factories had been designed with welfare in mind, private factories were outdated in design, while their managers were set in their ways. As standards were raised, employers saw production and morale improve. So, did a factory's reputation, which made it easier to recruit workers.

The Ministry of Munitions and the unions avoided the question of men's welfare during the war to avoid misunderstandings over working practices. Instead, it was left to factory owners to deal with any issues, while the Ministry only became involved if the workers took industrial action. However, it was noted that men were always willing to share any improvements that were put in place for the women they worked alongside.

Little was done to improve the working conditions of the many boys who worked in factories and the main issue was a shortage of supervisors who could keep them busy and out of trouble. By the time of the Armistice there were approximately 250,000 boys working in controlled establishments. Many were put onto semi-skilled work because they had a career ahead of them, while girls were left on unskilled work because they did not.

HM Principal Lady Inspector of Factories sent female inspectors into the National Factories, looking to help the women, girls and boys, who had never worked in a factory before. To begin with women workers did not like the caps and overalls they had to wear but they soon accepted them as the uniform of a munition worker.

By April 1916, there were female supervisors in all the National Factories but they often faced resistance from their managers, the foremen and the shop stewards. Over time they received training, so improvements were standardised and some even organised works committees towards the end of the war.

Welfare Outside the Factory[3]

Many welfare supervisors organised activities outside working hours to give its employees something to look forward to. They also encouraged comradeship and fostered friendships, especially for those working away from home.

From the beginning of 1917, the Health of Munition Workers' Committee helped local authorities, voluntary agencies and other organisations to set up activities. The Treasury offering grants to organise sports clubs, concerts, dances and scout troops. Financial support for trips to the cinema or the theatre and weekend trips was also given.

The Health of Munition Workers' Committee looked at other welfare issues, such as accommodation, travel, recreation and medical care. It also appointed female police officers to investigate antisocial behaviour and alcohol issues. The whole point of these activities was to improve life outside the factory, in the belief that it improved morale inside.

The weekly sick pay, paid under the Insurance Act was insufficient, so the Ministry of Munitions' Welfare Section set up an emergency fund to supplement it. Workers and welfare supervisors also collected funds to help workers who were injured or taken ill. Factories allowed pregnant women to do lighter tasks, such as making fuses or overalls, while a few even set up maternity homes. The Ministry of Munitions had paid grants to over forty nurseries before it decided against opening more, believing it was unhealthy to take small children on the long journeys to and from work.

Health Issues in the Workplace[4]

Attitudes to accident prevention and health awareness improved during the First World War due to problems with handling TNT, a new high explosive that was believed to be harmless.

Workers were inhaling the fumes and touching the dust in the early days of filling shells. Many were struck down by liver disease, which led to anaemia and jaundice. It also turned their skin a yellow-orange colour, which led to the nickname, Canary Girls. The first death of a TNT factory worker was recorded in January 1916. The number had risen to ten a month while 10 per cent of workers were off sick by the summer of 1916 when Home Office inspectors started conducting examinations, finding the factories to be dirty.

In March 1917, the TNT Committee introduced new rules in conjunction with research carried out by Guy's Hospital in London. Medical officers collected information from the smaller factories, while the National Filling Factories employed medical superintendents to keep records. Every worker had a regular medical and anyone taken ill was sent to hospital.

The women were put on alternate working periods, with a higher level of supervision. They had to wear protective equipment and their overalls were washed regularly. Mechanical filling, better ventilation and regular cleaning reduced the sick rate down to 1 per cent. Despite the improvements, it was noted that workers could suffer from TNT sickness long after leaving a factory.

Workers were forbidden from eating where the TNT was handled and they washed before eating in canteens. They were provided with milk and a dietary allowance, while they were encouraged to get exercise and fresh air by taking part in outdoor games.

At the same time, the Welfare and Health Section looked at other health issues:

- First aid equipment was installed.
- Medical rooms were set up.
- Health workers were appointed to improve safety and hygiene, especially in the factories making explosives and gas.

Companies were also obliged to cover medical costs and pay compensation for injuries under the Workmen's Compensation Act 1906.

The lessons learned from TNT sickness made factory owners aware that working with gas was dangerous, so similar precautions were implemented. Again, factories had a first aid station and medical staff on call, while employees were checked every fortnight. Despite the precautions, filling shells with gas proved to be more dangerous that working with TNT. Although there were few deaths, many workers needed time off to recover due to inhalation or skin irritation. Again, they were admitted to a local hospital and received sick pay while they recovered.

Works Canteens[5]

Chancellor David Lloyd George's launched an alcohol prohibition campaign early in 1915. New regulations issued as an amendment to the Defence of the Realm Act resulted in the reduction in drinking hours. Many public houses near to munitions factories, shipyards and military camps were closed.

Employers were banned from deducting money from employee's wages for food, while few factories had canteens or messrooms in 1914. Religious, temperance and women's associations tried to collect money for works canteens but few were successful because most people believed that munitions and shipyard workers were well paid. Meanwhile, many managers argued that it was impractical to set up canteens in their factories.

The Ministry of Munitions set up the Canteen Committee in January 1916 to open canteens in controlled factories. Some failed because it was impossible to feed everyone in the short break times, while others lost money due to poor organisation and rising food prices. Again, a lack of space or a shortage of kitchen equipment prevented many from opening a canteen.

The German submarine campaign reduced imports of many foodstuffs, so the Munitions (Food) Committee stepped in to make sure canteens had enough. The Ministry of Munitions' Labour Department became involved when compulsory rationing was introduced in April 1918. Two thirds of factories had eating facilities by the end of the war, with over 900 canteens feeding 1 million workers every day. Drinking water in the workplace had also been made compulsory.

Workers' Housing[6]

There had been a housing shortage around the armaments factories before the war and there were already issues by the time the Ministry of Munitions took over in June 1915. So, it set up a Housing Department to check factory staff numbers against the available accommodation. It also appointed the Bourneville Trust's property management agency, Barlow and Applet, to inspect properties, arrange repairs and deal with difficult landlords and tenants.

The Director of Housing Management wanted to keep married men at home and move single men nearer to their factory. However, the armament districts were already 22,500 housing places short and while work started on temporary accommodation, shortages of labour and materials delayed work. So, hostels were set up in public buildings or in large wooden huts with sleeping cubicles and communal amenities. The

Ministry of Munitions' Welfare Section started checking hostels in 1917 and while they were cheap solutions, they were unpopular because there was too little privacy and too much discipline. Even so, over 40,000 men and women had stayed in one by the end of the war.

While the Defence of the Realm Act was used to take over unoccupied premises for workers' accommodation, the Armaments Committee soon discovered that landlords were raising their rents. One city where housing had been a problem for some time was Glasgow. Many people had moved from the Highlands and from Ireland, looking for work before the war. Shipworkers and their families were crammed into dilapidated tenements along the River Clyde, while 10 per cent of Glasgow's housing stock lay empty because it was owned by speculators.

Like everywhere else across Britain, rents rose faster than wages and the Scottish Federation of Tenants' Associations and the Glasgow Women's Housing Association tried to stop evictions. Trouble started in April 1915 when women attacked the police while sheriffs evicted a soldier's family in Govan. A rent strike across the district resulted in demonstrations and violent confrontations across the city during the summer of 1915. Over 20,000 tenants were refusing to pay their rent by November and the trade unions eventually threatened to call strikes if the evictions continued.

Legal action against rent strikers was halted, while the State Secretary of Scotland Thomas McKinnon Wood asked the Cabinet to help. It agreed to freeze rents at pre-war levels and the Rents and Mortgage Interest Restriction Act 1915 was given Royal Assent in December 1915.

Meanwhile, investigators had been looking for lodgings for munition workers, while mayors issued appeals for accommodation. Billeting committees looked at overcrowding problems, while Labour Exchanges and Labour Advisory Committees made lists of available housing. The Advisory Committee on Women's War Employment also helped.

Many munition workers led dreary lives. Each shift started and ended either with a long walk or a journey on busy public transport.[7] By early 1916, the Inland Transport Department was trying to improve journeys, matching timetables to shifts or organising extra services. Platforms were built alongside the sidings that ran into the factories, while tram and bus routes were extended or modified. Meanwhile, wives were either making munitions themselves or looking after lodgers and their children. Couples rarely saw each other and they had little privacy in their cramped accommodation.

Organisations looked after new arrivals in a town, until they found accommodation. For example, the Travellers' Aid Society was set up to deal with women workers in May 1917. They met new arrivals at the station and gave them a night in a clearing hostel before they were allocated lodgings. Many youngsters had never been away from home before, so they preferred to stay in hostels for company and were looked after by a variety of associations.

The Central Billeting Board was set up in May 1917 to compile property lists and carry out inspections. Its staff also fixed rents, assigned tenants and dealt with complaints. The Billeting of Civilians Act gave it the power to force landlords to take in munitions workers but it also gave them protection from unreasonable tenants.[8]

The Central Billeting Board often encountered overcrowding and many workers shared apartments with strangers or rented a single room for their family to save money.[9] Shift workers sometimes shared beds, taking turns in what was known as Box and Cox (named after a Victorian comedy play in which an unscrupulous landlady rents out the same room to two tenants). Others chose to sleep on canteen floors rather than pay greedy landlords.

The housing situation became more challenging after the Increase of Rent Act froze rents in April 1918. Many landlords decided it was not worth renting rooms, while others stopped taking in lodgers because of food shortages. Altogether, the lack of housing eventually forced the Ministry of Munitions to make it illegal for landlords to evict munition workers.

Rising costs, as well as labour and material shortages, left nearly 1,500 houses incomplete by the end of the war. Meanwhile, a continuing housing shortage meant that some temporary houses and hostels continued to be used for many years after the war.

New Housing Schemes[10]

Housing schemes were built next to some of the large factories but the Treasury banned permanent housing unless it would be needed after the war. Just four grants were given to local authorities, while a few loans were given to Controlled Factories or National Factories and the money was recovered from their profits. A few companies helped finance a housing scheme because they intended to buy the properties after the war.

Houses, bungalows and hostels were built for 18,650 families and 5,350 single men and women around the Royal Arsenal. Vickers built 840 houses close to its shipyard in Barrow-in-Furness and another 500 houses next to its Erith and Crayford factories in Kent. There were other permanent housing schemes in Glasgow, Queensferry and Coventry. The Ministry of Munitions' Housing Section managed several permanent housing schemes but the rents were too high, so many workers refused to live in them.

Over 11,800 temporary timber houses were built for those who worked at the Coventry Ordnance Works and the nearby National Filling Factory. Around 3,500 temporary houses were built for those working for Thomas Firth's and Hadfields in Sheffield. Over 1,200 were built around the Austin Motor Company factories in Longbridge and Lickey in Birmingham, while another 1,000 were built close to Dudley's National Projectile Factory in the West Midlands. A village was also built for the 2,700 workers employed at Kynoch's explosive works on the River Thames.

The Gretna Townships[11]

The Ministry of Munitions wanted a large cordite factory and it chose an isolated site at Gretna on the Scottish border. A temporary town was ready by the end of 1916 while 980 houses and 188 hostels had been completed by the winter of 1917-18.

The workforce peaked at 24,000 workers and up to 7,000 family members lived with them in the Gretna and Eastriggs townships. Workers had access to a hospital and churches, while their children attended schools. An active social scene revolved around recreation grounds, meeting rooms, music halls and a cinema. The factory never stopped, so events were organised for workers on all three shifts.

Gretna was a highly organised community and access to trains to nearby Carlisle were restricted, while the canteens were banned from selling spirits to limit drunken behaviour. Law and order were kept by a police force, while a fire brigade dealt with over 200 incidents; fortunately, none of them were catastrophic.

Gretna employed 11,000 women and the welfare superintendent welcomed up to 200 every day to the site. They came from all walks of life and the welfare staff helped to make hostel life as comfortable as possible.

The Elizabethville Colony[12]

During the early months of the war, 100,000 Belgian refugees escaped to England. Some of them had engineering skills and the Belgian Minister of State *Monsieur* Émile Vandervelde asked if they could do munitions work in July 1915. They were sent to a shell factory built by Armstrong Whitworth's in Birtley, near Gateshead. It was run by the Belgian government and the 4,000 workers slept in sheds until a colony called Elizabethville, named after their queen, was ready. The workforce included 1,000 skilled Belgian soldiers who had recovered in British hospitals and they were joined by another 500.

The factory started production in February 1916 and it was run under military regulations, while the workers wore their uniform. While married men were joined by their families, no single women were employed. There were social and recreation amenities but life was monotonous and the workers were banned from the local pubs, resulting in a riot in December 1916. Most of the Belgians were repatriated when the war ended.

PART VI

The Weapons

Chapter 28

The Artillery

Making Field Guns and Howitzers[1]

The War Office always contracted at least two factories to make each calibre of artillery piece, so it could fall back on one if the other experienced a problem. During the early months of the war, it gave financial assistance to experienced gun makers, so they could expand their premises. They, in turn, relied on many subcontractors to make the components, while railway companies made gun carriages and limbers.

The 18-pounder was the standard field gun and they were made by the Royal Arsenal, Beardmore's, Armstrong Whitworth's and Vickers at the beginning of the war. The Bethlehem Steel Corporation in Pennsylvania in the United States was also contracted but it delivered its guns nine months late, while a fire at its factory in November 1915 increased the delay. Thomas Firth's, Cammell Laird's, Walter Somers of Halesowen and A. Harper, Sons and Bean of Dudley (both in the West Midlands) all made 60-pounder guns. Armstrong Whitworth's built a new gun shop, while Hadfields National Projectile Factory made them later in the war. The Royal Arsenal, Vickers, and Beardmore's made the first 6-inch guns but GHQ wanted more, so the Coventry Ordnance Works and the Nottingham Ordnance Factory were contracted.

The Coventry Ordnance Works made a lot of 4.5-inch howitzers after opening a new plant in the spring of 1916 and it would send 400 to Russia. Vickers designed the 6-inch howitzer and the first ones arrived on the Western Front in the spring of 1915. Beardmore's and the Coventry Ordnance Works followed; some were sent to Russia, Belgium, Italy and Greece. Dick, Kerr's of Kilmarnock, Mather and Platt's of Salford and Rees Roturbo's of Wolverhampton also started making them in the autumn of 1917.

The Royal Arsenal, Beardmore's, Armstrong Whitworth's, and Vickers made 8-inch howitzers. The pro-German owners of the Midvale Steel Company in Philadelphia in the United States refused to make them, so new owners took over and accepted a contract in November 1915. However, the howitzer was soon superseded and the surplus were sent to Russia. The large calibre artillery pieces included the 9.2-inch howitzer, the 9.2-inch gun, the 12-inch howitzer and larger. They were made by Beardmore's, Armstrong Whitworth's, Vickers and the Coventry Ordnance Works.

Manufacturing Issues[2]

The three parts of the British Army were at different stages with their artillery when the Ministry of Munitions took over in June 1915. The BEF was equipped with modern guns and howitzers but the Territorial Force divisions were deploying with obsolete models. The New Armies' divisions had less than a quarter of the 4,800 artillery pieces they required, delaying their deployment and leaving the crews with no time to train.

Lloyd George returned from the Boulogne Conference on 19 and 20 June 1915 with the news that the BEF needed more heavy guns and howitzers. It resulted in the publication of Munitions Programme A, which proposed that the BEF would need 7,240 artillery pieces by March 1916. GHQ then published Munitions Programme B, which suggested it would need just 2,525 artillery pieces. While it was a more realistic target, it was still doubtful if the gun manufacturers could make them in time. Lloyd George added the requirements for the other theatres, such as Gallipoli, resulting in Munitions Programme C, which required 4,600 artillery pieces.

There were concerns that companies were making promises that they could not meet and that many artillery pieces would be delivered late, if at all. Over half the artillery pieces and shells had to come from the United States, leaving the Treasury concerned about the cost. Meanwhile, a few wondered where all the trained gun crews were going to come from.

Experience on the front line meant that GHQ's demands kept changing. The Battle of Loos in September 1915 proved that the 6-inch howitzer was a valuable weapon but shortages of skilled labour and machine tools meant only one third would be delivered on time. The French experience at Verdun, early in 1916, resulted in more orders for 8-inch and 9.2-inch howitzers and the BEF made good use of them on the Somme in the summer. The prolonged campaign provided plenty of evidence of the work artillery was expected to do and the effects it had on the guns. Prolonged use wore out some barrels far quicker than expected and several National Factories had to switch to relining them over the winter of 1916-17.

Events outside the Ministry of Munitions' control then affected gun production in the spring of 1917.[3] There were discussions to be had with the United States, when it entered the war, while Russian demands for munitions ended when it dropped out of the war. It was also clear that the War Office's required less artillery pieces than originally estimated, requiring in less replacements. However, GHQ was asking for more long range guns, so it could increase its counter battery fire.

The Ministry of Munitions had to meet each challenge in turn and while some companies switched from making guns and howitzers to repairing them, any surplus artillery pieces were sent to the French or Italian armies. Pressure on the munitions industry eased when the War Office promised to shorten its bombardments in February 1918. However, it faced a major setback when 975 artillery pieces were lost during the German spring offensives on the Somme and the Lys. It would require another reorganisation of the gun factories to replace them.

The gunners' final challenge was having to adapt to the open style of warfare of the final advance. Minister of Munitions Winston Churchill said that 1919 was going be the 'highest point in weight of metal' but the war ended on 11 November 1918. The number of guns made during the war were as follows:

- 1,367 60-pounder guns.
- 6,926 18-pounder guns.
- 236 6-inch guns.
- 3,437 4.5-inch howitzers.
- 863 8-inch howitzers.
- 3,007 6-inch howitzers.
- 631 9.2-inch howitzers.
- 108 12-inch howitzers.

Total: 16,749 artillery pieces and 20,971 carriages.

Gun and Howitzer Designs[4]

Munitions Design and the Ordnance Committee designed smaller calibre guns and howitzers, while Vickers, Armstrong Whitworth's, and the Coventry Ordnance Works designed the larger artillery pieces. The Ministry of Munitions formed a Gun Section to control the supply of guns on behalf of the Munitions Supply Department, when it took over in June 1915.

Gun factories submitted weekly progress reports before the Ministry deployed supervisors to them during the buildup to the Somme in the spring of 1916; weekly meetings were held throughout the campaign. Infinite contracts were then issued at the end of the campaign to encourage companies to continue making guns and howitzers.

The Gun Section joined the Ordnance Supply Department in October 1916, which, in turn, expanded into the Shell and Gun Manufacture Department four months later. It often modified guns in accordance with GHQ's wishes, such as adding air recuperators and oil buffers and upgrading the breech mechanism. It designed new mechanical devices, so the gunners could make quicker calculations and fitted illuminated equipment to make it easier to use the guns in the dark. The department also had to deal with suggestions to improve shells, such as fitting streamlined noses and false capped bases to increase ranges.

Repairing and Relining Artillery Pieces[5]

Guns and howitzers lasted a long time in 1915 because of the shell shortages. Spare parts were delivered with each gun and howitzer while the Royal Arsenal's Gun and Carriage Department dealt with any repair work. However, adequate stocks of shells during the 1916 Somme campaign meant that they soon wore out, reducing their range and accuracy. It could take up to three months to return an artillery piece to Britain to reline and test, so repair work had to be programmed carefully.

The 18-pounder and the 4.5-inch howitzer could fire 13,000 shells before they needed repairing. The 9.2-inch howitzer needed attention after firing 7,000 shells, while the 60-pounder could only fire 4,000. It required skill and patience to make the inner linings of the barrels from the layers of steel and wire. However, relining a gun only took half the resources required to make a new one, so repairs became more important, the longer the war went on.

The Ministry of Munitions set up the Gun Parts Committee to build up reserves and distribute spare parts. More attention was also paid to taking care of guns, including the use of reduced charges and improved driving bands. Spare barrels were ordered in bulk, while new factories were contracted to help the Royal Arsenal keep on top of relining barrels and repairing carriages. Eventually, artillery batteries started detaching worn out barrels from their carriages, so they could be sent separately to be repaired. At the end of 1916, a workshop opened in Southampton to deal with minor repairs, while major repairs were forwarded to the original manufacturer.

Beardmore's, Armstrong Whitworth's, Vickers and the Coventry Ordnance Works became involved in repairs in the autumn of 1916. Seven National Projectile Factories also converted to National Ordnance Factories in early 1917 to start relining them:[6]

- Hunslet National Shell Factory in Leeds worked on 18-pounder guns.
- Hadfields in Sheffield worked on 60-pounder guns.
- Cammell Laird's Nottingham factory worked on 18-pounder and 6-inch guns.
- The Coventry Ordnance Works worked on 4.5-inch howitzers.
- The National Projectile Factories at Cardonald, Lancaster and Dudley were soon repairing 800 guns a month between them.

The number of guns repaired during the war were as follows:

- 293 60-pounder guns.
- 3,957 18-pounder guns.
- 594 4.7-inch guns.
- 217 6-inch guns.
- 30 12-inch howitzers.
- 318 9.2-inch howitzers.
- 413 8-inch howitzers.
- 950 6-inch howitzers.
- 943 4.5-inch howitzers.

Total: 8,943 artillery pieces and 2,230 carriages repaired.

Chapter 29

Making the Shells

Starting Shell Manufacture[1]

Originally, the high grade steel required for shells was made by the open hearth process in which iron ore and scrap steel were mixed slowly during the smelting process. Before the war, contractors bought shell steel from the only two firms that could meet the high specification. It was made from iron ore with a low sulphur and phosphorous content because high levels made it brittle. Most of Britain's iron ore had too much of both, so it was imported from Spain and Sweden. The War Office had shell contracts with William Beardmore's, Armstrong Whitworth's, Vickers, Cammell Laird's, Thomas Firth's and Hadfields, as well as the Royal Arsenal and the Projectile and Engineering Company in London.

By mid-October 1914, it was clear pre-war munitions estimates were inadequate, so orders for ammunition were increased. Again, advances were offered, so firms could expand their premises, while subcontractors were engaged to make components. New contracts had also been agreed with Babcock and Wilcox of Renfrew, Dick, Kerr's of Preston, J. and P. Hill's of Sheffield and Rees Roturbo of Wolverhampton by the end of the year.

The Armaments Output Committee was appointed to buy forgings for the companies in March 1915. While the Royal Navy required just 7,500 tons of shell steel a month, the BEF's demand increased to 150,000 tons. Britain would also send 50,000 tons a month to France because German troops had captured the country's iron ore deposits in Lorraine at the beginning of the war.

Trench warfare was soon outstripping ammunition estimates, so new sources were needed. Leicester companies formed a cooperative group to make shells in January 1915 and the War Office placed its first order in March. It was impressed with the idea, so the Board of Trade exhibited munitions items in towns and cities across the country. Dozens of companies offered their services and both the Royal Arsenal and Armstrong Whitworth's showed companies how to organise factories and trained their workers. The Armaments Output Committee also sourced raw materials, tools and machinery.

Steps had also been taken to find overseas sources. The Shell Committee organised production across Canada, while orders were placed with the Bethlehem Steel

Corporation, the Washington Steel and Ordnance Company, and the E.W. Bliss Company in America.

The Ministry of Munitions took over responsibility of shell production in June 1915 and the Armaments Output Committee became one of its departments. It launched three new schemes to stimulate shell production, only to discover there were shortages of labour and machinery.

Boards of Management were told to organise companies into cooperative groups. They were to set up National Shell Factories to assemble components made in smaller factories and workshops. It also planned to build National Projectile Factories to make large scale shells and National Filling Factories to fill shells of all calibres. The Ministry of Munitions would pay for them, while experienced companies built and managed them.

The new factories needed extra shell steel and forgings. So, following tests in November 1915, the British Army said it would accept acid Bessemer steel which was made by smelting iron ore, for its high explosive shells. It meant six more foundries could make shell steel and the Ministry provided money to extend their furnaces, while financing two new ones.

The Ministry of Munitions asked J.P. Morgan to source shell steel across the United States and Canada. It soon discovered the American and Canadian companies were having difficulties meeting the specification and only one third of shells they had promised had been delivered. Even so, Lloyd George promised French Under-Secretary for War Albert Thomas that Britain would increase production, when they met in Boulogne on 19 and 20 June 1915.

Shell deliveries increased slowly during the summer of 1915 and the Royal Arsenal's inspectors were sometimes accused of being too critical. So, modifications were introduced to make production easier, while the inspection tests were reviewed to see what tolerances could be relaxed. The Ministry of Munitions also paid companies to inspect their own shells to reduce the pressure on the Royal Arsenal.

The number of shells that had to be made was determined by the number of guns ordered by GHQ. Programme A only needed 250,000 shells for the field guns but Programme B increased the number to 1.46 million, following discussions with the French in July 1915. In September, Programme C raised it to 3.29 million because it covered the deployment of all the New Army divisions. The Ministry of Munitions always sent two estimates for shells to the Army Council, with the highest number being what it aimed to make, while the lowest number was what it expected to make.

Shell Manufacture in 1916[2]

The Ministry of Munitions built up a reserve of shells over the winter of 1915-16, ready for the Somme campaign. Progress on the National Projectile Factories was slower than expected, so Lloyd George met the company managers on 8 April 1916 to hear about their problems. While they discussed possible solutions, he made it clear that he did not want their factories to become 'a city of refuge for men who were avoiding their duty.'

The number of guns that could be made and the daily expenditure of rounds, defined the ammunition programme. While the plan was to have enough shells by March 1916, only 57 per cent of small calibre shells and 27 per cent of large and medium calibre shells had been delivered. The eventual arrival of shells from the United States and Canada and the completion of the National Filling Factories meant that the BEF had enough shells by the end of June 1916. The preliminary bombardment on the Somme used 1.5 million shells and it was two days longer than expected due to bad weather. Another 250,000 were fired on 1 July 1916, leaving Fourth Army's reserve dangerously low.

Another issue was that GHQ wanted far more 18-pounder shrapnel shells than expected. They were better for cutting wire because they did not crater the ground, while the development of the creeping barrage required large amounts.

Both the BEF and the Ministry of Munitions collected a lot of valuable data relating to munitions during the Somme campaign. The Allocation Department had just completed its winter shell programme at the end of September 1916, when GHQ asked for revised shell programme based on recent experiences. While the number of small and medium calibre shells fired had been double what was estimated, the quantity of large calibre shells fired had been correct.

Recently promoted Field Marshal Sir Douglas Haig wanted the BEF to have a reserve of 10 million shells for the spring campaigns in 1917, while the Army Council wanted another 4 million shells for other theatres. It also wanted to take as many fit men as possible out of industry to replace the losses on the Somme. The question was could the Ministry of Munitions make enough shells and find enough men?

A complicated management arrangement had coordinated the work of shell factories throughout 1916. The Director of Area Organisation controlled the Boards of Management, who, in turn, ran the National Shell Factories and the cooperative groups of small factories. Meanwhile, the National Projectile Factory Executive controlled the National Projectile Factories. To add to the complication, the Leeds factories were controlled by the Leeds Board of Management but were run by the National Projectile Factory Executive.

Shell Manufacture in 1917[3]

By the end of 1916, all the National Factories were up and running, and most of the production problems had been ironed out. So, the Ministry of Munitions put 4,000 factories making shells and components under the new Shell and Components Committee. Statistics from the Somme campaign showed that shell production could be reduced while gun and howitzer repairs had to be increased. The factories that wanted to reduce shell production were allowed to do so. Others switched production, including several National Projectile Factories, to make aircraft parts, trench warfare supplies, railway wagons and artillery pieces. The changes resulted in 30 per cent fewer large calibre shells, while the number of small and medium calibre shells remained the same.

The shell programme for 1917 predicted that the National Factories would need 350,000 tons of steel a month but Britain's steel works could only make 160,000 tons. The plan was to import 190,000 tons a month but the German submarine campaign cut the amount to 130,000 tons. Steel also had to be switched to shipbuilding, reducing the shell programme down to 310,000 tons, while the amount of ammunition shipped to France was reduced from 195,000 tons a month down to 150,000 tons.

Fortunately, an unconnected event over two years earlier, allowed the Ministry of Munitions to maintain its output of shells. German warships had fired on seaside towns in the North and North East of England, such as Scarborough, Whitby, Hartlepool and West Hartlepool in December 1914. Shell fragments had been analysed, proving that German shells had a higher sulphur and phosphorus content than the War Office and Admiralty allowed. The metallurgists' discovery was used by the Ministry of Munitions to argue that British iron ore could be used. They agreed and deposits across the North West of England and Scotland were exploited.

A convoy system, involving warships protecting the merchant ships, reduced maritime losses in the summer of 1917, so the steel industry was able to reorganise itself. More shell steel was ordered from the United States and Canada, so that British steel could be used in the shipyards. It was delivered in bars and then cut into shell length pieces in billet breaking yards. The decision had been taken because it was easier to ship bars of shell steel than plates of ship steel.

The Shell and Components Manufacture Executive Committee was replaced by the Munitions Council in September 1917 and it had a several requests from GHQ to deal with. It wanted less 18-pounder shells because there was a shortage of guns but more 6-inch shells, which had to be imported from the United States. It also wanted more long range shells and chemical shells, which were made in British factories.

Shell Manufacture in 1918[4]

By the end of 1917, Britain was struggling to get financial credit in the United States, so the War Cabinet Committee wanted to cut the amount shell imports. However, Secretary of State for War Edward Stanley predicted that the Germans would attack on the Western Front, using troops released from the Eastern Front, where Russia had recently dropped out of the war. So, the tonnage of steel imports was reduced by cutting back on other items rather than munitions.

Spring 1918 proved Stanley correct, when two huge attacks hit the British sector on the Somme in March and on the Lys in April. In both cases the line held but large numbers of guns and howitzers were lost, while 190,000 tons of ammunition were either fired or abandoned. Meanwhile, the Ministry of Munitions was being told to cut costs, while replacing the losses. American imports came to an end in the spring of 1918 as Britain transferred its business to Canada because it preferred to be in debt to its dominion.

Fourth Army fired over or 1 million shells (40,000 tons) a week, nearly half of them were 6-inch shells, when the BEF's counteroffensive started on 8 August 1918. The quantity doubled to 2 million shells (80,000 tons) a week as Third Army joined the advance. However, the greatest bombardment of the war was during the attack on the Hindenburg Line and east of Ypres, when 2.5 million rounds were fired by four of the BEF's armies in just three days.

The switch to semi-open warfare during the final six weeks of the war required far more shells than expected because the whole of the BEF was pushing forward at once. The rapid advances also required far more small calibre shells than usual because the heavy guns could not keep up with the infantry.

Making Shell Components[5]

A shell is made up of many components and factories required continual deliveries of non-ferrous metals, to make everything from brass fuses to copper driving bands and lead shrapnel balls. There were shortages of everything when the Ministry of Munitions took over in June 1915 and the smallest problem interrupted shell production. So, Lloyd George appointed Sir Eric Geddes as Deputy Director General of Munitions Supply and he took immediate steps to secure imports and build up reserves. The Ministry also bought supplies from France and Switzerland over the winter of 1915-16, so the country had enough to cover emergencies.

Despite controls being imposed over supplies, shortages continued. So, new designs were tried and different metals were substituted. These modifications would eventually save £12 million (£710 million today).

The components of a shell act together to detonate the explosives at the right time. High explosive shells initially used the No. 44 percussion fuse, which was designed to explode on impact, sending shards of the steel casing through the air. The No. 106 graze fuse was introduced early in 1917 and it reacted to the change in speed when the shell hit soft ground. The firing pin and detonator made contact, causing the shell to explode.

Shrapnel shells used time fuses that detonated after a predetermined time. It was set by rotating a graduated ring on the nose of the shell, with one click equalling a sixth of a second, which was 50 metres (yards) in flight. A high quality explosive compound called Tetryl burned around the nose for the chosen time, before burning down a central ignition tube, called a gaine. It then detonated the bursting charge at the base of the shell, scattering the lead bullets in the shell casing like a shotgun blast.

Initially, shrapnel shells were armed with a No. 80 time or percussion fuse that would either explode in flight or on impact; whichever the gun crew had chosen. The No. 80/44 fuse was a time and percussion fuse, introduced to cut wire in the autumn of 1914. However, many failed to explode and they were known as blinds. The gunners blamed the problem on the new high explosive mix, called amatol. However, tests proved that shells were suffering from setback: a failure to arm through the shock of firing. It then took another month to find out why the exploder containers at the base of the shell, were splitting.

The No. 100 fuse replaced the No. 80/44 fuse in August 1915. The modified No. 101 fuse, introduced in March 1916, was blamed for premature explosions in the breech of the 18-pounder gun. The problem was eventually tracked down to the gaine, so a shorter one with a different detonator was tested and approved. The remaining No. 100 fuses were converted into No. 102 fuses.

There were also production problems to sort out, such as when one company used scrap metal to make shells, to save money. Another occurrence of too many premature explosions during the winter of 1916-17 was traced back to the Coventry Filling Factory. Poor supervision had led to the fuses being fitted upside down.

Increasing Fuse Production[6]

To begin with, fuses were made at the Royal Arsenal or by the four armaments firms. However, contracts were soon awarded to the Raleigh Cycle Company in Nottingham and the Sterling Telephone and Electric Company in London. Boards of Management were then asked to engage everyone from clock manufacturers to electricians to gramophone makers to make fuses.

American imports arrived late and there was a huge problem when 400,000 Canadian shells arrived unexpectedly without fuses in the autumn of 1915. The Canadian inspection regime was improved while extra ones were sourced from Switzerland. Eventually, a new fuse plant was opened at the Royal Arsenal in June 1916, ahead of the Somme campaign.

Aluminium shortages meant that fuses were made from brass from the autumn of 1915. Cast iron was then used when deliveries from the United States became irregular in the autumn of 1916. The Ministry of Munitions had an acceptable stock of components by the summer of 1916, so it started distributing them to the factories that needed them most. It also opened the National Component Factory at Tipton in the West Midlands.

Time and percussion were complicated devices, so the Royal Arsenal, Armstrong Whitworth's and Vickers made as many as possible, while the rest were imported from the United States. Britain was making enough by the spring of 1917, so the imports were kept as a reserve. The Cambridge Scientific Instrument Company was trying to recreate a German clockwork fuse when the war ended.

Specialised Shells[7]

Early tests with white phosphorous, incendiary and thermite shells failed. Chemical shells were first tested in July 1915 but the Army Council refused to try them until the

Germans used them at Verdun in the spring of 1916. It then took many months of tests to find out how to make them work as the explosion on impact dispersed the gas.

The demand for smoke and incendiary shell increased to 225,000 shells a month in the spring of 1917, so factories were told to double their shifts. Later in the year, the requirement for chemical shells increased, however, cast iron and converted high explosive casings replaced the double skinned casings due to a steel shortage. Scrap steel from the National Shell Factories and National Projectile Factories was melted down as the demand for gas shells rose to over 1 million a month in 1918. The factories eventually made the following quantities during the war:

- 6.9 million chemical shells.
- 2.3 million smoke shells.
- 550,000 incendiary shells.

A Summary of Shell Production[8]

The monthly rate of production of shells increased from 49,000 a month in 1914 to 6.25 million by 1916 but it plateaued at 7.25 million during the last two years of the war:

- Ordnance Factories made 6.7 million (4 per cent).
- National Shell Factories made 20.2 million shells (12 per cent).
- National Projectile Factories made 20.2 million shells (12 per cent).
- Cooperative groups made 45.4 million (27 per cent).
- Private companies made 75.7 million (45 per cent).

A list of some of the larger shell factories is given below:[9]

- Armstrong Whitworth's employed 2,450 in Glasgow.
- Singer Manufacturing Company also employed 13,100 in Glasgow.
- Armstrong Whitworth's also employed 52,500 in Newcastle.
- Foster, Blackett and Wilson's employed 1,800 near Gateshead.
- Dobson and Barlow's employed 3,150 in Bolton.
- Platt Brothers and Company employed 6,000 in Oldham.
- Ferranti and Company employed 2,700, also in Oldham.
- Armstrong Whitworth's employed another 9,000 in Manchester.
- Beyer, Peacock and Company employed 2,350 in Manchester.
- Lancashire Ordnance Accessories Company employed 2,400 in Accrington.
- Howard and Bullough Company employed 4,800, also in Accrington.
- British Insulated and Helsby Cables employed 4,200 in Prescot.
- Fairbairn, Lawson, Combe, and Barbour employed 2,700 in Leeds.

- Greenwood and Batley Company employed 4,900, also in Leeds.
- Mather and Platt Limited employed 3,000 in Salford.
- Component Munitions Company employed 3,050 in Birmingham.
- A. Harper, Sons and Bean employed 5,500 in Birmingham.
- Patent Shaft and Axletree Company employed 3,400 in Wednesbury.
- Richard Hornsby and Sons employed 2,700 in Grantham.
- Kryn and Lahy employed 2,400 Belgian refugees in Letchworth.
- George Kent Limited employed 6,750 in Luton.
- Projectile and Engineering Company employed 2,500 in Battersea in London.
- Holland, Hannen and Cubitt's employed 6,000 in Camden in London.
- W. and G. Du Cros Limited employed 2,500 in Acton Vale in London.
- Pelabon employed 2,300 Belgian refugees in Richmond in London.

A total of 258.4 million empty shells were made during the war:

- 63 per cent (162.8 million) were made in Britain.
- 37 per cent (95.6 million) of empty shells were imported.

Approximately 217 million completed shells were made:

- 196 million rounds were made in Britain.
- 21 million were imported.

The shells were different calibres:

- 154 million (60 per cent) were small calibre.
- 56.5 million (21 per cent) were medium calibre.
- 48 million (19 per cent) were large calibre.

Making ammunition accounted for more than half of the Ministry of Munitions' total expenditure, peaking at £915 million a year (£26.5 billion today). While production halted as soon as the Armistice was declared, stores all over Britain and in the BEF's dumps were left filled with shell casings and shell components. All that could be done was to break them up and melt them down in the furnaces.

Chapter 30

Personal Weapons

Making Revolvers[1]

Infantry officers were armed with revolvers made by Webley and Scott Limited. Demand increased until the company's factory in Birmingham employed 1,150. The Ministry of Munitions inherited a stock of 5 million .455 bullets for the Webley and Scott revolver in the summer of 1915. While an additional 90,000 revolvers had just been ordered, the War Office reported that the BEF only needed 11.5 million rounds a month because expenditure was lower than estimated. By the summer of 1917, over 8.5 million rounds a month were being made for the .455 pistol and the .45 Colt pistol, used by pilots.

Rifle Supply[2]

The British Army used the Short Magazine Lee-Enfield (SMLE) Mark III rifle, which had been in use since 1907 and had been sighted for the Mark VII high velocity ammunition since 1911. Initially, the Royal Small Arms Factory at Enfield Lock (RSA), the London Small Arms Company (LSA) and the Birmingham Small Arms Company (BSA) made, resighted and repaired the rifles. They also made chargers, a clip that held five rounds, making them easier to load. While they could make or repair 9,000 rifles a month between them, they were all tested at Enfield Lock before they were stored at Weedon near Northampton. The three companies also made bayonets, scabbards and cavalry swords.

The British Army owned 475,000 Mark III rifles and 320,000 obsolete Mark I rifles on the outbreak of war but it soon needed a lot more for the Territorial Force and the New Armies. BSA was busy making Lewis guns, so the LSA was given a grant to extend its premises. Contracts for bayonets were given to Vickers, Sanderson Brothers and Company, and Samuel Newbould and Company, both of Sheffield, the Wilkinson Sword Company, and James Chapman and Sons, both of London, and Robert Mole and Sons of Birmingham.

Winchester Repeating Arms Company, Remington Arms Company and the Imperial Contracting Company also accepted contracts to make rifles in the United States. While they promised 2.7 million rifles, all three struggled to get enough labour, plant and materials for their factories. They then blamed delays on modifications to the rifles, even though they had asked for them to make production easier.

Meanwhile, several initiatives had been put started in Britain, including a contract for Vickers to make more at its Crayford factory in Kent. The Standard Small Arms Company (SSA) was set up in Birmingham to make the difficult parts of the rifle, while subcontractors made the easy parts, so they could be assembled at Enfield.

Enfield and BSA resighted over 150,000 rifles, while another 50,000 were imported from India. Approximately 130,000 Arisaka rifles were bought from Japan and while they were a different calibre, they were useful for training. The Admiralty even tried a bold plan in place to get 400,000 rifles and 900 million rounds from Brazil, only to see if fail in the spring of 1915.

The British Army had 1.15 million rifles in its possession when the Ministry of Munitions took over in June 1915.[3] It had also issued 400,000 obsolete or different calibre rifles to the New Armies for training. Imports from the United States were expected to arrive in the autumn, so BSA switched part of its production to the weapons the BEF was desperate for: machine guns.

The Ministry of Munitions introduced two ideas to increase the manufacture of rifles. One involved the factories exchanging surplus parts and the other invited companies to make the simple parts, while specialist manufacturers focused on the complicated parts. Many workshops were employed and they sent their parts to Enfield, where 1,600 women assembled them into rifles, in what was called the Peddled Scheme. Modifications that simplified production were soon introduced, making it easier for factories to make the Mark III* version.

The rifle situation became serious over the winter of 1915-16 due to a combination of factors:

- Poor organisation at the LSA factory delayed its opening.
- Unsatisfactory American machinery arrived late at the BSA factory.
- Vickers was still building its factory in Crayford.
- None of the rifles promised by the United States had arrived.

Meanwhile, the War Office had asked Sir Samuel Hughes, Minister of the Canadian Militia and Defence, to arm the Canadian Expeditionary Force (CEF) with 10,000 rifles, however, the Ross Rifle Company was mistakenly contracted to make 100,000.[4] While delays in delivery were blamed on the usual issues, the rifles proved to be intolerant to mud and British made bullets. It meant all the Canadian divisions had to be armed with Lee-Enfield rifles as soon as possible. Further tests in the spring of 1916 had the same results, so Ross rifles were only used for training purposes until the factory closed.

There were also problems with the first deliveries from the United States because the cartridge was difficult to insert and extract. The War Office refused to accept them for active service, as did Russia, so they were restricted to home use. It meant some of the Territorial Force divisions deployed overseas with obsolete Mark I Lee-Enfield rifles, while the deployment of the some of the New Army divisions was delayed.

All that could be done was to reduce the number of rifles given to the divisions preparing to go overseas from 17,000 to 15,500. Meanwhile, the Ministry of Munitions set up the Rifle Components Pool, which stored spare parts for any factory to use. The British factories struggled on, making nearly 500,000 rifles a month, which was never enough to build up a reserve. Fortunately, wastage was far lower than expected, so there were just enough to keep up with demand.

By the summer of 1916, all three American gun companies were experiencing financial difficulties, so the War Office wanted to cancel the orders.[5] However, the Ministry of Munitions did not want to sour relations with other American munition companies, so the delivery dates were extended and orders were reduced. Fortunately, standards improved and over 1.2 million rifles had been accepted by the time the United States went to war in April 1917. The American government also bought the British plant and materials in the three rifle factories and they started making Springfield rifles for the AEF.

Meanwhile, production in the British factories suffered due to the engineers' stoppage in May 1917, while there were further industrial troubles at LSA.[6] A fire then damaged the British Gun Barrel Company Works. Even so, there was a surplus of rifles by the start of 1918, meaning that the rifle factories could start making replacement parts for machine guns.

So many rifles were lost during the German spring offensives that it reduced the reserve from 448,000 to 196,000. It meant that production had to be stepped up again and the Ministry of Munitions took over Standard Small Arms Company in Birmingham and Greener in Chippenham, renaming them National Rifle Factory No. 1 and No. 2.[7]

Nearly 4 million rifles were made in Britain during the war, with the RSA making half of them.[8] The factory also made the following:

- 666 machine guns.
- 500,000 ammunition belts.
- 425,000 bayonets.
- 52,000 cavalry swords.
- 1.5 million scabbards.

The workforce peaked at 8,600 men and 1,550 women. Meanwhile, BSA made 1.58 million rifles, while LSA made another 364,000. Over 1.36 million were imported, with 90 per cent coming from the United States and the rest from Canada. Altogether nearly 5.32 million rifles were made for the British armed forces and its allies.

Chapter 31

Machine Guns

Increasing Firepower[1]

Each infantry battalion was equipped with just two Maxim or Vickers machine guns in 1914. The value of the weapon was soon appreciated and the Machine Gun Corps was formed in September 1915. It was organised into companies, each with four Vickers machine guns, while the infantry battalions received eight Lewis machine guns in exchange. The number of Lewis guns had increased to thirty-six by the end of the war, while each division had a machine gun battalion armed with sixteen Vickers. It meant that the number of machine guns per infantry division had increased from only 24 to over 400. Large numbers were also used to arm tanks and aircraft.

The manufacture of machine guns rose from 57 a month in 1914 to over 11,500 a month by 1918, many of them for the RAF. Altogether, Britain's factories made over 72,000 heavy machine guns and 168,000 light machine guns for its armed forces and those of its allies.

Heavy Machine Guns[2]

The Maxim machine gun was a belt-fed weapon, which was being phased out in 1914 because the gunmetal water jacket was too heavy. It could fire up to 500 .303-inch rounds per minute to around 2,800 metres (yards). The Royal Small Arms Factory in Enfield made 666 before production stopped in March 1917.

The Vickers machine gun had been adopted in 1912 but only 100 had been made when the war began. It was another belt-fed weapon, with a similar firing rate and range, however, the steel water jacket was much lighter. The company eventually employed over 12,000 men and women at Crayford and Erith in Kent but while the two factories were close together, they never cooperated.

The BEF was asking for many more machine guns by the time the Ministry of Munitions took over in June 1915. So, it contracted Vickers to make 12,000 machine guns by July 1916 and gave advances to help it extend its works. It also retrieved skilled factory employees from the armed forces and they were joined by skilled men from the northern textile factories, who helped them set up the plant. The Colt Manufacturing Company in America was contracted to make another 6,000.

Production at Vickers increased from only 22 machine guns a month in 1915 to over 1,800 by the end of the war, with Crayford making four times as many as Erith. Altogether, nearly 39,500 machine guns were made. One in three machine guns used by the BEF was a Vickers.

Light Machine Guns[3]

The Lewis machine gun and the Hotchkiss machine gun were both lighter models, which fired magazines that did not need cooling. It used a circular magazine, which held forty-seven .303-inch rounds and could be sighted to around 2,000 metres (yards). They were made by the 3,100 employees at the Raleigh Cycle Factory in Nottingham. Lewis guns were used in tanks and aircraft later in the war and a Mark II magazine, which held ninety-seven rounds was made for aircraft.

BSA was testing the Lewis gun when war broke out and while the first ones were ordered in September 1914, the BEF was soon asking for as many as could be made. The factory expanded to 15,000 employees and they made the guns under license to the *Armes Automatiques Lewis* until a direct contract was issued in August 1918. The number of Lewis guns made every month increased from 300 in 1916 up to 5,200 by 1918. Over 133,000 were made during the war, making every second machine gun in the British armed services a Lewis gun.

The Hotchkiss machine gun was being used by the French army in 1914 and it used a strip magazine capable of firing up to 250 rounds per minute. The Admiralty ordered 1,000 guns in February 1915, so the company relocated plant and staff from France to Coventry and it was making 700 a month by October 1915.

The French army took half the guns to begin with, while some were used by the cavalry and the Royal Flying Corps (RFC). They were also used in tanks until they were replaced by the Lewis gun in November 1916. However, the factory kept making 200 guns a month in case BSA encountered a problem making Lewis guns. Production had increased to 1,000 a month by 1918; over 35,000 were made during the war.

Repairs and Spares[4]

The original focus was to make as many machine guns as possible but they soon started breaking down because only a few spare parts had been sent out with each gun. For example, the Vickers machine gun had 400 parts and they wore out at different rates, so problems started to be reported during the 1916 Somme campaign. It resulted in the Royal Small Arms Factory at Enfield having to repair up to 400 machine guns a week. Meanwhile, the Lewis gun required more magazine replacements than BSA could make, so the Raleigh Bicycle Factory in Nottingham made extras.

Unfulfilled Plans[5]

The Admiralty ordered 900 Madsen machine guns from the Danish Recoil Rifle Syndicate in Denmark as early as May 1915. However, the Army Council preferred the Lewis and Hotchkiss, while the RFC rejected the gun because it could not fire upside down. Exporting many machine guns across the North Sea was too risky, as were plans to move the factory to England and so further orders were cancelled in April 1916.

The National Machine Gun Factory in Burton-on-Trent had not been finished when the war ended.[6] There was also a plan to set up two National Factories in Birmingham to make the Farquhar-Hill automatic rifle. However, orders for 100,000 were cancelled when the war ended.

Chapter 32

Small Arms Ammunition

Increasing the Supply of Bullets

The .303-inch Mark VII bullet had a lead core and a pointed aluminium tip. The .303-inch Mark VI had a rounded nose, which was used by the Admiralty. The War Office had 29 million bullets at the start of the war. While the Royal Arsenal could make 3.5 million a month, private companies could make another 9 million.[1] Greenwood and Batley of Leeds, Greenwood s of London and Birmingham Metal and Munitions, Kynoch and Kings Norton Metal Company (all from Birmingham) were asked to double their production. On top of that, an order to supply 20 million 7.65 millimetre cartridges for the Belgian army was dealt with.

By March 1915, it was clear that extra capacity was needed to supply the Territorial Force and New Army divisions preparing to deploy overseas. Kynoch, the Birmingham Metal and Munitions Company, and Eley Brothers Limited of London were given advances to extend their factories but the others were unable to do so. While a new contract was given to Rudge-Whitworth Limited of Coventry, no one else was able to start making cartridges because it required specialist plant and skilled labour. While orders were placed with four American companies, they would deliver late, while the Canadian Ross Rifle Company failed to deliver anything.

Despite the issues, nearly 644 million .303-inch Mark VII bullets had been delivered by July 1915, with 85 per cent of them being made in Britain. Birmingham had become a major centre for making rifle and machine gun ammunition:[2]

- Kynoch's employed 5,250 men and 9,375 women.
- Birmingham Metal and Munitions employed 4,325 men and 7,100 women.
- Rudge-Whitworth's employed 2,125 men and 4,050 women.
- Kings Norton Metal Company employed 2,350 men and 3,050 women.

Machine guns were being sent to France with 50,000 rounds and were being supplied with another 10,000 per month.[3] While new rifles were despatched with 400 rounds, they only needed around 90 per month as far less were being used in the trenches than expected.

The Ministry of Munitions increased demand to 550 million a month ahead of the Somme offensive. Paper tips were used when aluminium ran short in June 1916.[4] While the German government complained that they contained bacteria, it was considered that they did not contravene the 1899 Hague Declaration nor the 1907 Hague Convention.

The BEF reported it had a large surplus of bullets when the Somme campaign ended, so production was reduced to just 130 million a month. Meanwhile, stocks in France were balanced at 250 million, while the reserves at home were set at 500 million. The surplus was sent to Russia or Romania.

There was talk of moving plant from the bullet factories to other ones, when the German offensives began in the spring of 1918.[5] So many bullets were used or lost, that production was restarted and workers were asked to give up their Easter and Whitsuntide holidays. Meanwhile, Kynoch's broke up millions of defective rounds, so the metal could be melted down and reused.

The total number of rounds made was as follows:[6]

- .303-inch Mark VII* rounds (British made): 7.36 billion.
- .303-inch Mark VII (American made): 862 million.
- .303 rounds (American made): 65 million.
- .256-inch rounds for the Japanese Arisaka rifle: 310 million.
- 7.62 millimetre rounds for the Russian Moison-Nagant rifle: 1.39 billion.

Government Cartridge and Small Arms Ammunition Factories[7]

The failure of American factories to deliver cartridges on time left the Ministry of Munitions needing to make 640 million a month. Existing factories were soon busy but four National Factories were completed late due to a shortage of labour and materials.

Birmingham Metal and Munitions Company opened No. 1 Cartridge Factory in Blackheath in Staffordshire and 3,000 women and 500 men were soon making 25 million a month. No. 2 Cartridge Factory was set up at the Royal Arsenal and its output was included in that of the main factory. Kings Norton Metal Company opened No. 3 Cartridge Factory in Blackpole in Worcestershire, where its workforce of 2,450 women and 785 men made 12 million a month. The 3,100 Belgian refuges employed by Eley Brothers were already making 7 million a month at its factory in Edmonton in north London, when it was asked to increase production. So, it built No. 4 Cartridge Factory to employ 1,100 women and 300 men. The National Small Arms Ammunition Factory opened in Coventry to make 850,000 a month.[8]

The Ministry of Munitions bought large amounts of cartridge cases from Canada until the Birtley Cartridge Case Factory and the National Shell Factory in Liverpool started making them. Many were collected from the battlefields and they were sorted at the Richborough Salvage Station in Kent. Up to 2.5 million were repaired every month.

The BEF's demand for bullets and cartridges had halved by the time the National Cartridge Factories started making them at the beginning of 1917, because the rifle had been used less than expected during the Somme campaign. Meanwhile, Russian orders ended following the Revolution in October 1917. So, the plant was moved to other factories, while the workforce was reduced to one shift. Further reductions resulted in No. 4 Cartridge Factory repairing aeroengines after March 1918.

Government Rolling Mills[9]

The initial demand for bullets and cartridges was matched with a need for 360 million cups per month. Cups made from brass and cupro-nickel were placed at the base of bullets to stop them melting when they were fired.

Cups needed large amounts of imported materials, so the Government Rolling Mill was built at Weston Park, close to Southampton docks. The factory was highly mechanised to minimise labour and while production started at the end of 1916, it was another nine months before it was completed. The workforce of 1,350 women and 750 men was then able to make 100 million brass cups and 80 million cupro-nickel cups a month.

However, demand for bullets and their cups had fallen by the time the factory was complete, so some of the workforce started making fuse stampings and quick fire strips.[10] The factory was due to be shut down when the Germans launched their spring offensives in 1918, so there was extra demand to replace what had been lost. By the end of the war, 148 million cartridge cases had been made by British factories, while another 21 million had been imported.

Armour Piercing Ammunition

The Royal Laboratory trialled the steel tipped Mark VIIS bullet but it proved to be unsatisfactory. However, the Kynoch Mark VIIP, which had a hardened steel centre and a cupro-nickel outer, was approved at the end of 1916. The Royal Arsenal and the Birmingham Metal and Munitions Company eventually took over production from Kynoch. Kings Norton Metal Company made the Mark VIIW, which had a bronze envelope and a hardened steel core.

Chapter 33

Trench Warfare Weapons

Organising Manufacture[1]

Major General Sir Henry Rawlinson summed up trench warfare when he said that it was 'causing a demand for all sorts of things which are not recognised by regulation.' GHQ's first request was for 'some special form of artillery which can be used with effect at close range in the trenches.' Then in December 1914, GHQ asked for short range projectiles that could be thrown. Comments such as these led to the Fortifications and Works Directorate looking at trench mortars and hand grenades.

The Directorate of Artillery provided advice, while the Engineer Munitions Branch asked the Royal Arsenal to work on the ideas coming from the front line. However, it took time to produce safe and effective trench weapons and they had to be fully tested before they could be mass produced. It also took time to find suitable factories and coordinate their work. Meanwhile, the soldiers were busy experimenting with dangerous homemade weapons.

The Royal Arsenal made all the trench warfare weapons and ammunition to begin with but it was soon overwhelmed with orders. The Ministry of Munitions formed the Trench Warfare Department in June 1915, to take over the supply of trench warfare weapons and ammunition. Fortunately, trench warfare weapons and ammunition were simple items, so the Boards of Management were encouraged to form cooperative groups, to make them. Prices were high to begin with because the work was experimental and urgent but they reduced once the designs and production methods were settled.

Demand changed with the seasons; for example, three times as many grenades and mortar bombs were required during the summer months. Stores were opened at the ports of Newhaven and Bristol, so trench warfare weapons and ammunition could be stockpiled ready for shipping.

The Trench Warfare Supply Department under went several changes, as its changed from dealing with novelty weapons to producing an important part of the BEF's arsenal. Its responsibilities were divided between the stores departments in July 1917, once the trench warfare weapons and ammunition had been standardised.

Hand Grenades[2]

GHQ started asking for grenades in December 1914 and the first ones were percussion models, which exploded on contact. The Royal Laboratory made No. 1 grenades, while the Cotton Powder Company made the Marten Hale's No. 2 grenade in Faversham until they were both reported to be unsafe. Meanwhile, the troops also made their own grenades, either by filling a jam tin with explosives or tying explosives to a hairbrush shaped wooden handle. They too were also dangerous to use.

The Ministry of Munitions took over grenade manufacture in June 1915 but it initially struggled to get enough components, particularly detonators. A confusing array of designs appeared over the next six months, including Ball, Lemon, Oval, Double Cylinder and Pitcher grenades. The No. 5 Mills bomb made them all obsolete and while many Oval and Ball grenades were sent to Russia, 1.5 million were dismantled, so the parts could be melted down.

The Mills No. 5 bomb was a Belgian design patented by William Mills of Birmingham. It had a segmented cast iron body, which split into pieces when the amatol exploded. Removing a pin released a lever and a steel plunger activated the short fuse. The design had been tested by April 1915 and factories switched over to making it once a reserve of the other grenades had been built up, in cast there were production problems.

The introduction of the rifle grenade gave the infantry control of a lightweight, short range weapon. Troops had made the Newton or Pippin rifle grenades in the field but production was stopped because they were dangerous. The Hale rifle grenade (No. 3) was a tube shaped device, which was segmented like the Mills grenade. A steel rod attached to the base was inserted into the rifle barrel and it was fired when the striker hit the detonator's percussion cap. Factories were soon making 300,000 per month.

The Mills rifle grenade (No. 23) was a Mills No. 5 grenade with a steel rod attached to the base. It was again slotted into the barrel and a rifle cup secured the lever and striker until it was fired by a blank cartridge. The base plugs were soon changed to cast iron and 1 million had been made by May 1916. The Mills No. 36 grenade used a discharger cup fixed to the muzzle, which increased the range, while a smooth bodied version, called the Steuart (No. 39), was introduced in the spring of 1918.

Most grenades contained high explosives; however, irritants were used in the early days of the war. Westonite grenades and Hillite grenades often leaked lethal gas, making them unpopular. Red and white phosphorus grenades produced smoke, while incendiary grenades were used to burn grass to remove cover.[3] Rifle grenades, which used different coloured smoke for signalling, were introduced at the end of 1916. A later design used a parachute that suspended a coloured smoke candle or coloured stars for daytime and nighttime signalling.

The demand for the Mills grenade had increased to 1.4 million a month by the summer of 1916 and their manufacture had become highly organised. While production had been simplified by the adoption of a combined hand and rifle grenade, large numbers still had to be stockpiled in Britain. The introduction of the 'Egg' No. 34 grenade, which was only half the weight of the Mills grenade, added to the storage problem. It meant that huge quantities of grenades would be left over at the end of the war.

Trench Mortars[4]

The BEF asked for a mortar after coming under fire from a German model called the *Minenwerfer* in September 1914. GHQ wanted a heavy model and a light model and while it asked for a quick solution, it rejected five designs. Meanwhile, the troops made their own mortars from iron pipes, shell cases and old French mortars. They were all dangerous.

The BEF had already adopted the 1.57-inch and 2-inch mortars by the time Wilfrid Stokes suggested his model in January 1915. A bomb was dropped down a seamless steel tube, so the percussion cap on the base hit the striker at the bottom. However, the War Office told the Royal Arsenal and Vickers to continue modifying the 1.57-inch and 2-inch models until they were perfected. The 4-inch Stokes mortar had been adopted to fire smoke and chemical bombs but it was proving difficult to make uniform casings.

The Ministry of Munitions transferred mortars from the Directorate of Artillery to its Trench Warfare Supply Department in June 1915. Minister David Lloyd George and Military Secretary Major General Ivor Philipps were both impressed with the 3-inch Stokes mortar, as were the Ordnance Board at the Shoeburyness range. GHQ was also impressed and was soon asking for 2,400 3-inch mortars and 750,000 rounds a month. So, a new range opened at Buxton in Derbyshire to proof them.

By May 1916, the BEF wanted to use the 3-inch mortar because the 1.57-inch, 3.7-inch and 4-inch were proving to be too heavy or too complicated. It took the factories time to change their machines and while the Admiralty armed their merchant vessels with the surplus 1.57-inch mortars, 500,000 rounds had to be broken up. A positive outcome was that using just one type of mortar halved the quantity of mortar bombs that needed to be stored.

The German-owned company British Mannesmann Tubes in Swansea, which made seamless tubes, was taken over. However, it took time to test the hot drawn tubes for the barrels because they required a high grade steel. There were also shortages of fuses and other components until the spring of 1916. A lack of inspectors even meant that some mortar rounds were sent to the front without being checked. Meanwhile, problems with premature explosions, resulted in a slower burning charge being introduced.

GHQ had been desperate for a mortar that would lob heavy bombs across no man's land, like the German *Minenwerfer*, for some time. While the Royal Arsenal was able to copy a captured one, GHQ wanted its own model. Armstrong Whitworth's 5-inch design was too cumbersome, so the Trench Warfare Department copied a French 9.45-inch model. Despite it being heavy and inaccurate, GHQ asked for 200 mortars in November 1915. It also asked for 150,000 150-pound vaned missiles, called Flying Pigs.

The Royal Arsenal also designed a 2-inch medium mortar that fired 50-pound cast iron round bombs. However, it had a low rate of fire, a limited range and was easy to spot. By June 1917, it had been replaced with the 6-inch Newton mortar, which overcame all these problems.

Many mortars and large amounts of ammunition were lost during the German offensives in March and April 1918. However, stocks were replenished in time for the summer counteroffensive. The 3-inch Stokes mortar proved to be useful during the final advances because a man could carry it with a sling. Mobile mountings were also made for 6-inch and 9.45-inch mortars.

By the end of the war, the BEF had been supplied with nearly 19,000 mortars and 16.36 million rounds. Over 11.5 million of the rounds had been made for the 3-inch Stokes mortar, with production peaking at 450,000 a month.

Trench Warfare Filling Factories[5]

The increasing demand for mortars and grenades required dedicated filling factories and five were up and running by early 1916. British Westfalite Company filled 3-inch Stokes mortar bombs in Denaby near Rotherham, peaking at 470,000 a month. Two factories were opened in Watford in Hertfordshire and they made a mixture of 2-inch, 3-inch and 9.45-inch mortar bombs. A reorganisation in August 1916 resulted in No. 1 Factory continuing to make mortar bombs, while No. 2 Factory switched to rifle grenades and chemical shells.

Blake Explosives Loading Company of Fulham was taken over at the end of 1915 following poor safety reports. It was converted into the National Bomb Filling Factory and peaked at over 350,000 grenades a month before it switched to making 430,000 3-inch Stokes mortar bombs a month in April 1916. Production briefly switched back to grenades and new machinery allowed each worker to fill 6,000 Mills grenades per shift. The factory started filling flares and signal cartridges in January 1917.

Thames Ammunition Works built a factory in Erith in Kent, on land seized from an Austrian under the Defence of the Realm Act. While it was soon making 110,000 2-inch trench mortar bombs a month, it too was taken over due to poor management. Gravity conveyors were installed so that women could handle 6-inch mortar bombs and the factory had made 1.1 million of each type by the end of the war.

Mortar bombs and grenades were both filled with chemicals for a time. Walthamstow Filling Factory made tear gas grenades, while the Royal Arsenal, Watford No. 1 Factory and the Ardol's in Selby made lethal gas bombs until Greenford opened in west London. Mortars had fired 800,000 gas filled bombs by the time artillery shells and Livens projector missiles replaced them.

The Trench Warfare Filling Factories were transferred to the Gun Ammunition Filling Department in May 1918, by which time the workforce had increased to 2,500 women and 500 men. They were all given extra work following the explosion at the National Filling Factory at Chilwell, Nottingham on 1 July 1918.

Catapults, Flamethrowers and the Livens Projector[6]

GHQ asked for two designs of catapults, which could throw grenades across no man's land, at the beginning of 1915. The Leach catapult had a range of 200 metres (yards) but accuracy depended on the quality of the rubber sling. The West Spring gun used springs to flick a throwing lever and while it was more accurate, the range was shorter. Both could be dangerous and they were replaced by the Stokes mortar and rifle grenades by March 1916.

A portable flame thrower had been suggested to GHQ in April 1915 but it proved to be complicated to make and too heavy to carry. The Germans successfully used flame throwers at Hooge, east of Ypres, on 30 July 1915 and while French designs were considered, they were again too heavy. The only time British troops used flame throwers was on the Zeebrugge Mole in April 1918, where the operators only had to move a short distance across flat ground.

Ruston, Proctor and Company of Lincoln made a static flamethrower called the Livens large gallery battery. It required a tunnel under the trenches and a high pressure gas pipe, which connected several oil pipes together. Hydraulic rams raised the nozzles, so they could spray burning oil across no man's land. However, the amount of time and labour involved to build one meant only a handful were built.

A Livens projector was composed of a row of lidless steel oil drums set at an angle in the ground. Mills grenades detonated black powder, which catapulted bundles of burning oily streamers across no man's land. It was tested at Porton Down and first used on Vimy Ridge in April 1917. Improved versions had a longer range and projectors were also used to fire lethal gas missiles. By the end of the war, 145,000 Livens projectors had fired over 400,000 flame and gas missiles.

Personal Protective Equipment[7]

By August 1915, GHQ wanted a steel helmet to protect a soldier's head. The Type A mild steel Brodie helmet was light enough but it rarely stopped shrapnel. So, the Type B, which was made of hardened manganese steel, gave better protection without increasing the weight of the helmet. The brittle alloy was difficult to cast but Thomas Firth's of Sheffield had soon taught others how to make them.

The first batch of Type B helmets were delivered in March 1916 and production at factories across Glasgow, Sheffield and Wolverhampton peaked at 450,000 a month until every soldier had one. In no time at all, the number of head wounds fell to less than one quarter. Approximately 7.25 million Brodie helmets were made, including 500,000 supplied to the AEF.

GHQ wanted a hand held shield to protect scouts or bombers in March 1915. However, it was impossible to make one both light enough to carry and tough enough to stop bullets. The Dayfield body protector, which included metal plates held in fabric pouches tied around the body (like a modern flak vest) was tried instead. Bulk manufacture started in June 1917 and 20,000 had been made by the time open warfare started the following summer.

Chapter 34

Optical Munitions

Finding New Sources[1]

High quality slabs of optical glass are shaped and polished into precise pieces, to accurately magnify a view in measuring instruments. The War Office referred to them as optical munitions. The infantry used binoculars and periscopes but the artillery required many instruments such as telescopic sights, rangefinders and instruments to find their targets. The Royal Navy also used directors, compasses, telescopes and rangefinders to find theirs.

An appeal for optical items at the beginning of the war resulted in the public offering 33,000 binoculars, compasses and instruments. However, the expanding BEF required many more and while some binoculars were made in Britain with imported parts, many more were imported whole. Some optical glass was imported from France but American sources were too expensive.

Britain had imported 80 per cent of its optical glass from Germany and Austria before the war and pre-war stocks ran out in the spring of 1916.[2] Chance Brothers and Company of Birmingham made 1,000 pounds of optical glass a month to an obsolete formula, until the Institute of Chemistry replicated the German formula, known as Jena glass. Chance Brothers could then increase its output to 14,500 pounds a month, while Wood Brothers Glass Company built a new factory in Derby. The Periscopic Prism Company could then expand production of optical munitions in Kentish Town.[3] The National Photographic Lens Factory in Enfield also started making lenses for the Hythe Gun Camera, which trainees used to learn about aerial combat during the final months of the war.

Potash was an important ingredient in making glass.[4] However, Britain had been importing 2,500 tons a month from Germany before the war. Most of it had been used to make fertilizer for the farming industry but the glass industry now needed a lot more. So, the North Lincolnshire Iron Company started making potash by adding salt to the dust from its blast furnaces. Meanwhile, the Ministry of Munitions built HM Potash Factory in Oldbury in Birmingham.

While Northampton Polytechnic trained women to make optical glass, employers and workers objected to employing them for some time.[5] By the end of the war, the optical glass industry had expanded twenty-fold and the Royal Navy and BEF had been issued with the following:

- 231,500 binoculars.
- 292,600 compasses.
- 344,725 ranging devices.

PART VII

Mechanised Warfare

Chapter 35

Shipbuilding

The Shipyards

There were over 160 shipyards around the coast of Britain and another 6 in Ireland. Local agreements controlled wages and working conditions until the Admiralty took control of labour matters in October 1916. It did so on the condition that it used the companies suggested by the Ministry of Munitions. As many as 3,000 men of different trades would work on a battleship and they could take as little as twenty-two months to as long as forty-two months to complete one.[1] Some were built by the Royal Dockyards, while the rest were built by private shipyards. The following private companies built dreadnoughts before the war:

- John Brown's on the River Clyde built six.
- Fairfield's on the River Clyde built four.
- Beardmore's on the River Clyde built two.
- Scotts' on the River Clyde built two.
- Vickers' in Barrow-in-Furness built six.
- Armstrong Whitworth's on the River Tyne built seven.
- Palmers' in Jarrow on the River Tyne built three.
- Cammell Laird's in Birkenhead built one.
- Thames Ironworks in London built one.

The Royal Dockyards organised squads around experienced men, while those in the private yards usually recruited from their families. In both cases, the foremen decided who would work. While there was little industrial unrest in the Tyne shipyards during the war, the Clyde shipyard workers held several stoppages relating to the cost of living and dilution.

Building a Warship

Work on a warship started with the Director of Naval Construction checking the plans drawn by the Admiralty's architect. Each shipyard had a huge loft, where scaled down parts of the ship were marked out on wooden moulds or on scrive boards laid on the floor. The dimensions were then scaled up, so steel plates could be ordered from foundries such as Beardmore, Armstrong Whitworth's, Cammell Laird's, Vickers and John Brown's. They were then transferred to the shipyard by train.

The flat plates were bent into shape before they drilled, sheared, planed, flanged and bevelled. Many were stiffened with bars that had been bent into shape by pinning them to huge steel slabs before they were heated up. They were then assembled on building blocks laid along the slipway.[2]

Work began with the keel, followed by the reinforced base of the hull. Derricks, tower cranes and overhead gantries lifted the huge plates into place, so gangs could pin them together. Riveting gangs followed up, heating up each one, before inserted it and hammered the end down. Private gangs were paid per rivet and they often used pneumatic machines, however, Royal Dockyard gangs were paid by the hour to hammer them in by hand. Next came the caulking gangs, who hammered iron strips into any gaps in the seams, sometimes using pneumatic hammers and sometimes by hand.

Once the hull was complete, cradles and dog shores (wedges) were installed to take the ship's weight off the building blocks. A local dignitary was invited to cut the rope which released the weights and knocked out the final dog shores. The huge crowds cheered, ships' sirens were blown and a band played as the hull slid down the greased slipway into the water.[3]

Work could then start on building the compartments that formed the base of the ship's superstructure. Below deck, accommodation for everyone from the captain down to the lowest crew member had to be kitted out. The galleys, sick bays, storage, water tanks, fuel storage, boilers and engine rooms also had to be equipped. Funnels, masts and a conning tower completed the superstructure.[4]

Most of the large calibre guns were made by Beardmore's, Armstrong Whitworth's, and Vickers. A completed barrel consisted of an inner lining and an outer jacket. They often weighed over 100 tons and they could take up to a year to make. Work started by forging the inner lining as an octagonal bar. Once it cooled a hole was drilled through the centre. A hollow mandrel was inserted into the hole and it was kept cool with water as the bar was reheated and squeezed to the required dimensions. The lining was planed and smoothed into the correct shape and then heated before it was put into an oil bath to harden (temper) the steel.

The inner lining was enveloped with many spirals of wire that were squeezed, giving the barrel extra strength for less weight. The tube was then given another bath in hot oil before it was rubbed smooth. An outer jacket was cast and shaped in the same way as the inner jacket. It was then heated and slid over the lining, so the two would form a homogenous tube as it cooled. The rifling, which made the shell spin in flight, was then carved inside the inner lining.

Warships required gun turrets and they were built over pits in a workshop. The largest ones took up to two years to make and they could end up weighing as much as

300 tons. Once complete, they were dismantled and taken by train to the shipyard, to be reassembled on the ship's deck.

A completed ship had to be put through several weeks of inspections and teams were on hand to address issues as soon as they were spotted.[5] Everything from the boilers to the refrigeration areas and from the ammunition hoists to the bulkheads had to be checked. The ship was then put through a series of manoeuvre exercises, which involved monitoring the engines at different speeds. The rudders and anchors were checked before the ship was put through speed trials. The turrets and barrels were examined to see they moved correctly, as was the shell handling equipment. Finally, the ship carried out firing tests before it was commissioned for service.

Royal Dockyards[6]

Shipbuilding was originally based in the south and the Royal Dockyards were situated in natural harbours. Chatham Royal Dockyard is on the River Medway in Kent and it had three basins, three slipways, five dry docks and four (wet) docks. It launched two cruisers and twelve submarines during the war. Pembroke Royal Dockyard is near Milford Haven in south-west Wales. It launched three cruisers and two submarines during the war. There was also a small repair dock at Sheerness, Kent.

Portsmouth Royal Dockyard in Hampshire had four basins, one slipway, four dry docks, thirteen (wet) docks and one floating dock. It launched seven dreadnought battleships between June 1906 and October 1913:

- HMS *Dreadnought*
- HMS *Bellerophon*
- HMS *St Vincent*
- HMS *Neptune*
- HMS *Orion*
- HMS *King George V*
- HMS *Iron Duke*
- HMS *Queen Elizabeth*

It also completed the battleship HMS *Royal Sovereign* in April 1915, followed by five submarines.

Devonport Royal Dockyard in Plymouth on the River Tamar in Devon had five slipways, nine dry docks, three (wet) docks and two basins. It launched five dreadnought battleships between August 1907 and November 1913:

- HMS *Temeraire*
- HMS *Collingwood*

- HMS *Centurion*
- HMS *Marlborough*
- HMS *Warspite*

It also completed two battlecruisers, HMS *Indefatigable* and HMS *Lion*. It launched the battleship HMS *Royal Oak* in October 1914, followed by five submarines.

Around 53,000 were working in the Royal Dockyards when war broke out but 8,000 enlisted over the next twelve months. They were replaced by many new workers, bringing the total workforce to 64,000 by the summer of 1916.

The Naval Ordnance Department was responsible for inspecting guns and ammunition; it also dealt with mines and torpedoes after 1917. The Admiralty set up the Board of Invention and Research to look at scientific issues in July 1915; it was replaced by a Director of Experiments and Research in January 1918.

The Directorate of Scientific Research and Experiment ran the Admiralty's Research Laboratory, the Royal Navy Physiological Laboratory and the Services Electronics Research Laboratory. The Directorate of Naval Construction ran the Admiralty's Experiment Works and the Naval Construction Research Establishment.

The Admiralty's Engineer-in-Chief organised the Fuel Experiment Station and the Engineering Laboratory. Warships needed to regularly visit a dry dock or graving dock to have their hull cleaned or repaired. There were suitable dry docks in Renfrew, Belfast, Hebburn, Liverpool, Birkenhead, Bristol and Southampton.

Private Dockyards[7]

The north-east coast of Scotland afforded few opportunities for large shipyards, so there were just six in Peterhead, Aberdeen and Montrose. There were two more in Dundee on the River Tay, including Caledon Shipbuilding, which employed over 2,500. There were another nine small shipyards along the Firth of Forth, with the majority in Leith, Edinburgh's port.

Scotland's centre of shipbuilding was the River Clyde.[8] There were seven small shipyards around the Firth of Clyde, where the river enters the Irish sea, west of Glasgow. Over 10,000 were employed by 4 large shipyards along the lower reaches of the River Clyde:

- Scotts Shipbuilding and Engineering Company in Greenock.
- William Denny and Brothers in Dumbarton.
- William Hamilton and Company in Port Glasgow.
- Clyde Shipbuilding and Engineering Company in Port Glasgow.

There were another thirteen small shipyards in the three ports.

The upper reaches of the River Clyde were lined with shipyards, large and small. Beardmore's eventually employed 16,000 between its three sites in Dalmuir, Paisley and Anniesland. It launched the battleship HMS *Ramillies*, the aircraft carrier HMS *Argus*, three cruisers and many other small military vessels during the war. John Brown's eventually employed 9,600 in Clydebank and it launched the battleships HMS *Barham* and HMS *Repulse*, the seaplane carrier *Pegasus*, two cruisers and many more military ships.

There were two large shipyards on the south bank in Govan. Fairfield Shipbuilding and Engineering Company eventually had 9,500 employees. Harland and Wolff Limited employed another 4,500 and it built the battleships HMS *Valiant* and HMS *Renown*, as well as three cruisers. Both companies built many destroyers and submarines.

Yarrow and Company, and Barclay, Curle and Company eventually employed over 10,000 from Scotstoun and they launched over eight small military ships and many cargo ships between them. There were another 16 smaller shipyards along the upper reaches of the River Clyde, working on small warships and merchant ships. G. and J. Weir's employed 6,200 making auxiliary equipment while Barr and Stroud Limited employed 2,200 making naval optical munitions; they were both based in Glasgow city.

The second largest shipbuilding area in Britain, was the North East, with many yards lining the lower reaches of the River Tyne, east of Newcastle.[9] Armstrong Whitworth's was by far the largest company along the River Tyne, employing 25,000 in three locations. While its original factory was in Elswick, it had recently opened its High Walker and Low Walker yards, downstream of the city. Between 1907 and 1913, the company launched the four battleships, HMS *Superb*, HMS *Monarch*, HMS *Agincourt* and HMS *Canada*. It had also launched the battlecruiser *Invincible*. The battleship *Malaya* was launched in March 1915, followed by a further two battlecruisers, two cruisers, nine submarines, the aircraft carrier HMS *Eagle* and many other smaller craft during the war. The number of employees at the three sites also increased to over 50,000, of which over 10,000 were employed in the company shipyards.

Palmers Shipbuilding and Iron Company launched the battleship HMS *Hercules* in 1910 and the battlecruiser HMS *Queen Mary* in 1912. Its workforce increased to over 10,000 during the war and they worked on the battleship HMS *Resolution*, a cruiser, eighteen destroyers, three monitors and two submarines. Meanwhile, R. and W. Hawthorn, Leslie and Company doubled its workforce to 6,000, while Swan Hunter and Wigham Richardson Limited employed over 10,000. They both built cruisers, destroyers, monitors, torpedo boat destroyers, sloops and submarines. Another sixteen shipyards worked on smaller naval craft, as well as merchant and cargo ships, along the lower reaches of the River Tyne.

There were fifteen shipyards along the River Wear, in Sunderland and the largest was William Doxford and Sons Limited, which employed over 4,000 building torpedo boat destroyers. There were ten dockyards in West Hartlepool (now Hartlepool) and Middlesbrough building small warships and cargo ships. Smith's Dock Company in Middlesbrough was the largest and it repaired many ships during the war.

The largest shipyard in the North West of England was Vickers in Barrow-in-Furness.[10] Its 16,000 employees had completed the battleships HMS *Vanguard*, HMS *Erin* and HMS *Emperor of India* and the battlecruiser HMS *Princess Royal* between 1909 and 1913. The workforce more than doubled to work on the battleship HMS *Revenge* and seven cruisers during the war. There were also small dockyards at Workington on the Cumberland coast and at Lytham St Anne's on the Lancashire coast.

Around 8,000 worked at Cammell Laird's shipyard in Birkenhead, on the River Mersey, before the war, completing the dreadnought HMS *Audacious* in 1912. However, the number increased to over 13,000 as the shipyard worked on five cruisers, eight destroyers and eight submarines. There were also two merchant shipyards on the River Mersey and even two on the River Weaver in Northwich. There were another three small shipyards working on merchant ships in North Wales: two on Deeside and the third in Anglesey. Cardiff Channel Dry Dock and Pontoon Company, Elliot and Jeffery Limited and John Shearman and Company employed 3,000 in their Cardiff shipyards.

The few ports on the rest of England's east coast dealt with imports, exports and fishing, so the few small shipyards were dedicated to maintaining the local fleets. There were ten small shipyards around Goole, Hull and Grimsby, along the River Humber. There were also four small shipyards in Great Yarmouth in Norfolk, two in Lowestoft in Suffolk and three on the River Colne near Colchester in Essex. Green and Silley Weir employed over 5,000 men in their shipyard in the Royal Albert Docks in London. However, there were only three small shipyards along the River Thames, east of London. There was another at Gravesend and one at Faversham, both on the north coast of Kent.

Bristol was mainly used for imports and there were only three small dockyards dealing with merchant ships along the River Severn. There were just four more in Devon and Cornwall. The biggest private employer along the south coast, was John Thornycroft in Southampton, with 4,600 employees. Harland and Wolff also employed another 2,500. Across the water on the Isle of Wight was J. Samuel White and Company, which employed another 1,000 employees. The two companies built destroyers and many other small craft between them.

The largest dockyard in the north of Ireland, was Harland and Wolff, home of the fateful RMS *Titanic*, which had been sunk when it hit an iceberg in 1912. Its workforce of 15,000 workers doubled during the war to build a battlecruiser, a cruiser, ten monitors, cargo ships and tankers. There were another five dockyards building merchant and cargo ships in Londonderry, Larne, Belfast and Dublin.

Shipping Materials and Equipment[11]

Beardmore's, Vickers, Armstrong Whitworth, and John Brown's had their own steel works, so they were able to equip their own ships. However, other companies relied on a range of specialist subcontractors:

- Twenty companies cast steel plates, sheets, bars and rods.
- Sixteen companies supplied power tools and hand tools.
- Nineteen companies sold engineering plant and auxiliary machinery.
- Thirty-seven companies made engineering components, including propeller shafts, chains, springs and tubes.
- Forty-six companies made engines, both to move ships and for pumps.
- Twenty-two companies made boilers and engine room equipment.
- Eleven companies making electrical equipment, including dynamos, generators, lamps and motors.
- Eight companies made ventilation, heating and refrigeration equipment.
- Fourteen companies made shells and gunnery equipment.
- Twelve companies made optical and communications equipment.
- Eighteen companies made anchors, lifeboats, propellors and torpedo nets.

Naval Mines[12]

The Admiralty used unreliable spherical mines and obsolete Russian mines, during the early years of the war. The H2 mine was a large floating steel sphere and contact with any of the spikes (called horns) set off the explosives inside. The mine sat in a cradle, called a sinker, as it sank to the sea floor. The water pressure then made it float upwards, as a chain turned the sinker into an anchor.

A cooperative group made the components, while the North British Locomotive Company assembled the mines. Meanwhile, W.R. Morris Motors Limited of Oxford and several Manchester cotton machine factories made the sinkers. The Admiralty started deploying H2 mines in the Heligoland Blight area in March 1917, to catch German ships leaving the River Elbe to enter the North Sea.

The Royal Navy's mining campaign against the German shipping lanes intensified as output increased to 4,500 mines and 3,300 sinkers a month. It started the North Sea Mine Barrage in June 1918, which stretched 250 miles from the Orkney Islands to Norway. Output was reduced when the Mines Group Section of the Admiralty took over in 1918 but nearly 50,000 H2 mines and 75,000 sinkers had been made by the end of the war.

Chapter 36

Tanks

Supply of the Mark I Tank in 1916[1]

After many discussions about designing an armoured vehicle, neither the Admiralty nor the Ministry of Munitions were willing to supervise the manufacture of what was being proposed. The Tank Supply Committee was formed on 12 February 1916 as the Army Council requested 100 tanks. William Foster and Company of Lincoln immediately offered its Mother Tank (Mark I), which was powered by a six-cylinder 105-horsepower engine, for a trial.

The Tank Supply Committee sourced armour plates from Beardmore's, Cammell Laird's and Vickers. Meanwhile, the Daimler Company of Coventry supplied the engines. William Foster and Company of Lincoln set about assembling twenty-five machines while the Metropolitan Carriage, Wagon and Finance Company of Birmingham built the rest.

The Army Council asked for another fifty machines on 21 April 1916 and the Ministry of Munitions made them a top three priority, aiming to have them ready by the end of July.[2] Half would be armed with 6-pounder guns supplied by Armstrong Whitworth's and they would be known as the male version, while the other half would be armed with machine guns made by Hotchkiss and Company of Coventry and they would be known as the female version.

However, there were differences of opinion over how the tanks should be used. The BEF intended to use them many times, which would require a repair unit. However, the Ministry of Munitions' Supply Department thought they would only be used once, like a 'projectile' and so it did not order any spare parts.

By mid-July, it was obvious that the tanks would not be available until the end of September. Even so, another 100 were ordered to stop the contractors switching to other work. The first batch crossed the Channel during the first week in August and they were followed by two tank sections at weekly intervals.

Forty-nine tanks were deployed on 15 September 1916 but only thirty-two reached their starting point. Many broke down, while others became stuck on the rough ground (known as ditching). The rest were overtaken by the infantry before they turned back, after running low on fuel and ammunition. General Julian Byng summed up the tank's performance by saying they were 'a useful accessory to the infantry, but nothing more.'

It did not help that the Army Council asked if 1,000 tanks could be ready for the spring 1917 offensive, only to cancel the request.

Despite the doubts, the battlefield experience had been useful and the crews were able to suggest modifications that could be made to the rest. The Tank Supply Department had to add the useful ones to drawings before getting the Army Council's approval. Only then could the details be forwarded to the factories. Tanks then had to be tested, both in Britain and at the central depot and repair shop in France.

Another forty Mark I tanks were only now nearing completion because the factories had been busy making spare parts for the tanks that had survived the Somme battlefield. William Foster assembled fifty Mark II tanks over the winter, while the Metropolitan Carriage, Wagon and Finance Company made a similar number of the Mark III tanks using thicker armour. In both cases, they were not delivered until April 1917, much later than expected, because they had been struggling to fit a more powerful 150-horsepower engine, made by Ricardo and Company of Manchester, into the tank.

The problem was finding enough companies to make all the components for such a complicated piece of engineering.[3] Uncertainty over how many would be made and whether there would be continuation orders made companies reluctant to become involved. It then took time to coordinate the making and assembling of the many components. It meant that tank parts were often put behind guns, mechanical transport and aircraft when it came to priorities. Two more railway carriage builders started assembled the tanks but there were always shortages of armour plate, engines, gears and bearings.

Supply of the Mark IV and the Whippet Tank in 1917[4]

By the beginning of 1917, Mechans Limited of Glasgow, Armstrong Whitworth's, Marshall, Sons and Company of Gainsborough, and the Coventry Ordnance Works had been added to the list of firms assembling tanks. Parts were inspected where they were made, while the completed tanks were sent to a central testing station in Newbury.

While Field Marshal Sir Douglas Haig wanted more tanks, he considered other items more urgent, such as artillery, aircraft and lorries. Manufacture was then delayed because the Admiralty needed steel to build ships to replace those lost to German submarines.

Meanwhile, there were problems making the complicated track links from a hardened steel alloy and over half would not fit together. There were also problems making enough spares because demand was far higher than expected. The lack of cooperation between the Supply Department and those who used the tanks also meant that it could take six weeks to make a tank ready for battle once it reached France.

Work had started on designing the Mark IV in October 1916 and William Foster's completed the first one in March 1917. It was built using hardened steel plates of Hadfields manganese alloy for the body, which gave better protection against armour piercing bullets without increasing the thickness of steel. Other improvements included better track rollers and a larger petrol tank, which was bolted to the rear, so the crew were not exposed to danger if it exploded. The gun sponsons had also been designed to be pushed in, so they did not have to be removed when the tanks were moved by rail. Lewis guns had replaced the Hotchkiss gun, while the 6-pounder gun had a shortened barrel.

Production was delayed by a lack of labour and while the first Mark IV's reached France in mid-April 1917, they had not been given a thorough inspection. It would require several weeks of checking and modifications before it was ready to go into action. It resulted in the Mark II and III training tanks being deployed at Bullecourt, with disastrous results.

Mark IV tanks were deployed for the first time on 7 June 1917, in support of the advance across Messines Ridge. The battle proved that the hardened steel plates worked. It was the same alloy that had been used to make the Brodie helmet and it gave the same protection for less weight.

Confidence in tanks diminished when they struggled to cross the soft ground around Ypres in the summer and autumn of 1917. The new Tank Directorate formalised communication, making it difficult for the Mechanical Warfare Supply Department, who knew how to build the tanks, to speak to the crews, who knew what needed to be modified. The problems were only addressed after a new committee started visiting France in October 1917 to liaise between the makers and the users, postponing the decision to start designing the Mark V.

Foster's had also designed the Medium Mark A tank, known as the Whippet, which could travel 80 miles with the help of two four-cylinder 45-horsepower engines made by J. Tylor and Sons and independent transmission gears. The tank was armed with four machine guns and was crewed by three men. However, delivery was delayed until October 1917 because it had been difficult to get enough ball bearings.

Expanding Production and the Mark V in 1918[5]

The Army Council had asked for an extra 1,000 tanks in October 1917. However, Haig asked for as many as possible after they broke the German line at Cambrai on 20 November 1917. The problem was finding enough factories with skilled labour to make them all. The companies involved in building tanks agreed to coordinate their efforts in December 1917 while they were given top priority for steel for the first time.

The Tank Corps was reorganised at the beginning of 1918, with machines being divided into heavy battalions, light battalions and supply companies. There were also plans to support them with gun carriers and communication tanks. However, constant breakdowns and shortages of spares, resulted in one in five fighting tanks needing to be replaced every month.

In May 1918, the Supreme War Council asked if 1,000 tanks a month could be built in 1919. It was a ridiculous amount, not just because of the huge amount of steel it would require; there was already a shortage of skilled labour. So, the Ministry of Munitions asked the tank manufacturers for a realistic figure.

Design of the Mark V had begun in October 1917 and the first ones left the Metropolitan Carriage, Wagon and Finance Company's factory in January 1918. The armour had been increased to 14 millimetres and it had better steering and improved braking. The epicyclic gears were far easier to use, the crew could operate the unditching gear from the inside and there was an observer's turret. The first ones reached the war zone in May 1918.

The Metropolitan Carriage, Wagon and Finance Company completed the first Mark V* in May 1918. It was 6 feet (2 metres) longer, allowing it to carry infantry or large amounts of stores; it could also cross wider trenches. The only problem with the Mark V was faulty ventilation, which sometimes overwhelmed the crew with engine fumes. Altogether 1,032 Mark V and Mark V* tanks were produced in 1918.

The Tank Corps was shattered after just three days fighting in August 1918. While the tanks had helped break the German line east of Amiens, many had been knocked out by hidden anti-tank guns, while others had been caught out in the open when the mist lifted. It meant that the Tank Corps needed every tank it could get its hands on, so a plan to hand Mark IV tanks over to the Allies had to be cancelled.

Tanks were again made priority because it was recognised that they could achieve far more with much less steel, manpower and transport than an artillery barrage. So, the Tank Board was formed and it organised a group of factories to make 100 tanks per month. The Metropolitan Carriage, Wagon and Finance Company also started producing the Medium B Whippet in September 1918. It could travel 85 miles and was powered by a 100-horsepower Ricardo engine. The main problem in 1918 was manpower. Time and again, skilled men were being conscripted, while a flu epidemic in the autumn made many workers ill.

The Final Advance, Autumn 1918

The Metropolitan Carriage, Wagon and Finance Company also built a self-propelled gun version, which carried an artillery piece and ammunition. Work also started on an infantry supply tank (Mark IX) and Armstrong Whitworth's made a few that could carry up to 10 tons of supplies. However, a shortage of engines meant the gun and supply tanks were abandoned and the obsolete Marks I, II and IV tanks were used instead.

By October 1918, all five armies of the BEF were advancing and they all wanted tanks. While they were useful, they were being knocked out or breaking down quicker than they could be built or repaired. Although 1,250 tanks had been assembled, over half were being repaired in French workshops, while dozens more were waiting to be shipped from England. The Tank Corps' contribution to the BEF's advance diminished by the day until they were only used in small numbers to support the infantry. It was about to run out of tanks when the Armistice was declared.

By the spring of 1917, 150 Mark I's and 100 Mark II and III had been made. Another 408 Mark IV fighting tanks and 249 supply tanks were also made. Also, 388 Mark V and 288 Mark V* tanks had left the factories by the end of the war, as well as 167 Whippet Mark A and 45 Mark B tanks.

Joint Supply with the United States[6]

The United States wanted to get involved in the tank programme when it entered the war, so the Inter-Allied Tank Bureau was set up in June 1917, followed by the Mechanical Warfare (Overseas and Allies) Department in November 1917. The plan was to build Liberty tanks, or Mark VIII tanks, at new factory at Chateauroux in France, with the first batch going to the AEF.

The plan was for American factories to supply the forgings, engines, transmissions and skilled labour, while Britain supplied the guns, ammunition and unskilled labour. However, there were mistakes on the drawings sent to the United States, while there were delays in building the French factory. The United States was then unable to send enough steel while Britain did not have enough spare labour. While the first Mark VIII Liberty tank was completed by the North British Locomotive Company in October 1918, it was the only one and it did not see service.

Chapter 37

Lorries, Cars and Motorcycles

Organising the Manufacture of Mechanical Transport[1]

The British Army had started using lorries in 1911 and it only owned a few by 1914. Potential owners had been offered a loan to buy a vehicle, on condition that they made it available to the armed services if the nation went to war. The Chief Inspector of Subsidised Transport kept a list and 700 were add to the 200 in service in August 1914.

The War Department organised the British Army's vehicles, while the Royal Naval Air Service (RNAS) dealt with the Admiralty's transport. They also maintained a list of suitable manufacturers, which the Mechanical Transport Committee contacted when war broke out. As a result, a mixture of army trucks, commercial vans, omnibuses and workshop lorries accompanied the BEF to France.

Lorries were put to work carrying goods and troops between the railheads and the refilling points behind the line, where horse drawn vehicles took over. The plan was to standardise the design of lorries, cars and motorcycles to make them easier to maintain and repair, however, it took time to implement. Over the months that followed, the War Office invested in the following:

- Fourteen types of 3-ton lorries.
- Four types of 30-hundredweight lorries.
- Six types of ambulances.
- Six types of cars.
- Two types of motorcycles.[2]

Vehicles were inspected where they were made and then stored at the Mechanical Transport Depot on Kempton Park. Some were imported from the United States and Switzerland. The War Office also bought armoured cars which were made by fixing steel plates and weapons to lorries.

The Ministry of Munitions took over in June 1915 and while demand for artillery tractors and mechanical transport increased, it was difficult to find anywhere to make them because the car factories were already busy.[3] It meant that one in three vehicles had to be imported from the United States. While Russia put in a huge order for 4,500 lorries and 8,000 cars, it was impossible to meet.

The Mechanical Transport Department was set up in September 1916 to deal with the design, inspection and supply of British Army vehicles; it took over the Admiralty's vehicles in April 1917. The Department of Requirements and Statistics started prioritising manufacture at the same time due to the shortages caused by the German submarine campaign. The Ministry of Munitions introduced licenses to limit the sale of vehicle chassis but it eventually had to ban all private manufacturing. It also made a register of vehicles and controlled the sale and purchase of any new ones.

The department was divided into design and supply branches when it joined the Ministry's Engines Group in August 1917. It also started having vehicles sent back to the manufacturer to repair because it was easier than trying to do it in France. Over time, the BEF became increasingly mechanised and developed a variety of designs. It used everything from motorcycle combinations armed with machine guns to lorries carrying water tanks, to trailers for hauling large aircraft. By the end of the war, it had acquired 66,000 lorries. The Ministry of Munitions had also exported the following to France, Russia and Italy:

- 42,500 bicycles.
- 18,000 motorcycles.
- 2,240 cars.
- 7,300 lorries and ambulances.

Providing Enough Spare Parts[4]

One broken part could put a lorry, car or motorcycle out of service, so it was important to supply enough spare parts and tools. The problem was the battlefield put extra stresses on vehicles, so it took time to work out what was needed to keep vehicles on the road. It took even more longer to acquire enough spares for the large number of imported American models. While new vehicles were eventually sent to France with a selection of commonly required spares, there were always shortages.

One factor that helped keep vehicles on the road was standardisation. While this was possible with the chassis and bodywork, each factory used a different engine design. Tyres were another problem, as the BEF's fleet expanded. It eventually required 80,000 tyres and inner tubes a week. Two thirds of them were imported from the United States and stored at Camden Town in London before they were shipped to France. Attempts were made to standardise tyre sizes to make it easier to keep the vehicles on the road.

All vehicles required bearings of different sizes and shapes but Britain had limited capacity to make them, leaving it relying on imports.[5] The expansion of the mechanical transport, aircraft and tank industries increased demand and while many coming from the United States were poor quality, all imports were in danger from the submarine menace. So, the few British ball bearing companies, such as the Hoffmann Manufacturing Company of Chelmsford and Skefko's of Luton, were asked to expand production.

The Ball Bearings Branch was set up in July 1917, following a crisis caused by the United States reducing imports when it entered the war. Hoffmann's was turned into a National Ball Bearings Factory and while home production increased to 229,000 a month, the rapid expansion of aerial and mechanical warfare meant it was 1918 before production reached satisfactory levels. Hoffmann's and Skefko's continued to make the most ball bearings, while Ransome and Marles Bearing Company of Newark and Rudge-Whitworth Cycles and the Electric and Ordnance Accessories, both of Birmingham, made specialist bearings.

The Motor Factories[6]

By 1918, British factories were making 1,800 lorries, 1,300 motorcycles and 425 cars a month. Many of them were given to the AEF, so it did not have to ship its own transport over from America. What follows, is a list of the larger vehicle manufacturers across Britain:

Glasgow

- Albion Motors employed 2,000 making lorries.

Manchester

- Crossley Brothers employed 3,200 making tank and aeroengines.
- Belsize Motors employed 5,600 making aircraft and lorry parts.

Birmingham

- Austin Motor Company employed 18,500 making lorries.
- Dunlop Rubber Company employed 8,175 making tyres.
- Metropolitan Carriage, Wagon and Finance Company employed 3,375 making wagons and tanks.
- Birmingham Railway Carriage and Wagon Company employed 2,800 making lorries.
- Joseph Lucas Limited employed 1,750 making electrical equipment.

Coventry

- White and Poppe Limited employed 8,900 making engines, motorcycles and aircraft.

- The Rover Company employed 1,450 making motorcycles, staff cars and ambulances.
- Triumph Cycle Company employed 1,400 making motorcycles.

London

- Ransomes, Sims and Jefferies Limited employed 5,100 making wagons and planes.
- C.A. Vandervell and Company employed 3,525 making electrical parts.
- Associated Equipment Company (AEC) employed 2,500 making lorries.
- F.W. Berwick and Company employed 2,200 making lorries and planes.
- D. Napier and Son employed 2,175 making lorry and aircraft engines.

Ruston, Proctor's employed 7,450 making engines in Lincoln, Marshall's employed 4,600 making wheels in Gainsborough, while Brush Electrical Engineering Company employed 2,375 making vehicles and locomotives in Loughborough.

By the end of the war, the British Army owned 34,000 lorries, including 19,360 imported from the United States. The complexity of keeping them running was enormous because each lorry had around 2,000 parts. The British Army also owned a selection of 59,000 cars, vans and ambulances of which 18,300 were American. It had to take the delivery of another 2,500 vehicles after the Armistice to complete outstanding orders.

Chapter 38

The Aircraft Industry

Working for the War Department[1]

The Military Aeronautics Directorate was divided into three sections at the start of the war:

- The first dealt with men and machines.
- The second dealt with experiments and testing.
- The third acquired materials and components.

The experiments section split into pre-inspection aircraft and stores after August 1915, while a design branch was added to check new designs and inventions.

A reorganisation in April 1916 resulted in several branches:

- Fighting Branch
- Equipment Branch
- Contracts Branch
- Supply Branch

The Contracts Branch was set up to make sure there were enough materials and components to build complete aircraft, while the Supply Branch dealt with aircraft design, engine production and materials acquisition. The Hastening Section helped factories accelerate production by improving cooperation.

Aircraft Supply, 1914 to 1916[2]

The number of British companies making aircraft increased to around thirty but they needed time to meet the requirements of the Royal Flying Corps (RFC) and the Royal Naval Air Service (RNAS). In the meantime, the War Department supplied parts and offered financial assistance, so they could expand their workshops and train new workers. Meanwhile, French designed aircraft, including Moranes, Nieuports and Spads, continued to fly with the RFC throughout 1915.

The French government stopped exported aircraft but it allowed the export of Gnome, Le Rhône and Clerget aeroengines; the Hispano-Suiza engine was also imported from Spain. So, British aircraft companies were asked to base their designs according to what engines were available. Nearly 4,000 aeroengines had been bought by the time there were enough British models in 1916.

The Admiralty's Air Department was organised into two parts in September 1915. The Organisation Branch dealt with the deployment of aircraft while the Construction Branch was again split into three sections:

- Aircraft and seaplanes
- Armaments
- Lighter than air craft (airships and kite ballons)

The Aeronautical Supplies Department eventually had to merge army and navy aircraft supplies to stop them competing.

The Admiralty eventually bought over 1,100 complete French aircraft, as well as many R-2 model Curtiss aircraft from the United States for training. It had a design office but its staff was often sent to the private factories to monitor their progress. There was also an engine testing facility, while complete aircraft were tested on the Isle of Grain in Kent. A RNAS test flight was based at nearby Eastchurch.

Aircraft Supply, 1917 to 1918[3]

By 1916, each squadron was begin equipped with the same model; for example reconnaissance planes, artillery spotter planes, fighters or bombers. The Admiralty also had seaplanes and boat planes for anti-ship, anti-submarine and observation work. Factories had to be organised to deal with the different loss rates for each type of aircraft because it was only 33 per cent for bombers, it was as high as 66 per cent for single seater fighters.

The Ministry of Munitions took over aeronautical supply in March 1917 and its staff faced a complicated task. Demand was increasing but many of the aircraft firms and their subcontractors were still inexperienced. While unskilled labour could be taught how to build the parts for an aircraft frame, skilled mechanics were required to build an aeroengine and they were in short supply.

The aircraft industry was still in the experimental stage and aeronautical and mechanical engineers were constantly pushing the limits of flight. However, the safety of the pilots was paramount throughout the test process and the Ministry of Munitions would not start mass producing a plane until a model had been thoroughly tested. It could take up to eight months to get an airframe from the design stage ready for bulk production and another three months to prepare a factory to make it. Aeroengines took could take twice as long to get from the drawing desk to the airfield.

The United States wanted to develop and build its own planes when it entered the war, so it stopped exporting goods and bought raw materials from France. It left Britain having to rely on its own material sources and factories to complete its expanding aerial programme.

The Air Board was raised to ministry status at the beginning of 1918 but it continued to control aircraft design. Meanwhile, the departments dealing with aeronautical supplies had been part of the Air Group since August 1917. They covered requirements, technical questions, production, inspections, contracts and finance. They also dealt with the private factories, the National Aircraft Factories and ten factories that had been set up to build bombers with imported parts.

Farnborough was renamed the Royal Aircraft Establishment in April 1918 to avoid an acronym confusion with the newly renamed Royal Air Force (RAF). Its workforce had grown to 4,200 and they had built 480 planes and repaired 2,300 engines by the end of the war.

By 1918, aircraft construction had top priority and 200 squadrons were planned by the autumn. That required the industry to build 3,500 planes and 4,000 engines a month.[4] While standardisation had reduced the number of aircraft types down to just thirteen, a huge workforce was still needed to make them. By the end of the war, there were over 200,000 workers, including 20,000 skilled tradesmen, employed by the aircraft industry.

British aircraft factories built over 17,000 single seater aircraft, 34,200 two seater aircraft and 430 bombers during the war. They also built 3,000 seaplanes, ship planes and boat planes. The country had also imported 3,000 aircraft from France and the United States.

National Aircraft Factories[5]

A plan to expand aircraft programme resulted in work starting on three National Aircraft Factories, each capable of making 200 aircraft per month in September 1917. Holland, Hannen and Cubitt's set up National Aircraft Factory No. 1 at Wadden near Croydon, to make DH.9 machines and starting in April 1918. However, poor management and stoppages delayed production, so the 1,250 and 850 men had only built 240 by the end of the war.

Crossley Brothers built National Aircraft Factory No. 2 at Heaton Chapel, east of Manchester, and 1,600 men and 940 women started building DH.9 and DH.10 aircraft in April 1918. However, there were problems with the Dragonfly engine and it took until October 1918 to get replacements.

The Cunard Steamship Company set up National Aircraft Factory No. 3 in Aintree carried out test flights on the racecourse north of Liverpool. While it employed 1,600 men and 1,050 women, there were often stoppages and many Irish workers left when the Registration (Amendment) Act came into force in February 1918. The first machine was completed in June 1918 but only a few Bristol Fighters had been made by the time of the Armistice.

Sopwith Aviation Company also rented a factory at Richmond in the summer of 1918. It proved difficult to get enough skilled labour for all the aircraft factories because they started work so late in the war. There was also a plan to build forty Handley Page bombers in five of Oldham's mills. Alliance Aircraft Company set them up but the parts did not arrive until August 1918 and few had been completed by the time of the Armistice.

Private Aircraft Factories[6]

What follows is a list of the larger factories making aircraft:

- William Beardmore's employed 4,400 near Glasgow.
- A.V. Roe and Company employed 2,800 near Manchester.
- Phoenix Dynamo Manufacturing Company employed 4,000 in Bradford.
- Clayton and Shuttleworth's and Robey's employed 6,600 in Lincoln.
- Grahame-White Aviation Company employed 3,200 in Bedford.
- Averys employed 3,000 in Birmingham.
- British and Colonial Aircraft Company employed over 3,000 made Bristol aircraft near Bristol.
- Gloucestershire Aircraft Company employed 2,200 in Cheltenham.
- Petters Limited employed 2,000 in Yeovil.
- Aircraft Manufacturing Company (Airco) employed 5,200 in Hendon.
- William Cubitt and Company employed 5,250 in Holborn.
- Harris Lebus employed 4,000 in Tottenham.
- Handley Page Limited employed 2,500 in Cricklewood.
- Whitehead and Company employed 1,950 in Richmond.
- Short Brothers made aircraft in Bedford, seaplanes in Rochester and balloons in Battersea in London; the company employed 3,000.
- Boulton and Paul Limited employed 2,850 making aircraft in Norwich.

The following companies made aeroengines and other parts for aircraft:

- Arrol-Johnston Cars Limited employed 2,100 women making aeroengines in Paisley.
- Rolls-Royce employed 4,100 making Eagle V12 engines in Derby.
- Siddeley-Deasy Motor Car Company and the Daimler Motor Company employed 11,500 making aeroengines in Coventry.
- W.H. Allen, Sons and Company employed 3,400 staff making aeroengines in Bedford.

- Hoffmann's employed 4,000 making ball bearings in Chelmsford.
- India Rubber, Gutta Percha and Telegraph Works Company employed 3,650 making electrical parts for aircraft in Silverton in London.

Testing and Inspections

To begin with, the RFC's test flight was based at the Central Flying School at Upavon in Wiltshire, before it moved to Martlesham Heath in Suffolk; weapons were tested at nearby Orford Ness on the coast. Once a new model had been tested, a few were sent to France to be tried by experienced pilots. Bulk production did not begin until they were satisfied.

On the outbreak of war, Farnborough focused on flight tests and final inspections to encourage private contractors around London, Bristol and Southampton to work on their models.[7] Farnborough's Inspection Department tried new designs and aeroengines, while the National Physical Laboratory at Teddington did small scale tests in Battersea Park. Contractors were soon asked to test their designs at their own factories.

The Inspection Department moved to London at the end of 1915 and its inspectors visited factories until test centres were opened in Glasgow, Manchester, Coventry and London. The department's Engine Branch checked the suitability of metallic materials, while its Aircraft Branch checked non-metallic ones. They were some of the first offices to employ female staff and before long half of its inspectors were women.

Problems in the Aircraft Industry

A few skilled craftsmen made small number of aircraft before the war. However, the industry expanded rapidly in both size and complexity in a relatively short time, requiring experienced men from the engineering and woodwork trades and women who were new to the work. Fifteen schools had to be opened to teach the many different trades needed to build aircraft.

Aircraft factories needed their own terms and conditions because there were no pre-war rates to base their wages on. For example, some metal parts required skilled workers to beat large sheets into complicated shapes, while others parts required unskilled workers to shape small pieces on a lathe. Meanwhile, woodworking was broken down into simple stages, so unskilled workers could make pieces with jigs and moulds that 'resembled toy making'.

By August 1916, the Special Arbitration Tribunal was recommending wages for the many jobs needed to build an aircraft. The Women's Trade Union Advisory Committee wanted the same rates for women, while Mary Macarthur of the National Federation of Women Workers thought that the aircraft industry was an 'ideal field for testing possible sex antagonism.'[8]

Despite wage increases, many workers felt that they were underpaid compared to those making shells, resulting in stoppages in the spring of 1917. Factories were also seeing their key men called up because their occupations were unprotected. While a minimum wage and weekly hours were eventually set, the industry remained unsettled until the Armistice, by which time 135,000 men and 67,000 women were making aircraft.

Control of Production

Aircraft needed everything from carbon and alloy steel parts for the engine to timber struts, linen, cotton and dope for the wings, to hoses and cables, to petrol and oil. The Inspection Department set up a Chemical Section at University College London, to examine samples of everything in May 1916. The Ministry of Munitions eventually extended its control, to make sure there were enough of everything.

Aircraft needed many small steel parts made from different alloys. The parts had to be precise and it was difficult to make them with the technology available, so many were rejected. The engine crankshaft, which turned the up and down motion of the cylinders in to the rotating movement of the propeller, is just one example. Only small quantities were required, so it was difficult to find contractors willing to make them.

Making Aircraft Engines[9]

The British aircraft industry had only developed two engines when war broke out. However, Green's 60-horsepower engine had insufficient power, while Beardmore's 120-horsepower engine was still being tested. So, two French engines, the 70-horsepower Renault and the 100-horsepower Gnome, were built under license by Rolls-Royce in Derby, the Wolseley Motor Company in Birmingham and the Aircraft Manufacturing Company (Airco) in north London.

Five companies started making the 90-horsepower RAF.1a aeroengine at the beginning of 1915, while over twenty more, many of them car engine manufacturers, became involved over the next two years. Although plenty of engines were being made, the increasing number of models made it difficult to balance the manufacture of the engines with the airframes.

While there were shortages of timber, linen and chemicals, aeroengines were always the limiting factor because they were also needed for transport, tanks and agriculture. The Ministry of Munitions had to set up the Petrol Engine Department to organise their production in January 1917. Even then, there were never enough of either British made or imported models. It took so long to design and test a new model, that by 1917, the Ministry decided to focus on the thirteen existing models and the companies building them.

Pilots favoured Rolls-Royce's 190-horsepower Falcon, which powered the Bristol F.2 fighter, and Rolls-Royce's 200-horsepower Eagle engine, which powered the Handley

Page O/100 bomber. They also liked the imported Hispano-Suiza and Le Rhône aeroengines. Bentley made the BR2 engine, while Beardmore's made the BHP engine; both were 230 horsepower.

While Mitchell and Shaw's built a National Aeroengine Factory in Hayes, poor management forced the Ministry of Munitions to take it over in October 1917. Clement Talbot Limited of Ladbroke Grove in London was asked to repair and make spares and engines for their rival Rolls-Royce but the management lacked interest. So, Rolls-Royce was instructed to take over the factory and the 2,000 workers were soon repairing 600 Eagle aeroengines a month. The Ministry of Munitions took over the Motor Radiator Manufacturing Company's factories at Greet in Birmingham and Sudbury in Suffolk in January 1918, following union opposition to dilution. The Greet factory made bomber radiators, while Sudbury repaired damaged ones.

While relying on a few types of aeroengines helped production, it could cause problems, such as with the Sunbeam Arab and the ABC Dragonfly. Shortages of parts also led to many engines being left incomplete and unfinished planes having to be put in storage. The problem increased when engines had to be sent to France to keep squadrons at full strength.

Producing Metallic Components[10]

Building aircraft required many different components and buys parts became more complicated as aerial warfare became more sophisticated. Eventually aircraft companies had to order what they needed through the Aeronautical Supplies Department.

Only the MEA Magneto Company and the Eisemann Magneto Company of London made the small generators that started the engine, during the early months of the war. Imported American magnetos were unreliable while stocks of German made Bosch ones had run out by the time British companies had worked out how to make reliable ones.

Carburettors controlled the air and petrol mixture to the engine. Only five companies made them until cycling and motoring factories were contracted to the expanding aircraft programme. Before long production had soared from 2,800 to 11,900 a month. Radiators stored the water required to cool the engine and aircraft manufacturers designed them to suit their design. They then subcontracted the work to a specialist motoring radiator firm.

Petrol was stored in a tank and the fear was that even the smallest leak would be fatal, either from fire or a fuel shortage. The Imber fuel tank had a rubber cover that sealed any holes in the tank. The stronger RE.8 design, which appeared in 1918, used a copper casing around a cage of aluminium tubing. Unfortunately, the copper perished the rubber cover, so it was replaced with steel.

Aircraft needed high quality petrol. Initially three-quarters of the supply provide was rejected but improved production methods reduced the amount to virtually zero. The planes also required large amounts of castor oil to lubricate the engines and additives to stop them freezing; 750,000 gallons per month of liquids were being used by the RAF by the end of the war.

The number of companies making propellors increased from five to sixty-eight during the war. It became increasing difficult to get long lengths of walnut and mahogany wood, so Oddy and Cleaver's of Leeds designed a propellor made from smaller lengths spliced together. Propellors were tested at Farnborough until a test-house was opened at Milton in Berkshire.

As aircraft became more complicated, pilots required more instruments, such as altimeters, airspeed indicators, bombsights and pressure gauges to help them fly. They were researched at the National Physical Laboratory and tested at the Royal Aircraft Factory before contracts were awarded. The central store at the Royal Aircraft Factory started assembling instrument kits for each plane and the number increased from 300 a month in 1916 to 6,000 by the end of the war.

Crafting Non-Metallic Components[11]

Most of the wood used to make aircraft was imported and the silver spruce, used in the wings, came from the United States and Canada. Later designs used short spars spliced together, which made the wood easier to source. Walnut wood from the United States and mahogany from British Honduras and Nigeria were used to make the propellers. The airframes required plywood and shaped birch veneers were stuck together with casein cement.

The Ministry of Munitions financed two wood kilns in 1918 to supplement the small number of private ones around the country. The Great Western Railway built one in Swindon in Wiltshire, while the London Brighton and South Coast Railway built the other at Worthing in West Sussex. Between them, they cured 24,000 cubic feet of British ash timber during the final months of the war.

Courtrai flax from Belgium was used to make aircraft fabric until it ran out in 1916. The Ministry of Munitions then took over the Irish flax crop, while a Flax Control Board took control of the country's mills and factories. Irish linen fabric was used until English and Scottish manufacturers were taught how to make plain fabric. The Ministry of Munitions stopped fabric being used for anything else in the spring of 1918 and 60 million yards of cloth had been used by the aircraft industry by the end of the war.

Tests early in 1918 proved that the linen made in Lancashire's cotton mills could be used on training planes. Dope was a lacquer painted onto the fabric to stiffen it up, prevent sagging and stop air passing through. A coloured varnish was added later to stop sunlight weathering the fabric.

A lot of canvas was required to make the hangars to keep planes safe from the weather. The structures became larger as the number of planes increased and soon fifty frames a week were being made to designs by Gaston Hervieu and Julien Bessonneau. Eventually, over 10 million square yards of canvas had been used to make hangars the end of the war.

Arming the Fighters[12]

While aircraft were unarmed during the early days of the war, pilots soon had a desire to use weapons. Pilots used pistols while observers used rifles, either to protect themselves or to attack observation balloons. Both the Admiralty and the War Office requisitioned machine guns for their aircraft until the Ministry of Munitions took over production of Vickers and Lewis guns.

The Lewis gun was popular because it was light and the Mark II drum magazine, with ninety-seven rounds was specially designed for planes.[13] Initially, they were placed on a William Foster mount on the top wing or on pusher planes (where the engine faced backwards) because it could not shoot though the nose propeller. They were eventually mounted on a Scarff ring, so the observer could rotate and elevate the gun with ease.

The Vickers machine gun was used on single seater fighter planes. It was used with Constantinesco and Colley interrupter gear, which used a piped oil pressure system to synchronise the trigger with the spinning propellor. While the gun was belt fed, aircraft models used William de Courcy Prideaux's disintegrating link system, so the cartridges separated as soon as they had been fired.

The use of machine guns with interrupter gear on aircraft required a higher quality of bullets than usual because misfires were dangerous. So, bullets were checked carefully before they were labelled green. Specially made bullets were soon being made and they were labelled red. By the end of the war, 9.5 million red label bullets a month were being made.

The RFC soon wanted tracer and incendiary ammunition, particularly to use against observation balloons and Zeppelins.[14] Aerators Limited invented the SPK Mark VIIT bullet, known as the Sparklet, which was adopted in the summer of 1916. However, they were difficult to make and the phosphorous trace was usually too short to start a fire in the balloons, so they were replaced by the improved SPK Mark VIIG bullet in the summer of 1917.

The Buckingham .303-inch incendiary bullet had a flat nose, which tore through fabric, so the phosphorous trace would set fire to the balloon. The explosive Brock bullet was used by anti-aircraft weapons against Zeppelins but it was again difficult to make. The explosive PSA bullet came next but it failed to detonate when it hit fabric, so it was replaced by the highly sensitive RTS bullet in March 1918. It was both incendiary and explosive and production had soon increased to 900,000 a month.

Arming the Bombers[15]

The next development was bombing and while the first RFC bombers carried 20-pound bombs, RNAS models could carry 112-pound ones. The B.E.2 bomber could carry 224 pounds while the DH.9A carried 460-pounds. The Short bomber entered service in

November 1916 and while it could carry 896 pounds, only a few were made. Far more Handley Page O/100 bombers were made and they could carry 1,792 pounds.

Aerial bombs relied on gravity and cast iron encased bombs were used against personnel. The detonator exploded when the bomb, setting off the bursting charge and scattering the casing as shrapnel. Steel alloy encased bombs were used against railways and buildings and their tail fuse allowed the bomb to burrow into the ground before exploding. Eventually, all bombs were fitted with both types of fuses.

Initially, the Royal Laboratory made a 112-pound bomb and the Cotton Powder Company made the 20-pound Hale bomb, but the Trench Warfare Supply Department took over production in August 1916.[16] A 230-pound bomb and a 180-pound armour piercing bomb appeared when heavy bombers came into service, while the 20-pound Cooper bomb replaced the Hale version.

Petrol bombs and powder bombs had been used to start fires since the early days of the war, while small incendiary bombs were introduced to destroy kite balloons in the summer of 1916. They were soon superseded by incendiary ammunition.

Baby incendiaries were filled with thermite at Roslin's gunpowder factory in Scotland. They were released from a drum and showered an area with burning missiles. A Handley Page 0/100 bomber could carry up to 16,000 tiny incendiaries but there was also a 40-pound version, which scattered burning phosphorous when it hit the ground.

The RNAS used 230-pound and 520-pound alloy cased bombs, which exploded underwater against submarines. Bombs with a strengthened nose which exploded on contact were used against ships.

Aerial bombs were simple to make compared to an artillery shell and the first ones were made by the Ordnance Factory and the Cotton Powder Company in Faversham.[17] However, as demand grew, the Bomb Committee contracted the Thames Ammunition Works in Slades Green and Roburite and Ammonal Limited of Watford to assemble them.

Several cooperatives were organised to make parts:

- 20-pound bombs were made in Walsall.
- 50-pound bombs were made in Edinburgh.
- 112-pound bombs were made in Leeds.

The National Projectile Factory in Lancaster assembled the 230-pound bombs, while Watford's No. 2 Trench Warfare Filling Factory made the 336-pound bombs.

The Royal Arsenal and the Explosives Loading Company were filling bombs until an explosion at Faversham killed 116 on 2 April 1916. The Trench Warfare Supply Department then filled them at its No. 2 Factory in Watford.

A large demand for bombs in 1917 coincided with a shortage of steel, so the 50- and 112-pound versions were given cast iron casings. Surplus trench mortar bombs were then converted into 230-pound bombs. By spring 1918, bombing had become so important that it was made into a priority item. The Gun Ammunition Department took over bomb supply when the Trench Warfare Supply Department was disbanded in June 1918.

The number of aerial bombs being made increased from 7,600 bombs (350 tons) a month in 1916 to 750,000 bombs (7,300 tons) a month in 1918. Huge stocks of bombs were left over at the end of the war.

Airships and Balloons[18]

The Admiralty stopped making airships after HM Airship No. 1 (*Mayfly*) broke up and crashed in 1911. However, it took over the War Office's seven airships on the outbreak of war and three patrolled the Channel when the BEF crossed in August 1914. It soon adopted a small non-rigid airship to protect convoys from submarines and a larger design used for coastal patrols. The Admiralty ordered sixteen rigid and seventy non-rigid airships at the end of 1917 but Beardmore's, Armstrong Whitworth's, Vickers and the Short Brothers had only completed a few when the Armistice was declared.

Kite balloons were used by the BEF for reconnaissance and artillery spotting. The Admiralty let ships tow them, so they could watch for submarines. A modified Belgian design was used until a French Caquot design, which was streamlined with tail fins, was copied in the autumn of 1916. Nurse and Feeder designs were also made.

Originally, three waterproof garments manufacturers made balloons but a dozen more were contracted when extra ones were required to protect London from air raids. The National Balloon Factory was opened at Bohemia Limited, a cinema firm in Finchley in London, at the end of 1917.

Parachutes[19]

The Admiralty was originally responsible for airship parachutes but the Ministry of Munitions' Aircraft Production Department took over responsibility for all parachutes in September 1917. Spencer parachutes were used by the crews of kite balloons but they were too big to be used in aircraft. The smaller Guardian Angel parachute was being tested when the Armistice was declared.

PART VIII

The War Ends

Chapter 39

The Armistice and Demobilisation

Planning for the End of the War[1]

The Ministry of Munitions had to reduce production at the start of 1918 because of a cut in the imports of raw materials and steel, so it tried to limit the effects of reduced work. It estimated that stopping all contracts suddenly would result in 110,000 workers being made redundant and the industrial cities, such as Glasgow, Newcastle, Sheffield and Birmingham, would be hit hardest. It was estimated that some men could be found jobs in steel works and shipyards but there was nothing for the women. They would have to go back home.

The objective was to issue redundancies piecemeal, so as not to be newsworthy. The Ministry started by reducing orders and telling factory managers to cut overtime to avoid unrest. Contracts were ended if there was a housing shortage around the factory, so workers on subsistence could be laid off and sent home.

Women were laid off first, while men who could find work elsewhere went next. Then the bad timekeepers and troublemakers were given their cards. Finally, a last man in and first man out policy was used. A slow release of workers meant that press interest in redundancies dwindled, especially as news of the Allied offensives started to dominate the news.

A Reconstruction Committee had been appointed in the spring of 1917 to consider how to close the munitions industry down when the war ended. The Munitions Council's Committee on Demobilisation and Reconstruction started studying the problem in November 1917. The Civil War Workers' Committee and the Labour Resettlement Committee became involved in the summer of 1918. Between them, they estimated that 2.2 million men and 878,000 women would be affected when the war ended and many would lose their jobs quickly.

The two committees also had to consider how to deal with the tens of thousands of returning soldiers, many of whom would be looking to return to their old jobs. As the final battles were fought, the Demobilisation Cabinet Committee started coordinating the work of all the Ministry of Munitions' committees, as they considered how to stop the production of munitions.

Stopping Work[2]

The Ministry of Munitions started making provisional plans for what should be done regarding munitions production when the war ended as early as 1916. It introduced termination clauses to continuous contracts and 'war break' clauses to any longer than three months.

The Ministry's initial plan was for factories to continue at full production for two weeks after the war ended, to give them time to complete their orders. They would then shut down their machines one by one. Some workers would clear up the factory, while the Ministry paid the wages of those leaving. It would also take possession of any leftover materials and components at cost.

In November 1917, the Demobilisation and Reconstruction Committee told its supply departments to prepare shut down instructions in case the war ended suddenly. It asked all the munitions factories to do the same in February 1918 and asked how long they required to stop work:

- Shell factories needed five weeks.
- Explosives factories wanted eight weeks.
- Aircraft factories required twelve weeks.

In July 1918, the Ministry of Munitions decided that it would be cheaper just to stop all work as soon as the war ended.[3] Contracts would immediately stop and companies would be compensated for their costs. The Munitions Contracts Board started planning for the end of production after the Allies broke through the Hindenburg Line at the end of September 1918. The Demobilisation and Reconstruction Committee then took over planning just before the Armistice was declared on 11 November 1918.

Special notices told companies to stop work and the Ministry assessed their claims for compensation, while letting them buy any materials left over. The Board of Managements dealt with outstanding invoices, made the payments, disposed of any surplus materials and then disbanded. It left over 555,000 tons of filled shells and huge quantities of other weapons and ammunition in the stores.

The Minister of Reconstruction considered replacing the Ministry of Munitions with the Ministry of Supply after the war. The Right Honourable Andrew Weir, Lord Inverforth MP, was appointed Minister of Munitions and Supplies, while Winston Churchill was replaced by The Right Honourable Alfred Milner, 1st Viscount Milner MP, as Secretary of State for War in January 1919. Around 80 per cent of the 21,700 munitions contracts had been terminated by the end of January 1919. The rest had ended by the time the Ministry closed its doors on 21 March 1921.

After starting with an emergency business solution in the summer of 1915, the Ministry of Munitions had caught up with the demands of Britain's armed forces by the end of 1916. It made sure that the Royal Navy could control the High Seas, while the BEF and RFC (later RAF) played their part in many difficult campaigns, culminating in the Advance to Victory in the summer and autumn of 1918. It also saw to it that Britain's allies were supplied with the munitions they needed.

Leaving Work[4]

Anyone who wanted to leave their job when the Armistice was declared on 11 November 1918 was allowed to go immediately. The War Munitions Volunteers were released just three days later, while the Army Reserve Munitions Workers were released on 25 November 1918. The rest of the workforce were put on two weeks' notice, as hours were reduced and factories started to shut down. Joint Industrial Councils found out what other work was available, while Labour Exchanges helped place workers. However, a suggestion to grant all munition workers a month's holiday pay, as a reward, was rejected. Instead, they would be entitled to up to thirteen weeks unemployment benefit.

Around 725,000 munitions workers had been given their cards by mid-January 1919 but nearly half the men soon found work, often in their old jobs. Meanwhile, all the female workers were made redundant, as agreed with the trade unions. They had stepped forward when the country needed them and now, they were no longer required. However, they had experienced life outside the family home and had proved that they could find a job and pay their own bills. The war had left women with an awareness that would affect the nation's working and social life.

The war had also furthered the cause of suffrage. Parliament had granted the vote to around 8.5 million women on 6 February 1918. However, it only included women over 30 who were registered property owners (or their husband was) or were university graduates. In other words, most of the women who had worked in the munitions factories were too young or too poor to be allowed to vote. They would have to wait another ten years until the Representation of the People Act, allowed all women over 21 to vote in July 1928.

Reinstating Pre-War Practices and Stabilising Wages[5]

A restoration of trade union customs and practices when the war ended had been promised by the Munitions of War Act back in July 1915. While plans were discussed on how to reinstate them in the autumn of 1918, everyone acknowledged that industrial relations had changed during the war, so a Bill to restore them was postponed.

Two days after the Armistice, Prime Minister David Lloyd Geroge and his ministers met with the employers' associations and trade unions. The government stood by its pledge, while the rest agreed to meet to discuss terms and conditions. They all also approved of maintaining wages at the current rate for six months, due to the high cost of living.

The Wages Temporary Regulation Bill ended compulsory arbitration for most problems but it would continue to be used to determine wage rates. The right to lock out or strike was also restored. While resuming union customs and practices took time to adjust to, legislation confirming they had been reinstated was passed in August 1919. A lot had been worked out but there was still a lot to discuss before the nation's industry settled down to the conditions of a post-war world.

Bibliography

Books

Arnot, R. Page, *A History of the Miners' Federation of Great Britain from 1910 Onwards* (George Allen & Unwin Limited, United Kingdom, 1952)

Pratt, Edwin A., *British Railways and the Great War: Organisation, Efforts, Difficulties and Achievements*, Volume I (Selwyn and Blount Limited, London, 1921) (Republished by Naval & Institute Press, Maryland, United States, 2020)

Thomas, Roger D. and Patterson, Brian, *Dreadnoughts: A Photographic History* (The History Press, Cheltenham, 2010)

Ministry of Munitions
Volume I, Industrial Mobilisation (His Majesty's Stationary Office)
Volume II, General Mobilisation (His Majesty's Stationary Office)
Volume III, Finance and Contracts (His Majesty's Stationary Office)
Volume IV, Supply and Control of Labour (His Majesty's Stationary Office)
Volume V, Wages and Welfare (His Majesty's Stationary Office)
Volume VI, Manpower and Dilution (His Majesty's Stationary Office)
Volume VII, Control of Materials (His Majesty's Stationary Office)
Volume VIII, Industrial Capacity and Equipment (His Majesty's Stationary Office)
Volume IX, Review of Munitions Supply (His Majesty's Stationary Office)
Volume X, Supply of Munitions (His Majesty's Stationary Office)
Volume XI, Supply of Munitions (His Majesty's Stationary Office)
Volume XII, Supply of Munitions (His Majesty's Stationary Office)

Websites

https://www.archive.org
https://www.gracesguide.co.uk
https://www.naval-history.net

Notes

Part I: Going to War

Chapter 1: Mobilisation
1. *The Miners: Years of Struggle*, R. Page Arnot, pp.57–59
2. *The Miners: Years of Struggle*, R. Page Arnot, pp.59–77
3. *The Miners: Years of Struggle*, R. Page Arnot, pp.78–101
4. *The Miners: Years of Struggle*, R. Page Arnot, pp.101–108
5. *The Miners: Years of Struggle*, R. Page Arnot, pp.108–110
6. *The Miners: Years of Struggle*, R. Page Arnot, pp.115–122
7. *The Miners: Years of Struggle*, R. Page Arnot, pp.173–181
8. *Ministry of Munitions*, Volume VIII, Part I, pp.1–32 and *Ministry of Munitions*, Volume VIII, Part II, pp.3–41
9. *Ministry of Munitions*, Volume VIII, Part II, pp.38–41
10. *Ministry of Munitions*, Volume I, Part I, pp.46–71
11. *Ministry of Munitions*, Volume I, Part I, pp.72–92
12. *Ministry of Munitions*, Volume I, Part I, pp.7–45
13. *Ministry of Munitions*, Volume I, Part I, pp.93–112

Chapter 2: Trouble Ahead
1. *Ministry of Munitions*, Volume I, Part I, pp.113–136
2. *Ministry of Munitions*, Volume I, Part II, pp.1–29
3. *Ministry of Munitions*, Volume I, Part II, pp.30–56
4. *Ministry of Munitions*, Volume I, Part II, pp.57–80
5. *Ministry of Munitions*, Volume III, Part III, pp.30–52
6. *Ministry of Munitions*, Volume I, Part II, pp.81–101
7. *Ministry of Munitions*, Volume I, Part III, pp.18–36
8. *Ministry of Munitions*, Volume II, Part II, pp.120–130
9. *Ministry of Munitions*, Volume I, Part III, pp.1–17
10. *Ministry of Munitions*, Volume I, Part III, pp.37–60
11. *Ministry of Munitions*, Volume I, Part III, pp.61–76
12. *Ministry of Munitions*, Volume I, Part III, pp.77–99

Part II: Organising and Industry

Chapter 3: The Administration
1. *Ministry of Munitions*, Volume II, Part I, pp.187–237
2. *Ministry of Munitions*, Volume II, Part I, pp.107–150

Chapter 4: The Ministers
1. *Ministry of Munitions*, Volume I, Part IV, pp.1–53
2. *Ministry of Munitions*, Volume II, Part I, pp.3–46 and *Ministry of Munitions*, Volume II, Part I, pp.151–159
3. *Ministry of Munitions*, Volume II, Part I, pp.47–74 and *Ministry of Munitions*, Volume II, Part I, pp.160–167
4. *Ministry of Munitions*, Volume II, Part I, pp.47–74 and *Ministry of Munitions*, Volume II, Part I, pp.168–173
5. *Ministry of Munitions*, Volume II, Part I, pp.75–106 and *Ministry of Munitions*, Volume II, Part I, pp.174–186
6. *Ministry of Munitions*, Volume III, Part I, pp.1–27

Chapter 5: Financing the Munitions Industry
1. *Ministry of Munitions*, Volume III, Part I, pp.28–47
2. *Ministry of Munitions*, Volume III, Part I, pp.48–92
3. *Ministry of Munitions*, Volume III, Part I, pp.131–156
4. *Ministry of Munitions*, Volume III, Part III, pp.81–111
5. *Ministry of Munitions*, Volume III, Part I, pp.93–130
6. *Ministry of Munitions*, Volume III, Part II, pp.1–15
7. *Ministry of Munitions*, Volume III, Part III, pp.1–30
8. *Ministry of Munitions*, Volume III, Part II, pp.16–35
9. *Ministry of Munitions*, Volume III, Part II, pp.36–63
10. *Ministry of Munitions*, Volume III, Part II, pp.64–111

Chapter 6: Commercial Control
1. *Ministry of Munitions*, Volume III, Part III, pp.53–80 and Volume VII, Part I, pp.1–13
2. *Ministry of Munitions*, Volume VII, Part I, pp.14–22
3. *Ministry of Munitions*, Volume VII, Part I, pp.44–71
4. *Ministry of Munitions*, Volume III, Part II, pp.144–160
5. *Ministry of Munitions*, Volume VII, Part I, pp.34–43
6. *Ministry of Munitions*, Volume VII, Part I, pp.22–33
7. *Ministry of Munitions*, Volume VII, Part V, pp.1–16
8. *Ministry of Munitions*, Volume VII, Part V, pp.16–18
9. *Ministry of Munitions*, Volume VII, Part V, pp.34–46
10. *Ministry of Munitions*, Volume IX, Part I, p.19

Chapter 7: Programming Munitions' Output
1. *Ministry of Munitions*, Volume IX, Part I, pp.1–48 and *Ministry of Munitions*, Volume X, Part II, pp.1–30
2. *Ministry of Munitions*, Volume X, Part III, pp.68–78
3. *Ministry of Munitions*, Volume X, Part III, pp.92–114

Chapter 8: Research, Testing and Inspections
1. *Ministry of Munitions*, Volume IX, Part II, pp.1–24
2. *Ministry of Munitions*, Volume VII, Part V, pp.34–46

3. *Ministry of Munitions*, Volume IX, Part II, pp.31–43
4. *Ministry of Munitions*, Volume IX, Part II, pp.68–86
5. *Ministry of Munitions*, Volume IX, Part II, pp.27–29 and 80
6. *Ministry of Munitions*, Volume IX, Part II, pp.87–109
7. *Ministry of Munitions*, Volume IX, Part II, pp.44–55
8. *Ministry of Munitions*, Volume IX, Part II, pp.56–67

Chapter 9: The Railways

1. *Ministry of Munitions*, Volume XII, Part V, pp.1–4
2. *British Railways and the Great War*, Volume I, Edwin A. Pratt, pp.54–119
3. *Ministry of Munitions*, Volume XII, Part V, pp.5–12
4. *Ministry of Munitions*, Volume XII, Part V, pp.18–30
5. *British Railways and the Great War*, Volume I, Edwin A. Pratt, pp.676–719
6. *Ministry of Munitions*, Volume XII, Part IV, pp.41–50
7. *Ministry of Munitions*, Volume XII, Part IV, pp.13–17
8. *Ministry of Munitions*, Volume XII, Part V, pp.31–40
9. *Ministry of Munitions*, Volume VII, Part V, pp.19–33
10. *British Railways and the Great War*, Volume I, Edwin A. Pratt, pp.472
11. *British Railways and the Great War*, Volume I, Edwin A. Pratt, pp.522–533

Part III: The Raw Materials

Chapter 10: The Coal Industry

1. *The Miners: Years of Struggle*, R. Page Arnot, pp.46–51
2. *The Miners: Years of Struggle*, R. Page Arnot, pp.51–54
3. *The Miners: Years of Struggle*, R. Page Arnot, pp.154–164
4. *The Miners: Years of Struggle*, R. Page Arnot, pp.164–170
5. *The Miners: Years of Struggle*, R. Page Arnot, pp.170–173

Chapter 11: Iron and Steel

1. *Ministry of Munitions*, Volume VII, Part II, pp.90–138
2. *Ministry of Munitions*, Volume VII, Part II, pp.1–25
3. *Ministry of Munitions*, Volume VII, Part II, pp.26–44
4. *Ministry of Munitions*, Volume VII, Part II, pp.45–53
5. *Ministry of Munitions*, Volume VII, Part II, pp.86–89
6. *Ministry of Munitions*, Volume VII, Part II, pp.54–67
7. *Ministry of Munitions*, Volume VII, Part II, pp.139–150
8. *Ministry of Munitions*, Volume VII, Part II, pp.66–75
9. *Ministry of Munitions*, Volume VIII, Part IX, pp.225
10. https://www.gracesguide.co.uk/Main_Page, see 1918 Directory of Manufacturers

Chapter 12: Non-Ferrous Metals

1. *Ministry of Munitions*, Volume VII, Part III, pp.1–8
2. *Ministry of Munitions*, Volume VII, Part III, pp.9–20
3. *Ministry of Munitions*, Volume VII, Part III, pp.21–49

4. *Ministry of Munitions*, Volume VII, Part III, pp.50–67
5. *Ministry of Munitions*, Volume VII, Part III, pp.68–88
6. *Ministry of Munitions*, Volume VII, Part III, pp.89–99
7. *Ministry of Munitions*, Volume VII, Part III, pp.100–108
8. *Ministry of Munitions*, Volume VII, Part II, pp.76–89
9. *Ministry of Munitions*, Volume VII, Part V, pp.47–62 and *Ministry of Munitions*, Volume VIII, Part IX, pp.216–221
10. *Ministry of Munitions*, Volume VII, Part III, pp.134–156

Chapter 13: The Explosives Industry

1. *Ministry of Munitions*, Volume VII, Part IV, pp.1–10
2. *Ministry of Munitions*, Volume X, Part IV, pp.1–21
3. *Ministry of Munitions*, Volume VIII, Part II, pp.42–86
4. *Ministry of Munitions*, Volume X, Part IV, pp.38–53
5. *Ministry of Munitions*, Volume VII, Part IV: 65–87 and *Ministry of Munitions*, Volume X, Part IV, pp.92–115
6. *Ministry of Munitions*, Volume X, Part IV, pp.2–4 and 100–112
7. *Ministry of Munitions*, Volume X., Part IV, pp.116–119
8. *Ministry of Munitions*, Volume VII, Part IV, pp.11–34
9. *Ministry of Munitions*, Volume X, Part IV, pp.22–37
10. *Ministry of Munitions*, Volume VII, Part IV, pp.35–64
11. *Ministry of Munitions*, Volume X, Part IV, pp.60–62
12. *Ministry of Munitions*, Volume X, Part IV, pp.54–60
13. *Ministry of Munitions*, Volume X, Part IV, pp.59–62
14. *Ministry of Munitions*, Volume X, Part IV, pp.77–91
15. *Ministry of Munitions*, Volume X, Part IV, pp.120–126

Chapter 14: The Chemical Industry

1. *Ministry of Munitions*, Volume XI, Part II, pp.12–26 and 29–32
2. *Ministry of Munitions*, Volume VIII, Part IX, p.226
3. *Ministry of Munitions*, Volume XI, Part II, pp.27–29
4. *Ministry of Munitions*, Volume XI, Part II, p.39
5. *Ministry of Munitions*, Volume XI, Part II, pp.33–39
6. *Ministry of Munitions*, Volume XI, Part II, pp.41–44
7. *Ministry of Munitions*, Volume XI, Part II, pp.47–48
8. *Ministry of Munitions*, Volume XI, Part II, p.40
9. *Ministry of Munitions*, Volume XI, Part II, pp.45–46
10. *Ministry of Munitions*, Volume XI, Part II, pp.52–54
11. *Ministry of Munitions*, Volume XI, Part II, pp.48–52
12. *Ministry of Munitions*, Volume XI, Part II, pp.34–36
13. *Ministry of Munitions*, Volume XI, Part II, pp.1–11
14. *Ministry of Munitions*, Volume XI, Part II, pp.54–55
15. *Ministry of Munitions*, Volume XI, Part II, pp.1–10
16. *Ministry of Munitions*, Volume XI, Part II, pp.58–64
17. *Ministry of Munitions*, Volume XI, Part II, pp.65–81
18. *Ministry of Munitions*, Volume VIII, Part IX, pp.226

Part IV: The Factories

Chapter 15: The Original Armaments Factory

1. *Ministry of Munitions*, Volume VIII, Part I, pp.1–32 and *Ministry of Munitions*, Volume X, Part V, pp.7–14

Chapter 16: The Ministry Steps In

1. *Ministry of Munitions*, Volume II, Part II, pp.21–28
2. *Ministry of Munitions*, Volume II, Part II, pp.14–20
3. *Ministry of Munitions*, Volume VIII, Part I, pp. 40–47 and 58–72; also *Ministry of Munitions*, Volume X, Part V, pp.15–21
4. *Ministry of Munitions*, Volume VIII, Part IX, pp.225
5. *Ministry of Munitions*, Volume VIII, Part I, pp. 73–83 and *Ministry of Munitions*, Volume X, Part V, pp.22–28
6. *Ministry of Munitions*, Volume X, Part V, pp.29–33
7. *Ministry of Munitions*, Volume X, Part V, pp.34–37

Chapter 17: The National Shell Factories and Cooperative Schemes

1. *Ministry of Munitions*, Volume II, Part II, pp.29–47
2. *Ministry of Munitions*, Volume VIII, Part II, pp.87–123
3. *Ministry of Munitions*, Volume II, Part II, pp.53–59
4. *Ministry of Munitions*, Volume II, Part II, pp.60–78
5. *Ministry of Munitions*, Volume II, Part II, pp.79–92
6. *Ministry of Munitions*, Volume II, Part II, pp.93–118
7. *Ministry of Munitions*, Volume II, Part II, pp.5–13
8. *Ministry of Munitions*, Volume II, Part II, pp.115-119
9. *Ministry of Munitions*, Volume II, Part II, pp.110–115
10. *Ministry of Munitions*, Volume II, Part II, pp.120–130
11. *Ministry of Munitions*, Volume II, Part II, pp.131–147
12. *Ministry of Munitions*, Volume II, Part II, pp.148–150

Chapter 18: The National Projectile Factories

1. Ministry of Munitions, Volume VIII, Part II, pp.124–147

Chapter 19: The National Filling Factories

1. *Ministry of Munitions*, Volume VIII, Part II, pp.148–184
2. *Ministry of Munitions*, Volume VIII, Part I, pp.84–90

Chapter 20: Tools of the Trade

1. *Ministry of Munitions*, Volume VIII, Part III, pp.36–71
2. *Ministry of Munitions*, Volume VIII, Part III, pp.1–35 and Part IX, pp.214–216
3. *Ministry of Munitions*, Volume VIII, Part III, pp.92–107

Chapter 21: American Imports

1. *Ministry of Munitions*, Volume II, Part III, pp.5–14

2. *Ministry of Munitions*, Volume II, Part III, pp.15–42
3. *Ministry of Munitions*, Volume II, Part III, pp.43–58
4. *Ministry of Munitions*, Volume IX, Part II, pp.27–30
5. *Ministry of Munitions*, Volume II, Part III, pp.59–80
6. *Ministry of Munitions*, Volume II, Part III, pp.105–113

Chapter 22: Canadian Imports

1. *Ministry of Munitions*, Volume II, Part IV, pp.1–22
2. *Ministry of Munitions*, Volume II, Part IV, pp.23–34
3. *Ministry of Munitions*, Volume II, Part IV, pp.35–43
4. *Ministry of Munitions*, Volume IX, Part II, pp.28–29
5. *Ministry of Munitions*, Volume II, Part IV, pp.44–55

Chapter 23: Cooperation with the Allies

1. *Ministry of Munitions*, Volume II, Part III, pp.53–79
2. *Ministry of Munitions*, Volume II, Part III, pp.5–27
3. *Ministry of Munitions*, Volume II, Part III, pp.28–52

Part V: The Workforce

Chapter 24: Increasing the Workforce

1. *Ministry of Munitions*, Volume IV, Part III, pp.1–25
2. *Ministry of Munitions*, Volume IV, Part II, pp.1–35
3. *Ministry of Munitions*, Volume IV, Part III, pp.44–47
4. *Ministry of Munitions*, Volume IV, Part II, pp.36–65
5. *Ministry of Munitions*, Volume IV, Part I, pp.17–30 and *Ministry of Munitions*, Volume IV, Part IV, pp.35–57
6. *Ministry of Munitions*, Volume IV, Part I, pp.1–16 and *Ministry of Munitions*, Volume IV, Part IV, pp.23–34
7. *Ministry of Munitions*, Volume IV, Part III, pp.26–55
8. *Ministry of Munitions*, Volume IV, Part II, pp.66–94
9. *Ministry of Munitions*, Volume IV, Part III, pp.56–86

Chapter 25: Agreeing Wages and Hours

10. *Ministry of Munitions*, Volume V, Part I, pp.1–28
11. *Ministry of Munitions*, Volume V, Part I, pp.212–219
12. *Ministry of Munitions*, Volume V, Part I, pp.29–37
13. *Ministry of Munitions*, Volume V, Part I, pp.91–120, 194–204 and 219–237
14. *Ministry of Munitions*, Volume V, Part I, pp.89–90
15. *Ministry of Munitions*, Volume V, Part I, pp.37–42
16. *Ministry of Munitions*, Volume V, Part I, pp.56–59
17. *Ministry of Munitions*, Volume V, Part I, pp.121–166
18. *Ministry of Munitions*, Volume V, Part I, pp.167–193
19. *Ministry of Munitions*, Volume V, Part II, pp.1–15

20. *Ministry of Munitions*, Volume V, Part II, pp.121–145
21. *Ministry of Munitions*, Volume V, Part II, pp.16–37
22. *Ministry of Munitions*, Volume V, Part II, pp.55–76
23. *Ministry of Munitions*, Volume V, Part II, pp.95–114
24. *Ministry of Munitions*, Volume V, Part I, pp.65–86
25. *Ministry of Munitions*, Volume V, Part III, pp.87–106
26. *Ministry of Munitions*, Volume V, Part III, pp.107–134
27. *Ministry of Munitions*, Volume V, Part III, pp.135–156
28. *Ministry of Munitions*, Volume V, Part II, pp.115–120

Chapter 26: Dilution of the Workforce

1. *Ministry of Munitions*, Volume IV, Part IV, pp.1–17
2. *Ministry of Munitions*, Volume IV, Part IV, pp.74–97
3. *Ministry of Munitions*, Volume IV, Part I, pp.31–50
4. *Ministry of Munitions*, Volume IV, Part I, pp.51–93
5. *Ministry of Munitions*, Volume IV, Part IV, pp.98–138
6. *Ministry of Munitions*, Volume IV, Part IV, pp.58–73
7. *Ministry of Munitions*, Volume VI, Part I, pp.1–13
8. *Ministry of Munitions*, Volume VI, Part II, pp.67—91
9. *Ministry of Munitions*, Volume VI, Part I, pp.45–63
10. *Ministry of Munitions*, Volume IV, Part IV, pp.23–34 and *Ministry of Munitions*, Volume VI, Part I, pp.64–67
11. *Ministry of Munitions*, Volume VI, Part I, pp.14–44
12. *Ministry of Munitions*, Volume VI, Part II, pp.72–76
13. *Ministry of Munitions*, Volume VI, Part I, pp.92–121
14. *Ministry of Munitions*, Volume V, Part I, pp.47–55
15. *Ministry of Munitions*, Volume VI, Part II, pp.1–16
16. *Ministry of Munitions*, Volume VI, Part II, pp.22–35
17. *Ministry of Munitions*, Volume VI, Part II, pp.36–55
18. *Ministry of Munitions*, Volume VI, Part II, pp.56–71
19. *Ministry of Munitions*, Volume VI, Part II, pp.72–78

Chapter 27: Welfare Arrangements

1. *Ministry of Munitions*, Volume V, Part III, pp.1–22
2. *Ministry of Munitions*, Volume V, Part III, pp.23–51
3. *Ministry of Munitions*, Volume V, Part III, pp.52–67
4. *Ministry of Munitions*, Volume V, Part III, pp.68–86
5. *Ministry of Munitions*, Volume V, Part IV, pp.1–21
6. *Ministry of Munitions*, Volume V, Part V, pp.3–20
7. *Ministry of Munitions*, Volume V, Part V, pp.41–43
8. *Ministry of Munitions*, Volume V, Part V, pp.33–40
9. *Ministry of Munitions*, Volume V, Part V, pp.44–57
10. *Ministry of Munitions*, Volume V, Part V, pp.21–32
11. *Ministry of Munitions*, Volume V, Part V, pp.68–77
12. *Ministry of Munitions*, Volume V, Part V, pp.58–67

Part VI: The Weapons

Chapter 28: The Artillery
1. *Ministry of Munitions*, Volume X, Part I, pp.6–27
2. *Ministry of Munitions*, Volume X, Part I, pp.28–44
3. *Ministry of Munitions*, Volume X, Part I, pp.80–95
4. *Ministry of Munitions*, Volume X, Part I, pp.45–56
5. *Ministry of Munitions*, Volume X, Part I, pp.57–95
6. *Ministry of Munitions*, Volume VIII, Part II, pp.194–196

Chapter 29: Making the Shells
1. *Ministry of Munitions*, Volume X, Part III, pp.79–91
2. *Ministry of Munitions*, Volume X, Part III, pp.25–43
3. *Ministry of Munitions*, Volume X, Part III, pp.44–54
4. *Ministry of Munitions*, Volume X, Part III, pp.54–67
5. *Ministry of Munitions*, Volume X, Part II, pp.41–63 and Ministry of Munitions Volume X, Part V, pp.29–71
6. *Ministry of Munitions*, Volume X, Part III, pp.1–24
7. *Ministry of Munitions*, Volume X, Part II, pp.30–40
8. *Ministry of Munitions*, Volume X, Part III, pp.92–114 and *Ministry of Munitions*, Volume X, Part III, pp.115–122
9. https://gracesguide.co.uk/Main_Page, *see* 1918 Directory of Manufacturers in Engineering and Allied Trades

Chapter 30: Personal Weapons
1. *Ministry of Munitions*, Volume XI, Part VI, p.26
2. *Ministry of Munitions*, Volume XI, Part IV, pp.1–14
3. *Ministry of Munitions*, Volume XI, Part IV, pp.15–28
4. *Ministry of Munitions*, Volume XI, Part IV, pp.51–54
5. *Ministry of Munitions*, Volume XI, Part IV, pp.41–51
6. *Ministry of Munitions*, Volume XI, Part IV, pp.29–40
7. *Ministry of Munitions*, Volume VIII, Part IX, pp.230–232
8. *Ministry of Munitions*, Volume XI, Part IV, pp.55–67

Chapter 31: Machine Guns
1. *Ministry of Munitions*, Volume XI, Part V, pp.1–8
2. *Ministry of Munitions*, Volume XI, Part V, pp.9–13
3. *Ministry of Munitions*, Volume XI, Part V, pp.13–18
4. *Ministry of Munitions*, Volume XI, Part V, pp.19–25
5. *Ministry of Munitions*, Volume XI, Part V, pp.16–18

Chapter 32: Small Arms Ammunition
1. *Ministry of Munitions*, Volume VIII, Part IX, p.222
2. *Ministry of Munitions*, Volume XI, Part VI, pp.15–18

3. https://gracesguide.co.uk/Main_Page, see 1918 Directory of Manufacturers in Engineering and Allied Trades
4. *Ministry of Munitions*, Volume XI, Part VI, pp.19–34
5. *Ministry of Munitions*, Volume XI, Part VI, pp.4–15
6. *Ministry of Munitions*, Volume XI, Part VI, pp.90–96
7. *Ministry of Munitions*, Volume XI, Part VI, pp.35–44 and *Ministry of Munitions*, Volume XI, Appendices, pp.105–106
8. *Ministry of Munitions*, Volume VIII, Part II, pp.185–193 and *Ministry of Munitions*, Volume XI, Part VI, pp.51–69
9. https://gracesguide.co.uk/Main_Page, see 1918 Directory of Manufacturers in Engineering and Allied Trades
10. *Ministry of Munitions*, Volume VIII, Part I, pp.48–49
11. *Ministry of Munitions*, Volume XI, Part VI, pp.70–77

Chapter 33: Trench Warfare Weapons

1. *Ministry of Munitions*, Volume XI, Part I, pp.6–33
2. *Ministry of Munitions*, Volume XI, Part I, pp.72–90
3. *Ministry of Munitions*, Volume XI, Part II, pp.82–91
4. *Ministry of Munitions*, Volume XI, Part I, pp.34–71
5. *Ministry of Munitions*, Volume XI, Part I, pp.121–129
6. *Ministry of Munitions*, Volume XI, Part I, pp.91–100
7. *Ministry of Munitions*, Volume XI, Part I, pp.100–104

Chapter 34: Optical Munitions

1. *Ministry of Munitions*, Volume XI, Part III, pp.8–44
2. *Ministry of Munitions*, Volume XI, Part III, pp.1–7
3. *Ministry of Munitions*, Volume VIII, Part IX, pp.223–225
4. *Ministry of Munitions*, Volume XI, Part III, pp.71–90
5. *Ministry of Munitions*, Volume XI, Part III, pp.91–115

Part VII: Mechanised Warfare

Chapter 35: Shipbuilding

1. *Dreadnoughts: A Photographic History*, Roger D. Thomas and Brian Patterson, pp.5–15
2. *Dreadnoughts: A Photographic History*, Roger D. Thomas and Brian Patterson, pp.26–35
3. *Dreadnoughts: A Photographic History*, Roger D. Thomas and Brian Patterson, pp.52–93
4. *Dreadnoughts: A Photographic History*, Roger D. Thomas and Brian Patterson, pp.94–97
5. *Dreadnoughts: A Photographic History*, Roger D. Thomas and Brian Patterson, pp.148–151
6. https://www.naval-history.net/WW1NavyBritish-Shipbuild03.htm#3
7. https://www.naval-history.net/WW1NavyBritish-Shipbuild02.htm
8. *British Shipbuilding Yards*, Volume 2, Norman L. Middlemiss, (Shield Publications, 1994)
9. *British Shipbuilding Yards*, Volume 1, Norman L. Middlemiss, (Shield Publications, 1993)
10. *British Shipbuilding Yards*, Volume 3, Norman L. Middlemiss, (Shield Publications, 1995)
11. https://www.naval-history.net/WW1NavyBritish-Shipbuild01.htm
12. Ministry of Munitions, Volume VIII, Part IX, pp.221–222

Chapter 36: Tanks

1. *Ministry of Munitions*, Volume XII, Part III, pp.1–16
2. *Ministry of Munitions*, Volume XII, Part III, pp.17–31
3. *Ministry of Munitions*, Volume XII, Part III, pp.32–44
4. *Ministry of Munitions*, Volume XII, Part III, pp.45–56
5. *Ministry of Munitions*, Volume XII, Part III, pp.59–70
6. *Ministry of Munitions*, Volume XII, Part III, pp.57

Chapter 37: Lorries, Cars and Motorcycles

1. *Ministry of Munitions*, Volume XII, Part IV, pp.1–6
2. *Ministry of Munitions*, Volume XII, Part IV, pp.7–12
3. *Ministry of Munitions*, Volume XII, Part IV, pp.13–33
4. *Ministry of Munitions*, Volume XII, Part IV, pp.34–47
5. *Ministry of Munitions*, Volume VIII, Part III, pp.72–91
6. https://www.gracesguide.co.uk/Main_Page, see 1918 Directory of Manufacturers

Chapter 38: The Aircraft Industry

1. *Ministry of Munitions*, Volume XII, Part I, pp.1–38
2. *Ministry of Munitions*, Volume XII, Part I, pp.39–59
3. *Ministry of Munitions*, Volume XII, Part I, pp.60–99
4. *Ministry of Munitions*, Volume XII, Part I, pp.155–164
5. *Ministry of Munitions*, Volume VIII, Part II, pp.197–213
6. https:///www.gracesguide.co.uk/Main_Page, see 1918 Directory of Manufacturers
7. *Ministry of Munitions*, Volume VIII, Part II, pp.38–41
8. *Ministry of Munitions*, Volume V, Part II, pp.89–95
9. *Ministry of Munitions*, Volume XII, Part I, pp.75–80 and 100–105
10. *Ministry of Munitions*, Volume XII, Part I, pp.106–122
11. *Ministry of Munitions*, Volume XII, Part I, pp.123–146
12. *Ministry of Munitions*, Volume XI, Part V, pp.2 and 4
13. *Ministry of Munitions*, Volume XI, Part V, pp.6–7
14. *Ministry of Munitions*, Volume XI, Part VI, pp.29
15. *Ministry of Munitions*, Volume XII, Part II, pp.1–9
16. *Ministry of Munitions*, Volume XII, Part II, pp.10–18
17. *Ministry of Munitions*, Volume XII, Part II, pp.19–29
18. *Ministry of Munitions*, Volume XII, Part I, pp.147–154
19. *Ministry of Munitions*, Volume XII, Part I, pp.154

Part VIII: The War Ends

Chapter 39: The Armistice and Demobilisation

1. *Ministry of Munitions*, Volume VI, Part II, pp.77–83
2. *Ministry of Munitions*, Volume III, Part II, pp.112–143
3. *Ministry of Munitions*, Volume II, Part I, Supplement, pp.1–43
4. *Ministry of Munitions*, Volume III, Part II, pp.84–88
5. *Ministry of Munitions*, Volume VI, Part II, pp.89–9

Index

A and B Areas 14
A and B Factories 10
acids 83-4
Acquisition of Land Act 1916 102
Addison, The Right Honourable Dr Christopher, MP 27-8, 169
Admiralty 40, 46, 50, 60, 68, 69, 83, 93, 106, 127, 148
  aircraft 6, 236, 243, 245
  labour 9, 141-2, 157, 165, 190, 217
  mines 86, 119, 121, 223
  ship design 217-20
  supplies 70, 76, 77, 82, 99, 120, 128, 129
  transport 231, 232
  weapons 196, 200, 201, 203, 209
Advance to Victory, July to November 58
Advisory Committee 12, 27
Aeronautical Supplies Department 236, 241
aircraft
  bombs 243-4
  fabric supply 242
  inspection 239
  numbers made 237
  production 240
  testing 239
  supply 235-7
  types 235, 240, 241
  weapons 243
  wood supply 242
Aircraft Manufacturing Company (Airco), London 238
Air Board 237
Air Department, Admiralty 236
Air Group 237
airships 6, 82, 236, 245
Aisne, River 7
Albion Motors, Glasgow 233
alcohol 176
Algeria 42
Allen, Sons and Company, W.H., Bedford 238
Alliance Aircraft Company, Oldham 238
Allied Maritime Transport Council 41, 42, 137
Allocation of Urgent Supplies Board 43
aluminium 73, 74-5
Amalgamated Society of Engineers (ASE) 10, 12, 144, 163, 167, 168, 169, 171
amatol 85, 86, 87, 88, 118, 119, 192, 208
American Expeditionary Force (AEF) 42, 57
ammonium nitrate factories 86-7
ammunition, tracer 243
Anglo-Persian Oil Company 76
Anti-Gas Department 91, 96
Ardol Limited, Selby 92, 95, 210
Arisaka rifles (Japanese) 196, 204
Armaments Output Committee 13, 14, 25, 107, 111, 145, 188
Armistice 20, 29, 41, 47, 87, 121, 137, 171, 174, 194, 229, 234, 238, 240, 245, 250, 251
armour piercing ammunition 205

Armstrong Whitworth's, Newcastle-upon-Tyne 6, 12, 13, 35, 51, 106, 108, 114, 120, 145, 155, 179, 183, 185, 186, 187, 192, 193, 209, 217, 218, 221, 223, 225, 226, 228, 245
Army Council 6, 10, 46, 31, 40, 45, 127, 145, 188, 189, 192, 201, 225, 226, 227
Army Reserve Munition Workers' Substitution Scheme 165-6, 167, 251
Arnold, Professor Oliver 123
Arrol-Johnston Cars Limited, Paisley 238
Asiatic Petroleum Company, Queensferry 85
Asquith, The Right Ho. Herbert, MP 4, 7, 10, 25, 27, 29, 32, 151, 163, 166
Associated Equipment Company (AEC), London 234
Aubers Ridge, battle (9 May 1915) 25
Austin Motor Company, Birmingham 178, 233
Austria-Hungary 28, 41
Australia 74, 75, 88, 92
A.V. Roe and Company, Manchester 238
Averys, Birmingham 238

Babcock and Wilcox, Renfrew 187
Badge Committee 150
Bagley's, London 85
Baldwins Limited, Swansea 71
Ball Bearings Branch 233
balloons 236, 238, 243, 244, 245
Baltic Sea 68
Barclay, Curle and Company, Scotstoun 221
Barr and Stroud Limited, Glasgow 221
Beardmore and Company, William 6, 164, 188, 238
Beardmore, John 164
BEF, see British Expeditionary Force
Bell Brothers, Middlesbrough 71
Belsize Motors, Manchester 233
benzol 69, 80, 84, 135
Bessemer steel 188
Bethlehem Steel Corporation, Pennsylvania 183, 187
Berwick and Company, F.W., London 234
Beyer, Peacock and Company, Manchester 193
Billeting of Civilians Act 1917 20
binoculars 213
Birmingham Railway Carriage Wagon and Finance Company 233
Birmingham Small Arms Company (BSA) 195, 196, 197, 200
Board of Invention and Research 220
Birmingham Metal and Munitions 203
Board of Trade 10, 13, 15, 22, 25, 41, 51, 64, 77, 142, 148, 151, 166, 187
Boards of Management, areas 15, 101, 102, 105, 117, 124, 188, 189, 192, 107
  Area 1 Office: North East England 106
  Area 2 Office: North West England and North Wales 106-7
  Area 3 Office: Yorkshire and Lincolnshire 107-108
  Area 4 Office: The English Midlands 108-109
  Area 5 Office: South Wales 109-10

Area 6 Office: South West England
Area 7A and 7B Offices: London 110-11
Area 8 and 8 Offices: Scotland 111-12
Area 10 and 11 Offices: Ireland 112
Bolckow, Vaughan and Company 58, 71
Boer War, Second 45
Black List 41, 146, 147
Blake Explosives Loading Company, Fulham 210
bleach 94
Bliss, E.W. Company 188
Booth, George 14
Boulogne Conference (June 1915) 184
Boulton and Paul Limited, Norwich 238
Brand, Robert 131
Bragley's, London 79
brass 74, 75, 191, 192, 205
Brazil 68, 196
British Army x, 43, 45, 79, 82, 96, 99, 166, 184, 188, 195, 196, 231, 232, 234
British and Colonial Aircraft Company, Bristol 238
British and Foreign Supply Association 81
British Dyes Limited, Huddersfield 83
British Expeditionary Force (BEF) ix, x, 5, 7, 25, 26, 27, 28, 45, 53, 57, 58, 76, 92, 110, 164, 165, 169, 171, 184, 189, 191, 195, 196, 199, 200, 204, 209, 210, 214, 225, 228, 231, 232, 245, 251
British Guiana 74
British Gun Barrel Company Works 197
British Insulated and Helsby Cables, Prescot 193
British Mannesmann Tubes, Swansea
British Tanker Company 77
British Thomson-Houston Company 13, 109
British War Mission 129
British Westfalite, Denaby 86
British Westinghouse, Manchester 57
broken squads 11
Brotherton and Company, Leeds and Liverpool 79, 86
Brown's, John, Sheffield and Clydebank 71, 108
Brunner Mond and Company, Northwich 84, 85, 86, 88
Brush Electrical Engineering Company, Loughborough 234
Building Works Department 99
Bullecourt, battle of (April 1917) 227
bullets 203-205
Burmah Shell Company 76
Byng, General Julian 225

Cabinet Committee on Munitions 7
Calais Conference (July 1915) 7
Cambridge Scientific Instrument Company 192
Cammell Laird, Birkenhead 6, 71, 108, 115, 131, 183, 186, 188, 217, 218, 222, 225
Canada 135, 137
    exports from 133
    importing from 26, 41, 57, 58, 74, 80, 84, 117, 132, 189, 190, 191, 197, 204, 242
    industry 131, 187, 188
    inspection of goods from 20, 52, 70, 124
Canadian Expeditionary Force (CEF) 196
Canadian Explosives Company, Ontario 131
Canadian Explosives Limited 87
Canadian Inspection Department 52
Canadian munitions, importing 132-3
Canadian Shell Committee 131
canary girls 175
canteens 176
Caporetto, battle of (November 1917) 70, 136
Cardiff Channel Dry Dock, Cardiff 222

Cargo Fleet Iron Company, Middlesbrough 71
Carron Company, Falkirk 71, 74
cars, motor 231-4
Cassel Cyanide Company, Glasgow 92
Castner-Kellner Company, Runcorn 92, 93, 94
castor oil 241-2
catapults 211
Central Advisory Committee 26
Central Billeting Board 177
Central Bond areas 52
Central Clearing House 16, 123, 124
Central Flying School 239
Central Munitions Labour Supply Committee 155, 156, 162
Central Munitions Stores 44
Central Statistical Conference 47
Chamberlain, The Right Honourable Neville, MP 28, 164, 167
Chance Brothers and Company, Birmingham 213
Chance and Hunt Limited, Oldbury 80, 83, 85, 93
Chancellor of the Exchequer 6, 12, 14, 25, 32
Chapman and Sons, James, London 195
Chatham Royal Dockyard, Kent 219
Chief Inspector of Small Arms 50
Chief Inspector, Royal Arsenal 50
Chief Superintendent of Ordnance Factories 50
Chemical Advisory Committee 91
Chemical Products Company, St Helens 84
Chemical Warfare Committee 54, 91
Chile 80, 83, 87
Chislehurst caves 6
chlorine gas 92
chloropicrin gas 84, 93, 94, 95, 96
Churchill, The Right Honourable Winston, MP
    First Sea Lord of the Admiralty 25, 29
    Minister of Munitions 3, 4, 20, 28-9, 33, 65, 70, 154, 155, 169, 171, 185, 250
Circular L.2 155, 156
Circular L.3 40, 152, 153
Civil War Workers' Committee 249
Clayton Aniline Company, Manchester 79, 83
Clayton and Shuttleworth's and Robey's, Lincoln 238
clean cut 29, 166-7, 170
Clement Talbot Limited, London 241
Cleveland Ironmasters' Association 106
Clyde Dilution Committee 164
Clyde Shipbuilding and Engineering Company, Port Glasgow 220
Clyde shipyards x, 111, 163, 164, 168, 171, 177, 220, 221
Clyde stoppages 144-5
Coal Controller 56, 64, 65
coal gas 77
coal industry 63-5
Coal Mines Act (1911) 63
coal tar 77
Cochrane and Company, Middlesbrough 71
coke 68, 69, 83
Coley and Wilbraham Limited 84
Colt Manufacturing Company 199
Colville and Sons, David, Glasgow 71
Committee of the Cabinet on Reconstruction 27
compasses 213
Component Munitions Company, Birmingham 194
contracts, awarding
    American 128-9, 131, 132
    British 34-6, 39-40, 41, 45-6, 50
    Canadian 132
controlled factories 11-12, 32, 143, 152, 154, 155, 163, 176, 178
convoys, shipping 43, 245

copper 40, 42, 73, 74, 75, 76, 109, 191, 241
cordite 7, 46, 73, 79-82, 87, 89, 118, 157, 178
cost of living 13, 28, 36, 65, 143, 144, 151, 152, 153, 156, 159, 168, 170, 217, 251
Constantinesco and Colley 243
Cotton Powder Company, Faversham 208, 244
Coventry 29, 51, 52, 109, 117, 121, 168, 170, 171, 178, 200, 203, 204, 225, 233-4, 238, 239
Crossley Brothers, Manchester 233, 237
Cubitt and Company, William, London 238
Cunard Steamship Company, Liverpool 237

Daimler Company, Coventry 225, 238
Danish Recoil Rifle Syndicate 201
Dardanelles Strait x, 38
Dayfield body protector 212
Denny and Brothers, William, Dumbarton 220
Defence of the Realm Act (1914) 7, 11, 12, 13, 19, 35, 39, 67, 79, 84, 161, 176, 177, 210
Demobilisation and Reconstruction Committee 249, 250
Department of Area Organisation 101
Department of the Master-General of Ordnance 6, 10, 45
Department of the Quartermaster General 6
Derby Scheme, for recruitment 147-8
detonators 79, 82-83, 208, 244
Devonport Royal Dockyard, Devon 219
Diamond Match Company 127
Dick, Kerr and Company, Preston 57, 125, 183, 187
dilution 161-4
Director General of Munitions Inspection 51
Director General of National Service 28, 167
Director of Army Contracts 6
Director of Artillery 49, 209
Director of Experiments and Research 220
Director of Fortifications and Works 49
Director of Naval Construction 220
Director of Naval Ordnance 49
Directorate of Scientific Research and Experiment 220
Directorate of Transport and Movement 55, 57
Dobson and Barlow, Bolton 193
Dock Battalions 43
Dominion Arsenal, Quebec 131
Dominion Cartridge Company, Quebec 131
Dorman Long and Company, Middlesbrough 71
Dowlais Ironworks 58
Doxford and Sons Limited, William, Sunderland 221
Du Cros Limited, W. and G., London 194
Dumas, Robert 13, 109
Dunlop Rubber Company, Birmingham 233
DuPont de Nemours and Company, Delaware 87
Dutch East Indies 75, 76

Early Wage Discussions 151
Ebbw Vale Steel, Iron and Coal Company, Ebbw Vale 71
Efficiency Branch 37
Eight Hours Act 4
Eisemann Magneto Company, London 241
Electric and Ordnance Accessories, Birmingham 233
Electric Power Supply Department 125
Electro-Bleach Company, Middlewich 92, 93, 94
Eley Brothers Limited, London 203
Elizabethville Colony 179
Elliot and Jeffery Limited, Cardiff 222
end of the war
  leaving work 251
  planning 249, 250
  stopping work 250-1

Enemies Contracts Annulment Act 1915
Engineer Munitions Department 91
Engineering Employers' Federation 3, 110
Engineering Laboratory 220
English Channel 59, 60, 135, 225, 245
enlistment 7, 11, 28, 71, 76, 149, 142, 166, 167, 169
equal pay rates 153-4
Equipment Branch 50
Ergite, Penrhyndeudraeth 85
Excess Profits Tax 143
Experimental Establishments 49
explosives 87-9
Explosives Loading Company, Faversham 118, 119, 210, 244
Explosives Supply Department 44
Explosives Supply Branch 80
exports, British 20, 41, 70, 81, 94, 135-6
Export Prohibition Act 67
exporting Rolling Stock 57-8

Factory Acts (1802) 173
factories
  discipline in 143
  equipping 123-4
  managing 102
  working in the 103
Fairbairn, Lawson, Combe, and Barbour, Leeds 193
Fairfield Shipbuilding and Engineering Company, Govan 144, 217, 221
Fair Wages Clause (1911) 152
Farquhar-Hill automatic rifle 201
Federated Engineering and Shipbuilding Trades Union 164
Ferranti and Company, Oldham 193
field guns 183, 185-6
Final Advance (September to November 1918) 228
Financial Secretary 27, 31, 32
fire protection 19
Firth and Sons, Thomas, Sheffield x, 6, 71, 108, 114, 178, 184, 187, 211, 220
flamethrower 211
Flavelle, Joseph 132
Foreign Office 41, 67
Foster, Blackett and Wilson, Gateshead 193
Foster and Company, William, Lincoln 225, 226, 243
Forward newspaper 163
Forwarding and Delivery Branch 58, 59
Fox's, Samuel, Sheffield 71
French, Field Marshal Sir John 25
Frodingham Iron Company, Scunthorpe 71
Fuel Experiment Station 220
fuses 121, 192

Gallipoli, *see* Dardanelles
gas
  types 93-5
  cylinders 94
  shells 95
  masks 96
gauges 124
Geddes, Sir Eric 57
George Kent Limited, Luton 121, 194
General Federation of Trade Unions 10
General Headquarters (GHQ) 31, 47, 54, 57, 92, 100, 165, 183, 184, 185, 188, 189, 190, 207, 208, 209, 210, 211, 212
Glasgow Iron and Steel Company, Glasgow 71
Glasgow rent riots 177
Glasgow Women's Housing Association 177

Gloucestershire Aircraft Company, Cheltenham 238
Gordon, Sir Charles 129
Government Rolling Mills, Southampton 74, 205
Graces Guide website of British industry ix
Grangemouth 60
Great Labour Unrest 3
Greece 183
Greenwood and Batley Company, Leeds 194
Greenwood's of London 203
Grahame-White Aviation Company, Bedford 238
grenades 208-9
   types 208
   numbers 208
Gretna, Dumfries 82, 157, 178-9
Groups, Ministry 20-22
grenades, numbers 208
Gun Ammunition Filling Department 91, 211
Gun Parts Committee 186
guncotton 1
Gunpowder Factory 5, 79, 81, 82, 83, 244

Hadfields Limited, Sheffield 6, 71, 108, 114, 178, 183, 186, 187, 226
Haig, Field Marshal Sir Douglas 189, 226, 227
Hamilton and Company, William, Port Glasgow 220
Hampshire, HMS 135
Handley Page Limited, London 238, 244
hangars, aircraft 242
Hardman and Holden Limited, Northwich 85
Harland and Wolff Limited, Govan, Belfast, Southampton 112, 221, 222
Harmsworth, Alfred 129
Harper, Sons and Bean, A. Birmingham 183, 194
Harris Lebus, London 238
Hawthorn, Leslie and Company, R. and W., Newcastle 221
health and safety 143, 159
health issues 175
Health of Munition Workers Committee 157
Heath and Sons, Robert, Stoke-on-Trent 71
helmet 211-12
Henderson, Arthur 12, 64
high explosives 81
High Explosives Committee 7, 79, 83, 84, 86
high-speed steel 16
Hill's, J. and P. of Sheffield 187
Hindenburg Line 191
Hitchens, Lionel 131
Hoffmann Manufacturing Company, Chelmsford 232, 233, 239
Holland, Hannen and Cubitt's, London 194, 237
Holliday and Company, L.B., West Yorkshire 84
Home Ore Supply Committee 68
Hotchkiss machine gun factory, Coventry 171
Howard and Bullough Company, Accrington 193
Hours of Labour Committee (see Sunday Labour Committee)
House of Commons 31
housing 176-7
Housing Department 176
Housing Schemes 178
howitzers 183, 185-6
Hughes, Sam 131, 132, 196
Hunslet Engine Company 57, 108

Imperial College London 91
Imperial Contracting Company, America 195
Imperial Munitions Board 132, 133

imports 41, 130, 133
   American 127-30
   Canadian 131-3
Increase of Rent Act (1918) 178
India 68, 83, 196
India Rubber, Gutta Percha and Telegraph Works Company, London 239
Industrial Council 11
Industrial Workers of Great Britain 4
Inland Waterways Transport Department 59
inspecting imported goods 52-3
inspection 49-5
Inspector of Royal Engineer Stores 50
Inspector of Steel 50, 51, 69
Iran 76
Iron and Steel Department 70, 75
iron ore x, 16, 41, 42, 56, 59, 67-8, 70, 71, 75, 133, 135, 187, 188, 190
Insurance Act 174
Inter-Allied Bureau of Statistics 137
Inter-Allied Council 129
Inter-Allied Munitions Council 29, 41, 47
Inter-Allied Tank Bureau 229
Inter-Departmental Contracts Committee 40
Inter-Departmental Oil Committee 77
International Supply Commission 136
Inventions Department 54
Italy 20, 27, 29, 42, 47, 68, 69, 70, 135, 136, 137, 183, 232

Japan 81, 135, 196, 204
Joint Committee of Finance and Contracts 40
Joint Hours of Labour Committee 157
Joint Industrial Councils 251
Joint Priority Board 29

Kings Norton Metal Company 6, 120, 121, 203, 204, 205
Kitchener, Field Marshal Lord Herbert 7, 8, 9, 12, 13, 14, 15, 25, 26, 27, 135, 141
Knickerbocker Trust 3
Kerensky Offensive, Russian 28
Kerr Stuart, Leeds 57
Kryn and Lahy, Letchworth 194
Kynoch Limited, Essex 82, 83

L (for Labour) Committee 171
Laboratory Stores Division 50
Labour Advisory Board 146, 158, 163
Labour Department 16, 29, 132, 152, 176
Labour Enlistment Complaints Committee 167
Labour Exchanges 10, 13, 15, 109, 141, 146, 162, 177, 251
Labour Gazette 152
Labour Party 10
labour, regulation of 142-3
Labour Resettlement Committee 249
Labour Supply Department 46, 163, 169
Lanarkshire Steel Company, Glasgow 71
Lancashire Engineers' Stoppage (May 1917) 168
Lancashire Ordnance Accessories Company, Accrington 193
Lance Blythe Limited, Lancashire 84
Langwith Byproduct Company, Mansfield 86
Law, Bonar 32, 33, 34
lead 75
Leaving Certificates, abolishing 169
Leeds Munitions Committee 105
Leicester 13, 14, 109, 187
Leitch and Company, John W., Huddersfield 79
Lever, Hardman 32

Index 267

lifting equipment 32, 51, 124
limiting profits 11-12, 37
Livens projector 92, 95, 210, 211
Lloyd George, The Right Honourable David MP
   as Chancellor 12, 31, 34, 144, 176
   as Minister of Munitions 7, 14, 19, 25-26, 46, 54, 64, 101, 107, 114, 128, 131, 143, 146, 155, 162, 163, 184, 191, 209
   as Prime Minister 32, 166, 167, 168
lock outs 22, 152, 252
London Metal Exchange 67, 74
London Small Arms Company (LSA) 195, 196, 197
London Transport 4
London and North Western Railway 57
Loos, battle of (September 1915) 88, 92, 94, 95, 118, 184
lorries 231-4
Lothian Chemical Company, Edinburgh 85
Low Moor Munitions Company, Bradford 84
Lubbock Committee 153
Lucas Limited, Joseph, Birmingham 233
Lunham and Moore, 128 43
lyddite (see picric acid)
Lys offensive (April 1918) 171, 184, 190

Macarthur, Mary 155, 239
machine guns
   Hotchkiss 52, 171, 200, 201, 225, 227
   Lewis 52, 199, 200
   Madsen 201
   making 199
   Maxim 199
   repairs and spares 200
   Vickers 52, 199-200, 243
machine tools 16, 39, 69, 108, 123-4, 130, 133, 142, 184
Mahon, Major General Reginald H. 13
manganese alloy steel 226
Mann, John 32
manufacturing issues, artillery 184
Marshall, Sons and Company, Gainsborough 226
Massachusetts 43
Mather and Platt Limited, Salford 183, 194
McKenna, The Right Honourable MP, Reginald 32, 34
MEA Magneto Company, London 241
Mechanical Engineer's Department 99
Mechanical Transport Depot 232
Mechanical Warfare (Overseas and Allies) Department 229
Mechans Limited, Glasgow 226
Mersey, River 4, 222
Messines campaign (June 1917) 47, 227
Metropolitan Carriage, Wagon and Finance Company, Birmingham 225, 226, 228, 233
Mexico 129
Middle East x
Middlesbrough 56, 58, 71, 87, 106, 222
Midland Railway Carriage Works, Birmingham 43
Midland Railway Company, Derby 74, 109
Midvale Steel Company, Philadelphia 183
Milner, Right Honourable Alfred, 1st Viscount Milner MP 250
Military Aeronautics Directorate 235
Military Service (No. 1) Act (1916) 149, 165
Military Service (No. 2) Act (1918) 171
Minenwerfer 209
mines, naval 223
Mineral Resources Development Department 40
Miners' Federation of Great Britain 3, 4, 5, 12, 64, 65
Minimum Wage 4, 240
Mining Association 64

Ministry of Blockade 41, 129
Ministry of Munitions staff 26
Ministry of Reconstruction 28
Mitchell and Shaw, Hayes 241
modifications 53-4
Moir, Ernest 128
Mole and Sons, Robert, Birmingham 195
Montagu, The Right Honourable Edwin MP 27
Morgan and Company, J.P. 8, 87, 127-8, 129, 136, 188
Morris and Company, H.N., Manchester 84, 85
Morris Motors Limited, W.R., Oxford 223
mortars, trench 209-10
motorcycles 231-4
Motor Radiator Manufacturing Company, Birmingham 241
Motor Rail 57
munitions committees x, 15, 102, 106, 107, 108, 111
Munitions Council 29, 33, 41, 47, 113, 129, 190, 240
Munitions (Food) Committee 176
Munitions Inland Transport Branch 59
munitions levy 34, 37, 143
Munitions (Liability for Explosions) Act 1916 89
munitions, moving 58-9
Munitions of War Act (1915) 13, 19, 22, 27, 34, 37, 64, 142, 143, 144, 151-2, 153, 155, 158, 161, 251
Munitions of War Amendment Act (1916) 148-9, 163
Munitions of War Amendment Act (1917) 154, 169
Munitions of War Committee 14, 25
Munitions Ordering of Work Regulations 157
Munitions Priority Committee 149
Munitions Stores Department 43
Munitions Railway Transport Branch 59
Munitions Requirements and Statistics Department 46, 47
Munitions Tribunals 143
Munitions Vote 31
Munitions Work Bureaux 146
Munitions Works Board 32, 70, 102
Munitions Workers' Enrolment Department 146

Napier and Son, D., London 234
Narvik 68
Nasmyth, Gaskell and Company 57
National Administrative Council of shop stewards 170, 171
National Advisory Committee on War Output 12
National Aircraft Factories 237
National Box Factories 76
National Cartridge Factories 205
National Component Factory, Tipton 192
National Concrete Factories 102
National Cotton Waste Mills 81
National Explosives Factories 91
National Factories 15, 20, 32, 35, 39, 70, 99, 118, 122, 125, 129, 145, 152, 154, 155, 162, 163, 164, 174, 178, 184, 189, 190, 201
   building the 101-102
   managing the 102
   working in the 103
   improving production in the 103-4
National Federation of Women Workers 5, 155, 239
National Filling Factories 93, 117-21
National Fuse Rectification Factory 76
National Gas Mask Factory 96
National Gauge Factories 124
National Gun Carriage Repair Factory 76
National Ordnance Factories 108
National Physical Laboratory 124
National Photographic Lens Factory 213
National Projectile Factories Executive Committee 103-13
National Projectile Factories 113-15

Birtley 114
Lancaster 114
Templeborough, Rotherham 114
Tinsley, Sheffield 114
Nottingham 115
Dudley, West Midlands 115
Hackney, London 115
Cardonald, Glasgow 115
Cathcart, Glasgow 115
Renfrew, Glasgow 115
National Registration Act 147-8
National Registration Card 167
National Rifle Factories 197
National Service Volunteers' Scheme
National Shell Factories 15, 27, 37, 102, 103, 105-13, 117, 123, 188, 190, 193
National Small Arms Ammunition Factories 204
National Spelter Company, Avonmouth 74
National Steel Billet Breaking Factory 70
National Tool Factories 124
National Transport Workers' Federation 5
National Union of Railwaymen 5
National Wood Distillation and Acetone Factories 81
Naval Construction Research Establishment 220
Naval Inspection Department 50
Naval Ordnance Department 220
Netherlands 74, 84
Neuve Chapelle, battle (10 March 1915) 8, 25, 45
New York 43, 76, 127, 128, 129
New York Stock Exchange 3
Newton, Chambers and Company, Sheffield 71
Nitrogen Products Company, Middlesborough 87
Nobel's Explosive Company, South Wales and Chittening 79, 82, 83, 85, 87, 93, 119, 120, 121
Non-Ferrous Council 67
North British Locomotive Company 57, 111, 223, 229
North East Coast Armaments Committee 13, 14
North Sea Mine Barrage 223
North Western Engineering Trades Employers' Association 145

Oddy and Cleaver, Leeds 242
Office of Works, HM 102
oil 76-7
optical munitions 213-14
Order 447 156
Ordnance Board 5, 13, 209
Ottawa Car Company, Ontario 131
Overseas Transport Department 42, 43, 83

Palmers Shipbuilding and Iron Company, Newcastle 217, 221
Pankhurst, Emmeline 155, 162
parachutes 245
Park Gate Iron and Steel Company, Rotherham 71
Paris Economy Pact 57
Partington Steel and Iron Company, Manchester 71
Patent Shaft and Axletree Company, Wednesbury 194
Pearson and Knowles Coal and Iron Company, Warrington 71
Peddled Scheme, rifles 196
Pelabon, London 194
Pembroke Royal Dockyard, southwest Wales 219
Petters Limited, Yeovil 238
Petrol Engine Department 240
petrol 76-7, 241
Periscopic Prism Company 213

Phoenix Dynamo Manufacturing Company, Bradford 238
Phosgene Gas (Carbonyl Chloride) 92
picric acid (TNP) 7, 79, 80, 82, 83, 84, 86, 87, 88, 94, 118, 121, 135
piece work 154
Platt Brothers and Company, Oldham 193
Plumstead marshes 6
poaching workers 16, 23, 143
Pontoon Company, Cardiff 222
Port Forwarding Department 43
Port Talbot Steel Company, Port Talbot 71
Portsmouth Royal Dockyard, Hampshire 219
Potash Factory, HM, Oldbury 213
power supply 124-5
Principal Lady Inspector of Factories, HM 174
Prideaux, William de Courcy
Priority Branch 39, 40, 70
Priority Committee 46, 147
Priority Work 149-50
Production Committee 11, 12, 143, 144, 151, 152, 153, 155, 156
Projectile and Engineering Company 6, 187, 194
propellants 73, 80-82, 89, 130, 133, 135
propellors 242
Protected Occupations Schedule 28, 167, 170, 171
Public Health Acts (1848) 173
Purchasing Department 129
push and go men 25, 46

quality problems 53

railways
  planning 55
  maintaining rolling stock 55-6
  maintaining the railway network 56-7
Railway Centralising Committee 58
Railway Executive Committee 58
Railway Materials Branch 56
Railway Materials Department 58
Railways Priority Committee 56
Rainham, Essex 8, 84, 89, 93
Raleigh Cycle Company, Nottingham 192, 200
Ransome and Marles Bearing Company, Newark 233, 234
Ransomes, Sims and Jefferies Limited, London 111, 234
Raw Materials Department 16, 73
Read Holliday and Sons, Huddersfield 84
Reconstruction Committee 249
redundancies 71, 252
Rees Roturbo's of Wolverhampton 115, 183, 187
Remington Arms Company, America 128, 195
Registration (Amendment) Act 1918 237
Regular Army 5, 7, 25
Release From the Colours Scheme 145, 162
Rents and Mortgage Interest Restriction Act (1915) 177
Repington, Lieutenant Colonel Chales à Court 25
Research Establishments 49
reserved occupations 147, 149-50, 167, 169
Reserved Occupations Committee 149
Restrictions of Imports Committee 71
revolvers 195
Ricardo and Company, Manchester 226, 228
Richard Thomas and Company, Abergavenny 71
Richborough Salvage Station 204
rifles 195-7
Rifle Components Pool 197
Robey's, Lincoln 238
Robert Graesser Limited, Wales 84

Index 269

Robert MacLaren and Company, Glasgow 74
Roburite and Ammonal Limited, Watford 86, 244
Rolls-Royce, Derby 238, 240, 241
Ross Rifle Company, Quebec 131 196
Rover Company, Coventry 234
Royal Air Force (RAF) x, 171, 199, 237, 240, 242, 251
Royal Aircraft Establishment 49, 237
Royal Arsenal 5, 10, 43, 49, 50, 51, 58, 76, 81, 88, 89, 95, 99-100, 105, 120, 124, 125, 128, 178, 183, 185, 186, 187, 188, 192, 203, 204, 205, 207, 209, 210, 244
Royal Commission on Mines 63
Royal Dockyards 4, 9, 153, 217, 219-20
Royal Dutch Shell 76
Royal Flying Corps (RFC) x, 200, 201, 235, 239, 243, 251
Royal Gun and Carriage Factory 5
Royal Laboratory 5, 50, 99, 110, 205, 208, 244
Royal Naval Air Service (RNAS) 231
Royal Navy x, 80, 82, 86, 88, 127, 188, 213, 214, 220, 223, 251
Royal Navy Physiological Laboratory 220
Royal Small Arms Factory (RSA), London 5, 195, 197, 199, 200
Ruston, Proctor and Company, Lincoln 211, 234
Richard Hornsby and Sons, Grantham 194
Rudge-Whitworth Coventry, Birmingham 203, 233
Runciman, Walter 64
Russia 20, 27, 28, 41, 44, 57, 68, 74, 80, 80, 86, 128, 135-7, 183, 184, 190, 197, 204, 205, 208, 231
Russian Revolution 29

sabotage 129
Saint Andrew's, University of 93
Salonika x
Salt Union, Northwich 86
Samuel Newbould and Company, Sheffield 195
Sanderson Brothers and Company, Sheffield 195
salvage 20, 76, 204
Scandinavia 42, 69
Scarpa Flow, Orkney Islands 60
Schedule of Protected Occupations 28
Scientific Advisory Committee 91
Scottish Federation of Tenants' Associations 177
Scotts Shipbuilding and Engineering Company, Greenock 217, 220
scrap metal 75-6
Secretariat 20
Secretary of State for War 7, 14, 25, 27, 190, 250
Select Committee of National Expenditure 33
semi-skilled workers (definition) 161
Senghenydd, Glamorgan 63
Services Electronics Research Laboratory 220
Sharp and Mallett Limited, West Yorkshire 84
Shearman and Company, John, Cardiff 222
Shell and Components Manufacture Executive Committee 101, 190
Shell and Components Executive Committee
Shells and Fuses Agreement (1915) 11, 151
Shell Conference 10
Shells
  manufacturing 187-93
  filling 117-8
Shelton Iron and Steel Company, Stoke-on-Trent 71
shift work 154-5
shipbuilding 217-23
Shipbuilding Employers' Federation 5, 144
Shipconstructors' and Shipwrights' Association 5
Shipping Control Committee 42
Shipping Priority Committee 42
shield 212

Shoeburyness, Essex 5, 49, 51, 209
Shop Stewards Stoppage (November 1917) 169-70
Short Brothers, Bedford, Rochester and London 238
Short Magazine Lee-Enfield (SMLE) rifle 195
Sicily 42, 80, 83
Siddeley-Deasy Motor Car Company, Coventry 171, 238
Singer Manufacturing Company 4
Skefko's, Luton 232, 233
skills terminology 161
skilled workers (definition) 161
Smith, Sir Hubert Llewellyn 148
Sneyd Bycars Limited, Stoke-on-Trent 93, 95
Somers, Walter, Halesowen 183
Somme campaign (July to November) 1916 27, 32, 39, 46, 54, 87, 94, 119, 164-5, 184, 185, 186, 188-9, 192, 200, 204, 226
Somme offensive, German (March 1918) 171, 184, 189, 190
Sopwith Aviation Company 238
South Metropolitan Gas Company, London 84
Spain 42, 67, 68, 71, 75, 80, 83, 188, 236
spare parts, vehicles 232
Special Brigade 91
Special Arbitration Tribunals 156, 239
Special Committee for Land and Buildings 32
spelter 42, 73-4
Spencer Chapman and Messel Limited, London 83
Spicer and Sons, James, London 96
stabilising wages 251
Standard Oil 76
Standard Small Arms Company (SSA), Birmingham 196
Stanley, Edward, 17th Earl of Derby 147, 190
starred jobs, see reserved occupations
Steel Company, Glasgow 71
steel production, 69-71
Steel Production Department 75
Sterling Telephone and Electric Company, London 192
Stettinius Sr., Edward R. 127
Stevenson, James 101
Stokes mortars 54, 108, 109, 135, 209-10, 211
Stokes, Wilfrid 209
stores 43-4
Stratton Works, Swindon 86
strikes 3, 4, 5, 12, 64, 143, 151, 152, 177, 208, 209, 252
submarine warfare 28, 29, 32, 36, 39, 40, 41, 42-3, 47, 56, 67, 68, 70, 77, 80, 83, 127, 129, 133, 135, 137, 157, 176, 190, 232, 236
subsidised transport 231
Summers and Sons, John, Chester 71
Sunday Labour Committee 157
Superintendent of Experiments 49
Superintendent of Research 49
Supply and Demand 45-7
Supply Department 225
Supreme War Council 227
Swan Hunter and Wigham Richardson Limited, Newcastle 221
Sweden 16, 42, 68, 187
Switzerland 20, 52, 74, 132, 191, 192, 231
Synthetic Products Company, King's Lynn 81

tanks 225-9
  Mark I 225-6
  Mark IV 226-7
  Mark V 227-8
  Mark V* tank 228
  Mark IX tank 229
  Whippet 227

Tank Corps 52, 227, 228
Tank Supply Committee 225
Tank Supply Department 226
tear gas 92, 95, 96, 210
Territorial Force 5, 7, 25, 45, 50, 106, 184, 195, 197, 203
tetryl 81, 82
Texas 43
Thames Ammunition Works, London 86
Thames Ironworks, London 217
Thomas, Albert 26
Thomas, David 128, 131
Thornycroft, John, Southampton 145, 222
time work 154-5
timekeeping 158-9
Times newspaper 25
tin 75
Titanic, RMS 222
TNT factories 84-6
toluol 68
tools 16, 21, 46, 68, 69, 123-4, 142, 187,
Trade Boards Act (1908) 155
Trade Card Scheme 28, 166, 167, 169
Trade Union Congress 10, 162
Trafford Park, Manchester 70, 76, 85
Transport Workers' Battalions 43
Transports, Shipping Controller and Tonnage Priority Committee 42
Treasury 6, 11, 31, 32, 33, 34, 36, 64, 127, 132, 174, 178, 184
Treasury Agreement (1915) 11, 12-13, 22, 36, 64, 151, 155
Treasury Conferences (1915) 151
Trench Warfare Filling Factories 210
Trench Warfare Department 91
Trench Warfare Supply Department 207
trench warfare weapons 208-11
Trenton, Ontario 87
Triumph Cycle Company, Coventry 171, 234
Triple Alliance (unions) 5
tritrotoluene (TNT) 7
Tyne shipyards x, 168, 177, 220, 221

Urgent Supplies Board 40, 43
union restrictive customs and practices
 reinstatement of 251-2
 suspension of 10, 12, 19, 22, 26, 37, 88, 144, 152, 161, 162, 163, 173
United Alkali Company, Widnes 92, 93, 94
United Society of Boilermakers and Iron Shipbuilders 5
United States enters the war 28, 42, 67, 87, 127, 129-30
United States 3, 43
 aircraft 236, 237, 241
 buying from 8, 25, 26, 57, 69, 131, 132, 133
 cost of imports 33, 36, 69, 105, 113, 204
 enters the war 28, 42, 67, 87, 124, 129, 136, 137
 inspection of goods 20, 22, 51, 52, 70, 124, 188, 196
 exports to Britain 41, 44, 80, 84, 102, 117, 123, 124, 127-30, 183, 184, 189, 190, 191, 192, 195, 196, 197, 199, 203
 exports to France 136
 exports to Russia 135
 export quantities 42, 70, 74, 75, 76, 79, 81, 87, 107, 119, 120, 130, 133, 197, 231, 234
 munitions industry 128-9
 shipping from 43, 77
 tank construction 229
 vehicles 231, 232, 233
unskilled workers (definition) 161
unskilled workers, training 164

Vandervell and Company, C.A., London 234
Vanguard newspaper 163
Verdun 184, 193
Vickers, Sheffield 6, 12, 13, 51, 71, 108, 114, 118, 119, 120, 184, 185, 186, 187, 192, 195, 209, 223, 226, 245
Vickers, Barrow-in-Furness, 6, 166, 217, 218, 222,
Vickers, Crayford and Erith 52, 178, 196, 199, 200
Vimy Ridge 211
Viviani, René 7
Vote of Credit 31

Wage Truce 151
Wages Administration 152-3
Wages Temporary Regulation Bill 252
War Cabinet Committee on Priorities 40
War Munitions Volunteers 146-7
War Office x, 10, 14, 15, 26, 45, 54, 55, 77, 92, 99, 109, 110, 120, 127, 128, 131, 135, 184, 195, 196, 197, 213, 231, 243
 pre-war and early days 6, 7, 183, 188, 203, 245
 finances 25, 31-5
 testing 49, 68, 190
 designs 51, 53, 209
 explosives 79, 82, 83, 86, 88,
 recruitment 141, 166, 172
War Priorities Committee
War Service Badge 23, 141-2, 149, 165
War Supplies Department 129
War Trade Department 41
Washington Steel and Ordnance Company 188
warship, building a 217-9
Watson, Laidlaw and Company 6
Webley and Scott Limited, Birmingham 195
Weedon, Northamptonshire 43, 44, 195
Weir, Right Honourable Andrew, Lord Inverforth MP 250
Weir, G. and J., Glasgow 111, 115, 144, 221
Welfare and Health Section 173
welfare inside the factories 173-4
welfare outside the factories 174
West Riding Chemical Company, Wakefield 93, 95
Western Front 7, 28, 29, 46, 57, 86, 183, 190
White and Company, J. Samuel, Isle of Wight 222
White and Poppe Limited, Coventry 121, 233
Whitehead and Company, London 238
Wigan Coal and Iron Company, Wigan 71
Wilkinson Sword Company, London 195
Wilson, President Woodrow 129
Winchester Repeating Arms Company, America 195
Wolseley Motor Company, Birmingham 240
Women's Social and Political Union 5, 155, 162
Women's Trade Union Advisory Committee 239
women's wages 155-6
Wood Brothers Glass Company, Derby 213
Woolwich see Royal Arsenal
Working Classes Acts, 1885 173
working hours 156
Workington Iron and Steel Company, Cumberland 71
Workmen's Representatives 12
Workmen's Compensation Act (1906)
Wood, Thomas McKinnon 177

Yarrow and Company and Barclay, Scotstoun 221
Ypres 7, 28, 47, 92, 94, 111, 115, 170, 191, 211, 227
Ypres, Third campaign (July to December 1917) 28, 47

Zeebrugge 211
Zimmerman Telegram 129
zinc 73-4